INDIA

INDIA

Globalization and Change

PAMELA SHURMER-SMITH

University of Portsmouth

A member of the Hodder Headline Group
LONDON
Co-published in the United States of America by
Oxford University Press Inc., New York

First published in Great Britain in 2000 by
Arnold, a member of the Hodder Headline Group
338 Euston Road, London NW1 3BH

http://www.arnoldpublishers.com

Co-published in the United States of America by
Oxford University Press Inc.
198 Madison Avenue, New York, NY 10016

British Library Cataloguing in Publication Data
A catalogue record for this book is available from the British Library

Library of Congress Cataloging-in-Publication Data
A catalog record for this book is available from the Library of Congress

ISBN 0 340 70579 5 (hb)
ISBN 0 340 70578 7 (pb)

1 2 3 4 5 6 7 8 9 10

Production Editor: Julie Delf
Production Controller: Iain McWilliams
Cover Design: Terry Griffiths

Typeset by J&L Composition Ltd, Filey, North Yorkshire
Printed and bound in India by Replika Press, New Delhi

What do you think about this book? Or any other Arnold title?
Please send your comments to feedback.arnold@hodder.co.uk

To Les Shurmer

CONTENTS

ACKNOWLEDGEMENTS

This book is dedicated to my father, Les Shurmer, lifelong socialist and activist. It doesn't begin to repay all that he has given to me.

The Lal Bahadur Shastri National Academy of Administration in Mussoorie made me an honorary professor and provided me with a base for research in 1995. It then provided me with a 'home' on many subsequent visits. I acknowledge a debt to the then Director, Dr N.C. Saxena and to all my colleagues there, particularly Harsh Mander, Santhosh Mathew and Nira Ramachandran and Professor H. Ramachandran.

I have received much warm hospitality, particularly from Harsh and Dimple Mander, Smita Gupta and Praveen Jha, Sulu and Santhosh Mathew, Naomi and N.C. Saxena. All of these people have also spent hours discussing contemporary India with me and have been generous with their introductions. I would like to acknowledge the help of 'Vasu' Srinivasan at Tilonia; 'Hirubhai' Sharma, Sudipto and Achira Chatterjee at Asha Gram; Ajit Bhattacharjea, Director of the Press Institute of India; Shekhar Singh of WWFN; Smitu Kothari of Lokayan; Jharana Jhaveri, video-producer; Madhu and Bharat Dogra, independent pamphleteers.

My Head of Department, Kelvyn Jones, has always provided support and intellectual stimulus. Laura McKelvie, who also loves India, persuaded me to write this book and then encouraged me when I wanted to give up. In many ways this is her book.

I can never express enough love or thanks to Louis, my husband, for just being there, for listening and reading, for telling me that the struggle is worthwhile or to John, my son, for being such a good friend and for sharing my passion for India.

I am grateful to the Faculty of the Environment Open Learning Centre of the University of Portsmouth which produced all of the maps and to Louis Shurmer-Smith who supplied these. I extend my thanks to Lokayan and the Centre for Science and Environment for permission to reproduce their cartoons and to SSi Ltd for their advertisement.

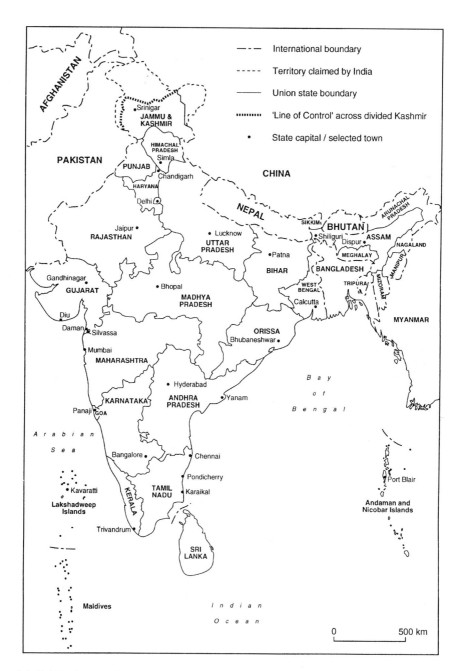

FIGURE I.1 Political map of India

Note: The international boundaries of India are neither authenticated nor correct.

INTRODUCTION

India's population is fast approaching a billion; this fact is easy to read but much more difficult to absorb – one thousand million people, each of whom sees the world in a slightly or radically different way from the others. This book contains about 100 000 words, so each word has to stand for 10 000 people. How can it possibly do justice to them? All it can do is generalize, exemplify and, most of all, introduce a country and its billion people, giving leads which will encourage more engaged knowledge.

When we generalize we are bound to do violence to subtlety and even to ignore the reality of some people altogether; but the alternative is to give up and to remain tongue-tied before a mass of detail. One has to blunder on and be ready to listen to the criticism afterwards. But there is another problem, that of authorship and authority. I am acutely aware of the criticism made by Madan (1994) that western academics have a tendency to raid India for data whilst obliging Indian academics to adopt western theory. As a white British national, I carry with me the baggage of an imperialist legacy; much that I observe in India is an outcome, direct or indirect, of an indefensible colonial encounter, set in train a quarter of a millennium ago, but still reverberating in our daily lives, whoever we are and wherever we may live. Indian readers, in particular, may well question my right to make any generalizations at all about contemporary Indian society and ask whether interpretation from outside is not just another round of cultural imperialism. I hope it will become clear as this book unfolds that my personal belief is that, in conditions of increasing influence of multinational firms and global institutions, it becomes an imperative that the ordinary people of the world make their own connections rather than slot into the globalizing strategies of powerful forces. I do not believe that we can afford exclusive nationalisms any longer. Although I shall be pleased if it attracts Indian readers, this book imagines a readership of interested outsiders, people who do not have much firsthand knowledge of India or the assumptions that Indian people take for granted. I ask Indian readers to be tolerant of the ignorance that exists in the West when I try to explain things which seem obvious to them; the colonial legacy means that India knows much more about the West – its values, practices and fashions – than the West appears to know about India.

This book addresses the state of India at the turn of the millennium. (Whose millennium? Whose calendar?) India is changing fast, but so is the rest of the world. Much of the change one experiences in India is certainly a part of the maelstrom referred to as globalization – that complex of American hegemony, transnational firms, flexible capital accumulation, new international division of labour, communications and information revolution, which has marked the later postcolonial era. I do not want to argue that India is simply responding to global pressures, with change always dictated from outside; instead, I shall concentrate upon the people of India as active (that does not necessarily mean willing) participants in the processes of world change. Events taking place in India are themselves contributory to globalization as the country participates in the increasing density of transnational interdependences.

India has long been integrated into the polity and economy of the wider world. Though the fashionable term 'globalization' ought to ring hollow in Indian ears, it echoes with a new resonance today because it is espoused by the category of Indian society which has more to gain from solidarity with its own class internationally than with its fellow countrymen. However, this globalization is accompanied by a thinning of internal solidarity. Élite Indians have increasing amounts in common (economically, politically and culturally) with English speakers elsewhere in the world, but suffer increasing distance from the mass of the national society. The same globalizing processes impact profoundly on the rest of the population too, even if the consequences are less easy to see. For the poor, the outcomes of globalization are not qualitative lifestyle changes and westernized consumer goods, but more of what went before: more rural indebtedness, more landlessness, more food shortages, more child labour, more casualization of work, more violence and intimidation.

When was India not intimately involved in global processes? Invasions, migrations, trade have been the essence of India's history and present identity. The Aryan invasions of autochthonous Dravidian peoples formed the template for the deepest and most intractable divisions within what was to become India; the Mogul invasions bequeathed a system of land tenure and administration as well as Islam; British imperialism left its imprint on virtually every aspect of life and was quite as cataclysmic politically, economically, socially, and culturally as the current wave of globalization. India has never been isolated; she has always been implicated in the affairs of the world.

This book quite categorically does not intend to rehearse the history of India, even though there is a tendency for accounts of

India in the present to dwell upon the past (Khilnani 1997; Bose and Jalal 1997) as if it were a country uniquely weighed down by its heritage. India's history is complex and fascinating but it is also hotly contested. Contemporary political claims are backed with historical, pseudo-historical and mythological 'evidence' about the conflicting rights and relationships of supposed invaders and autochthones and the amateur historian easily falls into pits dug by present-day combatants, as will be shown in Chapter Eight. When, occasionally, I refer to the past, it will be to show how the present makes use of it, rather than to offer a causality of the present.

The major divergences in Indian society are based around unequal access to resources and this book will constantly confront this. The bulk of Amartya Sen's work rests upon this fundamental principle and Sen has alerted the economics profession to the realization that inequality of capabilities and the corresponding inability to exercise a meaningful range of choices is as important as mere differentiation of income levels. He shows that genuine and effective access to education, health care, democratic political institutions, and infrastructural provision (such as pure drinking water) are as much subject to unequal distribution as is income. He also draws attention to the importance of gender equality as an indicator of well-being (Sen 1987, 1992, 1999; Dreze and Sen 1995). His interest in entitlements emerged from the gradual realization as a child that the Bengal famine of 1943 struck unequally and he found himself worried by the persistent question as to why some people should be trapped in their destitution, whereas others could shape their lives. Sen absolutely believes in the possibility of freeing people from this trap by enhancing their capabilities through the exercise of democratic processes and freedom of expression. In the 'gloomy science' of economics Sen remains an optimist, but one with a clear view of reality.

When thinking about inequality in India, it is necessary to realize that conceptions of social class developed in western conditions do not exhaust all the possibilities of privilege and exclusion. Class, in the sense of position in the economic processes of production and consumption, is an important concept in India as elsewhere, but the ways in which classes emerge in India have to be seen in the light of local principles of differentiation translated into inequality of power and prestige. More than anything else, this means taking account of communities which focus upon caste, religion and region. It also means being aware of gender differences emerging from variously structured patriarchal kinship systems. But the influence is two-way; changing class configurations mean that caste, religion, region, gender and kinship are not fixed attributes either.

It is easy to exoticize India by concentrating upon the differences from the affluent West, but I am of the unshakable belief that students of 'other' cultures have a duty to acknowledge the continuities and similarities which make communication and understanding possible. If one reifies culture and concentrates on 'tradition' and local differences, the problems of people in other countries can often seem inevitable and the people more foreign than they really are.

OUTLINE OF THE BOOK

I have chosen to present India from a perspective which emphasizes the internal inequalities of wealth and power and then links these to contemporary global processes, suggesting that the commonalities of interest of equivalent social strata in different countries are more significant than either the cultural differences between countries or the cloak of apparent cultural similarity thrown over the conflicting elements of any one country. Chapter One will focus on the outcomes of India's New Economic Policy, introduced in 1991 as the consequence of the acceptance of a World Bank loan and a Structural Adjustment Programme. This implies a consideration of the consequences of 'liberalization' and a shift from centralized planning to a free market. Much of the rest of the book hangs on the implications of this shift.

Chapter Two concentrates on the sector of society which benefits most from economic liberalization: the affluent, English-educated, cosmopolitan, urban élite. Although this is a small fraction of the whole, it is highly audible and visible; it dominates the media, politics and society and its interests are widely represented. This leads us on, in Chapter Three, to the aspiring sector of society, the urban middle class, struggling to acquire the advantages of membership of a globalized new service class but often squeezed by the pressures of the market. Then, in Chapter Four, there is consideration of the forgotten people, the urban poor, doomed to a life of marginality and illegality – occupants of slums, denied public utilities, because municipal authorities have never provided sufficient official housing or planned for the poor in the mushrooming cities. These people are the backbone of the unorganized sector of the economy, casual workers in unregulated industrial units.

Chapter Five looks at rural India, where three-quarters of the population lives. It dispels any illusion of unchanging tranquillity and considers the consequences of capitalized farming, rural indebtedness, and displacement of tribal people and small cultivators. However, it also derives hope from the fact that India still has a considerable rural population of small farmers and that new forms of local government, combined with local social movements, may be able to provide the catalyst for effective rural development.

Cutting across the divisions between urban and rural and also across social classes are the categories of gender and age; although these are referred to in the earlier chapters, they form the focus of Chapter Six. There is probably no aspect of life more subject to sweeping generalizations and gross essentialization than gender and age, but both are socially constructed and thus subject to change. Much of the characterization of age and gender emerges from the prevalent family form and the chapter considers the ways in which different socio-economic niches develop different forms of the family, sometimes with surprising outcomes. India has more formal provision for the democratic representation of women than any other country in the world, and women have been singled out as the major agents of social 'uplift'; however, they score badly on the development indicators – literacy, income, life expectancy. India also has an appalling record of child labour and low school attendance, both linked directly to family poverty.

In Chapter Seven, crime and corruption are examined. No society exists without these elements and criminal practices always mould themselves around the dominant economic, social and political structure; as India changes, the patterns of its illegality and the uses of violence also change. India is concerned about the pervasiveness of both petty and grand-scale corruption and conscious of its international rating as one of the top 10 most corrupt societies. Its press publishes regular comment, blaming corruption on the legacy of feudal relations, or British inspired bureaucracy, or western influenced consumerism, depending upon the ideological position of the writer. The chapter explores the nexus of politics, bureaucracy, business and organized crime, concluding that the configuration of these elements reflects legitimate systems.

Religion and caste are important to understanding contemporary India; however, these are multifaceted rather than monolithic. They have a personal and philosophical side to them but they are also things which change in the light of economic, social and political pressure. Caste, in particular, permeates the whole book, but communal issues form the specific subject matter of Chapter Eight. This is, perhaps, the most important chapter in the book, but it had to be delayed until other more mundane aspects of life could be established. In their present *avatars*, both religion and caste are used as forces of a divisive communalism which is constantly manipulated by political groups and could tear India apart. The chapter also recognizes the importance of the secular and anti-communalist counter movements, including the emergence of an anti-nuclear movement.

Chapter Nine looks at the tension between centralist and regionalist forces in Indian politics. Decentralization is a plank in the platform of liberalization and the rolling back of the power of the state[1] which forms a major part of the Structural Adjustment Programme; but decentralization is also a response to regionalist aspirations. The individual States which make up India see themselves in frequent conflict with the Union Government; State-level politicians can have greater influence than those at the centre. The old Indian nationalism of Congress and the Independence struggle can no longer be relied upon as a rallying force as narrower nationalisms dangerously emerge.

The fall-out from many of the economic, social and political problems in India can be seen in the impact upon the environment and this is the subject matter of Chapter Ten. There are industries with high levels of effluent; polluted rivers; choked cities; deforestation; large and inappropriate hydro-electric schemes all in the name of economic development. India imports toxic waste and accepts polluting industries because it has been forced to accept growth at any cost. Of course, the costs do not fall evenly, neither do the benefits. Whilst India has serious environmental problems, it also has a flourishing and sensitive ecological movement which operates at both grass-roots and national level. Some of the most notable social movements are configured around environmental issues which have a direct impact on people's lives and livelihoods.

Chapter Eleven contemplates the people everyone loves to hate, India's bureaucracy, but shows that, under pressures of liberalization and also new caste-based power structures, it is adapting in unexpected ways. It is becoming less élitist, more market orientated and is learning to side-step the various reforms which sought to curtail its powers. Parts of it are also becoming more deeply involved in serious corruption and white collar crime. With all its faults, the state bureaucracy is currently the only effective means whereby welfare and rural development can be delivered. Rumours of the demise of the Civil Service in the 'new' India have been much exaggerated and the chapter backs calls from more socially-conscious elements of the service for radical internal reform rather than increased privatization.

A short final chapter addresses the phenomenon of emigration and its impact back on Indian society. It is a mark of the upper classes' espousal of globalization that a period of work in the West is coming to be a typical stage in a professional man's career. People from the élite sections of society are training and preparing for employment abroad. They see themselves as part of a mobile international service class, seeking the greatest advantage globally. A large part of their motivation derives from the high salaries to be earned outside India, but there is also the lure of the anticipated western middle-class lifestyle. When they return, they reinforce not only the cultural changes which are already well established in the major cities, but also the local divisions of wealth. In addition to this professional migration, there are migrations of men as labourers and technicians particularly to the Gulf, this time with the sole aim of earning better wages, which they send home to improve the livelihood of their families. Though very different from one another, both categories are targeted with generous schemes to persuade them to invest their overseas earnings in India. They contribute handsomely to India's invisible exports but it is also becoming clear that expatriate groups, nostalgic for home, are a major moral and financial reinforcement of communalism back in India.

BACKGROUND TO INDIA

India is not just large (3 165 596 sq. km.), it is also immensely varied, both in terms of its physical geography and human attributes. The physical geography and climate I will leave to others; suffice to say that we are thinking of a country which includes the snowy wastes of the high Himalaya, the hot dry desert of Rajasthan, the Deccan Plateau, the Indo-Gangetic Plain, lush tropical coastal regions, the densely forested North East, the eroded badlands of the Chambal Valley. There are the great life-giving rivers – the Ganges, the Cauvery, the Narmada, the Krishna. India has a monsoon climate, with hot wet summers and cooler, dry(ish) winters, separated by two searing hot dry months in May and June. Most of Indian agriculture is rain fed and the success or failure of the monsoon makes more difference to the national income than any other single variable.

But just as impressive as its physical variation is the variation in modes of living. It is easy to fall into the purple prose of the travelogue, talking of contrasts between old and new, subsistence-based tribespeople versus software engineers, mud huts versus skyscrapers, counterpoising pictures of young women in traditional dress and western fashions. The central thesis of this book is that all of this apparent difference is equally a part of the contemporary India and that there are no people who are the fossilized remains of an earlier 'traditional' society. Those who are poor, illiterate, powerless are as much members of the great global process as those who reap its benefits. The small peasant farmer today is very different from his predecessors because the total economic context has changed – his landlord is likely to live in a city, not to be present as a rural patron; his more successful neighbour may be producing an exotic crop, such as strawberries, for the global market and may be seeking to force him off the land in order to expand his own holding; the local money-lender may now have indirect connections into organized crime; the local politicians may demand his support with the backing of 'armies' paid for by large-scale business; even arranging his daughter's marriage may be becoming difficult because a cash dowry is demanded now by men of his community. All of these things are outcomes of the increasing integration of India in the global marketplace, and are new problems he has to face, even if in a photograph he might still appear to be a 'timeless' figure.

Because of this variation and integration, India is a good place to contemplate globalization; every aspect of the world system is present in this one national system, from the billionaires to those who die of starvation. One would have to be deliberately myopic not to be able to see the connections in the processes at work and the relationships which emerge. Here one can observe the outcomes of all those key concepts – 'new international divisions of labour', 'flexible modes of production', 'just-in-time methods', 'deregulated markets' – and they are not always pleasant to look upon, not just because of the poverty but also because the

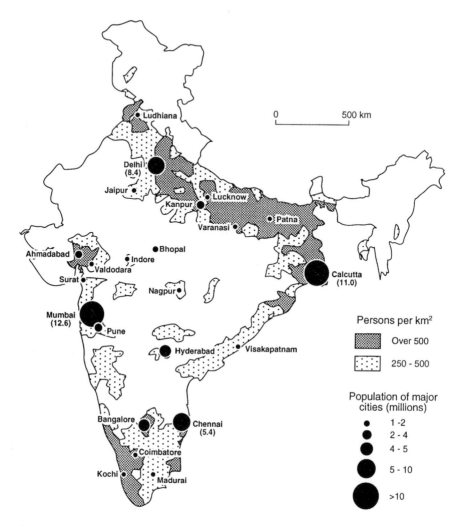

FIGURE 1.2 Population density and distribution
Data source: CSO (1997)

power and the affluence co-exist alongside it, rather than spaced out onto the other side of the globe. India makes one confront the joint realities of globalized production and consumption; it is all there, from primary production, through manufacturing, finance, commerce, research and development, media, all the way to specialization in conspicuous consumerism. In the new international division of labour there are people in India to fill every niche and, when trying to make sense of all this, conflicts are more interesting than mere contrasts.

MAJOR CONCEPTS

Caste

One cannot get very far towards an understanding of India without confronting the notion of caste although, arguably, far too many western orientalists have made caste unnecessarily complicated and imbued the concept with almost mystical qualities of antiquity, ritualism and inevitability, none more so than the French structuralist anthropologist Louis Dumont (1970). It is a pity that the British ever adopted the sociologically sloppy term 'caste', which was used by the Portuguese for the whole range of concepts of differentiation and hierarchy they encountered in India. It is an even greater pity that, with their scientistic impulse, they decided to force it artificially into a 'system'. The problem with the word is that it rolls together several different ideas about social differentiation into a single entity – but caste does not exist in the singular, it is many different things.

Caste refers to what are taken to be traditional notions of social differentiation in Hindu society. The simplest way to start to clarify the confusion is to recognize that behind the single European word are two separate terms for two different ways of conceiving of inequality of status, wealth, power and differentiation of communities. These are *varna* and *jati*. *Varna* refers to *categories* of characteristics (not to *groups* of people); *jati* refers to corporate groups.

Varna is described in the Vedic scriptures (the Sanskrit word literally means 'colour', but people probably used it metaphorically to imply difference, rather than to refer to racial characteristics). If we go back to the *Laws of Manu*, the ancient scriptures which explain the imagined origins of Hinduism and prescribe behaviours and duties, we find that the first question asked by the sages of Manu, the law-giver, is 'Sir, please tell us properly and in order, the duties of all [four] classes' (tr. Doniger and Smith 1991, p. 3). Eventually he tells them:

To protect this whole creation the lustrous one made separate innate activities for those born of his mouth, arms, thighs and feet. For priests he ordained teaching and learning, sacrificing for themselves and sacrificing for others, giving and receiving. Protecting his subjects, giving, having sacrifices performed, studying and remaining unaddicted to the sensory object are ... for a ruler. Protecting his livestock, giving, having sacrifices performed, studying, trading, lending money and farming land are for a commoner. The Lord assigned

only one activity to a servant: serving these other classes without resentment.

A man is said to be purer above the navel: therefore the Self-existent one said that his mouth was the purest part of him, the priest is the Lord of this whole creation according to the law because he was born of the highest part of his body ... (ibid. pp. 12–13)

So there we have it – *brahmins* (from the mouth of God); *kshatriyas* (from his arms); *vaishyas* (from his thighs) and *shudras* (from his feet). Later Manu tells us that there is no fifth category, because the people who do not spring direct from God are outsiders, the untouchables, beneath the feet. Of course this is a *brahminical* interpretation of the origin of inequality and I would not expect you to assume that the account is anything other than allegorical.

> *The Laws of Manu*, like all other works we have from the ancient period in India, was composed by members of the social class (*varna*) called Brahmins or 'priests'. Indeed, the text is not only *by* priests but to a large extent *for* priests. The subject of the rules of *dharma* laid out here is often the householder priest. (Doniger and Smith 1991, p. xxiii)

This ability to keep a principle operational for at least four thousand years is a tribute to one powerful category's tenacity of the will to construct and control knowledge.

Varna represents a system of categories which are justified in terms of notions of supernatural purity and pollution; it enjoins people to accept the fate which they have been born to and it imposes broad bands of differentiation across society. Although it is obvious that what is outlined is an economic/political/social system, it is justified as the will of God and incorporated into religious ideology. We find that even Gandhi, the champion of the oppressed, accepted the inevitability of the system of *varna* and sought not to undermine it but to ameliorate the conditions of those in the inferior positions and outside, calling the 'untouchables' *harijans* – children of God. It is the notion of *varna*, more than anything else, which has caused many people from the most stigmatized ranks of Indian society to reject Hinduism altogether (and also to reject as patronizing the term *harijan*).

Jati are named, hereditary, endogamous (intramarrying) *groups* of people who regard each other as more or less equal in status. They are all associated with traditional occupations or positions of privilege and in the past one's *jati* would have unambiguously determined one's role. The *jati* probably emerged from tribal type kinship-based groupings which gradually crystallized into specialist roles in feudal systems of production and distribution. The various *jati* were functionally interrelated in traditional villages under the *jajmani* system, whereby *jati* of landowners, tillers, carpenters, barbers, potters, priests and so on formed organic wholes but where the various groups were locally arranged in a hierarchy of wealth and prestige. The crucial point is that birth determined one's whole status in society. As an individual one could not (normally) escape this no matter what one's abilities – *jati* determined one's occupation, occupation did not determine one's *jati*. Today everyone is still born into a *jati*, but is not obliged to follow the occupation associated with it (Kolenda 1997). The traditional occupations are still usually performed by members of the relevant group, because these are the people who will have been taught the appropriate skills and have access to useful networks, but modern occupations like factory worker, driver, clerk, computer programmer may recruit from many different communities. This does not mean that people doing different jobs cease to be members of the *jati* they were born into nor that they do not expect to marry people from the same group; indeed *jati* membership is one of the main reasons for the continued practice of arranged marriage (and arranged marriage is one of the main reinforcements of *jati*). I would agree with Andre Beteille (1997) that *jati* is of far more significance than *varna* in contemporary India as the political aspects of caste take precedence over the religious.

Although caste is a Hindu concept, it permeates non-Hindu sections of society. Changing the religious affiliation of a group or forming break-away religions has long been a device for escaping from caste, but it is invariably short-lived, since caste-based status invades Sikhism, Islam, Christianity, and Buddhism.

There are plenty of classic anthropological accounts of *varna* and *jati* and the relationship between the two. Bailey's (1957) *Caste and the economic frontier* is overly simplified and decidedly functionalist, but gives case studies which show the interaction of the principles of *varna* and *jati* as groups renegotiate their position in village hierarchies. Adrian Mayer (1960) presents a closely worked study of the ways in which avoidances and alliances are made according to *jati*. Both have been highly influenced by the work of M.N. Srinivas (1962), and as a consequence pick up the same *brahminical* perspective on caste which suffuses most academic accounts until the very recent past. Inherent in this view is that, within the logic of caste, the *brahmins* really are inherently superior to all others and that upward social mobility is possible only by emulating their practices through the process of Sanskritization. For a summary and evaluation of anthropological theories of caste, one can do no better than refer to Quigley (1993). For considerations of the contemporary implications of caste it is interesting to compare the very differently motivated collections of Fuller (1997) and Srinivas (1996).

'Untouchability'

The most insidious aspect of caste is the notion of 'untouchability', the idea that some people are inherently disgusting, polluting and unworthy, forced to live literally outside the main community, deemed capable of contaminating water and cooked food with their touch, or by sharing vessels, denied access to the wells used by 'clean' castes, refused education, banned from the temples. We have stories of 'untouchables' having hot metal poured into their ears because they dared to hear the scriptures or blinded because they presumed to try to read (a *brahmin* monopoly). They could be attacked with impunity and their women came to expect rape (ideas about ritual impurity seemed to disappear in this context).

The prohibition of 'untouchability' was written into the Indian constitution (whose main author was Ambedkar, the leader of the 'untouchables') but that does not mean that it has ceased to exist. Caste-based violence is still routine in many rural areas and the many daily insults of avoidance are still practised, as is harrowingly documented in the Human Rights Watch (1999) publication, *Broken people*. The Union Government recognized the phenomenon in passing the 1989 Scheduled Castes and Scheduled Tribes (Prevention of Atrocities) Act, which outlawed practices which were a product of this institutionalized contempt. However, as Human Rights Watch indicates, convictions are almost impossible, given the pervasive structures of intimidation combined with the caste composition of the police and the courts.

Box I Scheduled Caste/Scheduled Tribe Prevention of Atrocities Act 1989 (extract)

---

1) Whoever, not being a member of a Scheduled Caste or a Scheduled Tribe–

  i) forces a member of a Scheduled Caste or a Scheduled Tribe to eat or drink any noxious substance;
  ii) acts with intent to cause injury, insult or annoyance to any members of a Scheduled Caste or a Scheduled Tribe by dumping excreta, waste matter, carcasses or any other obnoxious substance in his premises or neighbourhood;
  iii) forcibly removes clothes from the person of a member of a Scheduled Caste or a Scheduled Tribe or parades him naked or with painted face or body or commits any similar act which is derogatory to human dignity;
  iv) wrongfully occupies or cultivates any land owned by or allotted to ... a member of a Scheduled Caste or a Scheduled Tribe...

shall be punishable with imprisonment for a term which shall not be less than six months but which may extend to five years...

Reservation

The Constitution sought to improve the plight of underprivileged communities through the extension of the British practice of reservation – positive discrimination whereby a proportion of government jobs, seats on democratically elected bodies, and educational places were set aside for members of the 'Scheduled Castes' (SC) (former 'untouchables', listed on a schedule) and 'Scheduled Tribes' (ST). Additionally, development schemes were targeted at these sections of society with the aim of 'uplifting' them. In 1992 the recommendations of the Mandal Commission were applied nationally and these 'privileges' were extended to a category known as the 'Other Backward Classes' (OBC); these are communities just above the 'line of pollution' which had traditionally performed low status and badly remunerated work. This policy is popularly referred to as 'Mandalization'; it is highly controversial and the basis of considerable inter-caste political enmity, particularly since the designation OBC is often accorded on the basis of a group's political clout, rather than its level of deprivation.

A major aspect of caste today is the combination of concern with the size of reservation quotas granted to the categories SC/ST and OBC with the desire on the part of politicians to mobilize caste-based 'vote banks'. Caste becomes an important political consideration (something akin to ethnic identity) whereby communities lobby for the advantages that politicians promise in return for support. People have long predicted the demise of caste, but, as Chapter Nine will show, it is an entrenched and vibrant feature of contemporary India.

Tribal people

A section of India's population is classified as 'tribal'. These are groups which traditionally have not been integrated into the caste hierarchy, but are loosely accorded much the same status as 'untouchables', though without the implication of inherent impurity. Tribal people are seen by others as simple and 'primitive' forest dwellers who are the descendants of the original population of India. They characteristically speak different languages or dialects from the rest of their State and generally have semi-subsistence economies. The tribal people are not, objectively, as different from the surrounding populations as is often assumed, and there is plenty of evidence for tribes becoming Hindu castes.

Religion

Just as caste assigns people to communities, so can religion. The outcomes of this will be considered later, but it is necessary to give some background to the religious differences of India. Official statistics are collected on religious affiliation, despite the fact that India is an avowedly secular society (i.e. religion and the state should be separated from one another). The 1991 census shows that Hindus constituted 82 per cent of the population;

Box 2 Scheduled Castes and Tribes as a percentage of State population		
	SC	**ST**
Andhra Pradesh	15.93	6.31
Arunachal Pradesh	0.47	63.66
Assam	7.40	12.82
Bihar	14.55	7.66
Goa	(n/a)	(n/a)
Gujarat	7.41	14.92
Haryana	19.75	0
Himachal Pradesh	25.34	4.22
Jammu & Kashmir	(n/a)	(n/a)
Karnataka	16.36	4.26
Kerala	9.92	1.10
Madhya Pradesh	14.55	23.27
Maharashtra	11.09	9.27
Orissa	16.20	22.21
Punjab	28.31	0
Rajasthan	17.29	12.44
Tamil Nadu	19.18	1.03
Tripura	16.36	30.39
Uttar Pradesh	21.05	0.21
West Bengal	23.62	5.59
Other States (NE)	1.48	61.83
Union Territories	17.82	1.71
ALL INDIA	16.48	8.08

Muslims 12.1 per cent; Christians 2.34 per cent; Sikhs 1.94 per cent; Buddhists 0.76 per cent and Jains 0.4 per cent; that leaves just 0.46 per cent for all others.

Unfortunately, this is far too simple. The category 'Hindu' is inflated, since all that it means is 'the religion of Indian people'. As Madan (1987) explains, 'It is outsiders, non-Indians, who have felt the need to give a name to these people and characterize their religion' (p. 143). Hinduism is not a single organized religion with one sacred text or doctrine; it has no unifying organizational structure; worship is not congregational. There is no agreement as to the nature of the divinity. Hinduism exists as a series of 'Great Traditions' of the religious experts and 'Little Traditions' – the local gods, beliefs and practices of the ordinary people. Some traditions have a high degree of philosophical abstraction, others are highly pragmatic. Although one generally refers to the idea of different sects to represent this variation, this is an intellectual convenience; it takes on a completely different complexion when one finds that many of the people classified as Hindus do not recognize the category as applying to themselves at all. The *dalit* intellectual, Kansha Ilaiah, starts his book *Why I am not a Hindu* (1996) with the words:

I was not born a Hindu, for the simple reason that my parents did not know that they were Hindus. This does not mean that I was born as a Muslim, a Christian, a Buddhist, a Sikh or a Parsee. My illiterate parents, who lived in a remote South Indian village, did not know that they belonged to any religion at all. People belong to a religion only when they know that they are part of the people who worship that God, when they go to those temples and take part in the rituals and festivals of that religion. My parents had only one identity and that was their caste. Their festivals were local, their gods and goddesses were local and sometimes these were even specific to one village. No centralised religious symbols existed for them. This does not mean that they were tribals .... They were integrated into the village economy. (p. 1)

Figure 1.3 Neo-Buddhists in Maharashtra

His book (which turns the notion of a caste system inside out) emphasizes the contrast between *dalit–bahujans* and Hindus, whom he defines as those who recognize the authority of the *brahmanical* priesthood, but this also implies those whom *brahmin* priests are willing to serve. (Foreigners often walk away from temples displaying the sign 'Admission to Hindus Only', and are then surprised when a friendly priest urges them to enter. They do not realize that 'Hindus Only' is primarily a prohibition on 'untouchables'.)

An anonymous article in the (far from deferential) publication *Dalit Voice* (1997) insists that Hindus are a religious minority in India, comprising only 15 per cent of the population. This is certainly a gross exaggeration in the other direction, but the idea is gaining ground that Hindu equates with higher caste. (*Dalit Voice* delights in calling the right wing BJP [*Bharatiya Janata* Party, tr. Indian People's Party] the '*Brahmins' Jati* Party'.) There is a very real politics of religion which intersects with the politics of caste and class. One may also question whether it is justifiable to include tribal peoples in the Hindu category; some observe elements of mainstream Hindu practice, others have entirely ancestral or tellurian religious beliefs.

It is arguable that the principal reason for the inflation of the Hindu category is to claim Hindu hegemony over the people of India and to establish a sense of national solidarity through unity in opposition to others. These 'others' are primarily Muslims but, to a lesser extent, Christians and sometimes Sikhs. Those who propagate the view that *Hindutva* (Hindu culture) means the *Indian* way of life would make foreigners of Muslims and Christians. Such people pretend to fear both the rate of growth of the Muslim population (from 11 per cent of the population in 1981 to 12.1 per cent in 1991 is hardly a takeover, even if the figures are correct) and the phenomenon of conversions of *dalits* and tribal people to Christianity (no figures available, but infinitesimal numbers). One needs, however, to recall that Muslims constituted about 25 per cent of the population of pre-Independence India and that the Partition of the subcontinent into Hindu-majority India and Muslim-majority Pakistan at Independence was accompanied by horrific violence which is not easily forgotten. Indeed it still continues along the Line of Control in disputed Kashmir. Partition left the Muslims in India a beleaguered minority, associated in too many people's minds with the neighbouring enemy.

Political structure

When India gained its independence from Britain in 1947 it unified the former princely States with British India, the provinces which had been ruled directly through the Colonial Office. It also relinquished to the separate new nation of Pakistan the border provinces (with the exception of Kashmir) which had Muslim majorities. The Indian border remains problematic – all maps published in India contain the caution, 'The international boundary of this map purports to be neither correct nor authentic' (or similar words); to do otherwise would be to accept an unaccepted *status quo* relating to the borders with Pakistan and China. (The recognition of the border which includes the States of the North East is not altogether uncontroversial, either.)

Independence conferred universal adult suffrage for the first time and, having been fully involved in the Independence Movement, women were included in government from the very beginning. India is a democratic republic, with a two-tiered Union Government, consisting of the lower *Lok Sabha* (People's Assembly) and the upper *Rajya Sabha* (States' Assembly). The members of the *Lok Sabha* are directly elected, representing national constituencies; the members of the *Rajya Sabha* are nominated by the State assemblies (the *Rajya Sabha* does not dissolve, it is a permanent assembly but members come up for renewal). A (largely ceremonial) President is Head of State but the Prime Minister is the Head of Government.

The Union comprises 25 States and seven Union Territories. Each of these has an elected *Vidhan Sabha* (Legislative Assembly) whose members are directly elected from smaller State constituencies and a Legislative Council, which is not elected. The representative of the Union at State level is the Governor (often a retired senior civil servant).

In both the *Lok Sabha* and the State legislatures a proportion (about a fifth in the case of the *Lok Sabha*) of constituencies are reserved for members of Scheduled Castes and Scheduled Tribes. At the constituency level this leads to considerable animosity but it means that no political party, whatever its ideology, can afford to ignore the 'backward' sections of society.

The relationship between Union and State is not always easy, given the huge regional variations within India and the fact that the government of a State may be politically opposed to that at the Centre. In a general State of Emergency (such as that declared by Indira Gandhi in 1975), State legislative assemblies are dissolved and total power is assumed by the Centre. Similarly, in the event of the Union Government deciding that the rule of law has broken down in any single State, it can dismiss the State government and impose President's Rule.

The Union Government assumes responsibility for such things as defence, foreign affairs, currency and wider matters of policy; the States are responsible (within the overall directives of the Union Government) for administration, law and order, education and welfare, development work, and public works. Both the Union and the States collect taxes but the Union raises the majority of income (through excise and revenue predominantly, but also through income and wealth taxes) and makes grants to the States. Both the States and the Union maintain permanent Civil Service, recruited by competitive public examination. The State governments have considerable power, particularly in matters of local administration and development, and are able to cause very different outcomes in the lives of the people of the State. To take two neighbouring examples, Bihar, with its legacy of feudal overlordship, has a political and administrative structure famously riddled with corruption and inefficiency, and its people score lowest on virtually all indicators of development and welfare, whereas West Bengal has implemented land reform to empower smaller farmers and has achieved both considerable economic and social progress and high levels of popular participation in governance (Chopra 1999).

Many political parties operate at both national and State level with increasing representation of regional parties in the *Lok Sabha*, demonstrating the growing tension between Union and State.

The States are divided into administrative districts, which in turn are divided into blocks (development units) which divide into villages. At each of these levels there is (supposed to be) a democratically elected council (*panchayat*) which reserves a proportion of its seats for Scheduled Castes and Tribes and which, in absolutely revolutionary fashion, reserves at least a third of each category of seat for women. In addition, a

Box 3 Political parties represented in the *Lok Sabha* 1998

Name	Description	Seats
Bharatiya Janata Party	Nat. Hindu. Right	182
Congress (I)	Nat. Sec. Middle	142
Communist Party of India (Marxist)	Nat. Sec. Left	32
Samajwadi Party	Nat. Sec. Soft Left	20
All-India Anna Dravida Munnetra Kazhagam	Reg. Tamil Nationalist (TN)	18
Rashtriya Janata Dal	Nat. Sec. Populist	17
Telugu Desam	Reg. Sec. Populist (Andhra)	12
Samata Party	Nat. Sec. Soft Left (UP)	12
Communist Party	Nat. Sec. Left	9
Biju Janata Dal	Nat. Sec. Populist	9
Akali Dal	Reg. Sikh Nationalist (Punjab)	8
Trinamool Congress	Nat. Sec. Middle	7
Shiv Sena	Reg. Hindu Right (Maharashtra)	6
Dravida Munnetra Kazhagam	Reg. Tamil Nationalist (TN)	6
Janata Dal	Nat. Sec. Populist	6
Bahujan Samaj Party	Nat. Sec. *dalit* rights (UP)	5
Revolutionary Socialist Party	Nat. Sec. Left	5

Key: Nat. = national party; Reg. = regional party; Sec. = secular

Notes: There are 12 further parties in the *Lok Sabha*, each with four or less seats; these are a mixture of national and regional parties. It is interesting to note that in contrast to the Hindu parties, the Muslim League has only two seats.

Two members are nominated by the President to represent Anglo-Indians

third of all Chairs of *panchayats* at each level are reserved for women and Chairs reserved for SC/ST in proportion to their number. The basic idea of this system of local government, known as *panchayati raj*, has deep roots in parts of India, but it was not enshrined in the Constitution until the 73rd Amendment was passed in 1992. *Panchayati raj* is important not just because of its gender implications but because it transfers democratic institutions right down to the lowest level of government. Formerly, practically all local decision-making was in the hands of State and All-India civil servants; now, with government closer to the people, it becomes possible for them to ensure that locally relevant schemes are pursued and also to monitor their effective execution. Optimists believe that *panchayati raj*, combined with the Right to Information about government works, will begin to crack the problem of pervasive corruption, favouritism and inefficiency. Pessimists point to the fact that SC/ST-led

panchayats come under attack from upper castes, citing the atrocity in which six Scheduled Caste *panchayat* members were hacked to death in Tamil Nadu in the run-up to local elections in 1997 (*The Hindu* 1997b).

Language

A great many languages are spoken in India and the language question is fraught with political implications, since the status of any language immediately privileges or disadvantages different categories of people. The Union recognizes two official languages: Hindi (written using *Devanagari* script) and English. Urdu is virtually the same language as Hindi, but is written in Persian script; since Partition it has become increasingly associated with Islam. Ahmad (1996b) shows how Hindu and Muslim writers came to deal themselves into separate camps, 'The two terms, *nation* and *community*, at once political and cultural, are the framing realities for [the] particular "mirror" which we call Urdu' (p. 202). In this case political difference has created language groups, rather than the more easily comprehended reverse.

Each State recognizes English in addition to its official State language. To a limited extent, the composition of the States reflects the pattern of the main regional languages, particularly since the States Reorganisation Act of 1956. There are additionally 1600 different languages, 400 of which are spoken by more than 200000 people; although many of these are mutually intelligible dialects, some are tribal languages with little overlap with the official State language.

The status of Hindi is problematic. Spate (1954) blithely assumed the demise of English as 'the language of administration, central or provincial, after a limited transition period of a few years' (p. 126) and felt that it could no longer be justified as the medium of instruction in universities. However, Hindi, the language of the northern States, is far from universally acceptable, since, as an Indo-European language, it has hardly anything in common with the Dravidian languages of the South. Its use as an official language advantages northerners (and this was made much of in propaganda terms when Deve Gowda, a Kanada speaker with no Hindi, became Prime Minister). Southerners use English as the national language and have a better command of it than all but the very best educated northerners. So, if Hindi favours the North, English favours the South.

English is spoken by only about 2 per cent of the population; it is the language of the educated élite who have attended English-medium schools (and others who have laboured to learn it). Its international advantages are obvious, but it is also the only *lingua franca* of the upper classes of the whole nation. It is the medium of instruction in the most reputable universities and institutes and, therefore, the language of academic books and journals. State schools and universities predominantly use the State language at undergraduate level, with English offered as a second language in the better ones, but Masters degrees are often taught in English. It is obvious that this is highly exclusionary, and reinforces class divisions, but it is difficult to see any way around it. In terms of media and literature, there is a thriving Hindi and regional language press whilst film and television tend to divide into Hindi, Tamil and, to a lesser extent, Telugu. The excellence of Indian literature in English needs no advertisement, but Rushdie and West (1997) give a very useful overview.

The speakers of the minority languages are at the greatest disadvantage. Children from tribal communities find it difficult at school and their parents are at the mercy of intermediaries when they need to make contact with officials. Official language recognition becomes one of many negotiating positions when a regional movement campaigns for the division of a State.

Development

On all indicators, India has made considerable improvements in standard of living

Box 4 Major State languages	
Andhra Pradesh	*Telugu & Urdu*
Arunachal Pradesh	*Monpa etc.*
Assam	*Assamese & Bengali*
Bihar	*Hindi*
Goa	*Konkani & Marathi*
Gujarat	*Gujarati*
Haryana	*Hindi*
Himachal Pradesh	*Hindi & Pahari*
Jammu & Kashmir	*Kashmiri & Urdu*
Karnataka	*Kannada*
Kerala	*Malayalam*
Madhya Pradesh	*Hindi*
Maharashtra	*Marathi*
Manipur	*Manipuri*
Meghalaya	*Khasi*
Mizoram	*Mizo*
Nagaland	*Konyak etc.*
Orissa	*Oriya*
Punjab	*Punjabi*
Rajasthan	*Hindi & Rajasthani*
Sikkim	*Nepali etc*
Tamil Nadu	*Tamil*
Uttar Pradesh	*Hindi*
West Bengal	*Bengali*

since Independence; life expectancy, infant mortality, literacy have all improved, but there is certainly no room for complacency and India ranks 139 (out of 174) on the United Nations Human Development Index for 1995, falling into the bottom category, 'Countries with Low Human Development'. Life expectancy at birth is now 58 years for men and 59 years for women (at Independence it was only 30) and, despite all the gloom which greets the rate of population growth, the birth rate declined from 41 to 32 per 1000 between 1951 and 1991. It very much depends on one's attitude to these things as to whether one sees an even more radically declining death rate (23 to 11 over the same period) as constituting a *problem* (I would regard it as an improvement).

The per capita income for 1996–97 was only Rs 10399 ($286) per annum. This, however, masks considerable internal variation in income levels as well as a substantial subsistence factor in the rural areas, but it is low by any standards. In India, poverty and affluence are more often presented on the basis of household than individual and an average household (according to the 1991 census) contains 5.52 people. In 1994–95 (the most

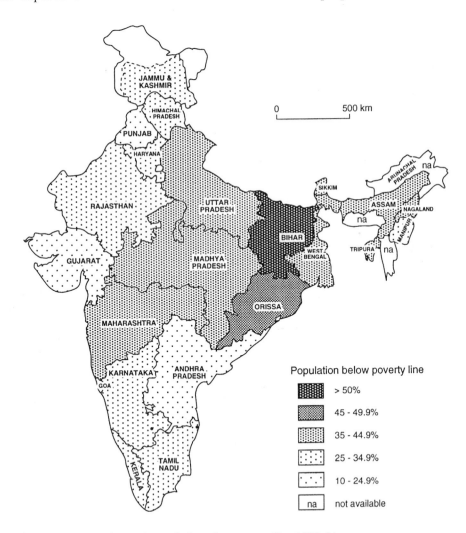

FIGURE 1.4 Percentage of population below the poverty line 1993–94
Data source: CSO (1997)

recent figures available) households by income tranches were divided thus:

Below Rs 22 550 – 53.6%
Rs 22 551–45 000 – 28.0%
Rs 45 001–70 000 – 11.2%
Rs 70 001–96 000 – 4.4%
Above Rs 96 000 – 2.9%
(Source: *Statistical outline of India 1997–98*. Based on NCAER data, p. 207)

Estimates vary as to the number of households falling below the poverty line but the *Statistical outline of India 1997–98* (p. 206) quotes this as being 35.97 per cent of the national population. The poverty line is calculated calorifically. It represents the ability to provide 2 400 calories per adult per day in the rural areas and 2 100 in the urban areas (this is commuted into a notional household annual income of Rs 6 400). The rural areas are much more susceptible to variations in standard of living, many more households dropping below the poverty line in bad monsoon years. Poverty amounts to malnutrition in an Indian context.

The major governmental attack on malnutrition comes in the form of the Public Distribution System (PDS), a nation-wide network of ration shops for which those registered as poor obtain special cards for the purchase of subsidized foodstuffs. The 1997 budget announced that each month households below the poverty line would be able to buy 10 kilos of grain at only 50 per cent of the government procurement price. However, the PDS is notoriously inefficient and corrupt, with considerable leakages; a World Bank study (1997) states that it costs the government Rs 7 to deliver one rupee's worth of subsidy to the poor through the PDS. The PDS works better in the urban than rural areas, but it acknowledges that the poorest of the poor are not the main beneficiaries. Other forms of poverty alleviation come in the form of programmes for rural women and children, guaranteed labour schemes, loans and grants for agriculture and to set up small businesses, often targeted at the Scheduled Castes and Tribes; but there are only infinitesimal and rare pensions and similar benefits.

Primary education and health care are free,

but both are sparsely provided. A remarkable official statistic informs us that 104.3 per cent (*sic*) of all children in the appropriate age band are enrolled in primary schools (*Statistical outline of India 1997–98*, p. 198). The explanation for this is that the teachers send in the returns for attendance but, given that much of the time the teachers do not attend themselves, it is hardly surprising that their information is nonsensical. The UN Human Development Index puts enrolment at 55 per cent for the first three years of schooling. The census gathers information on literacy; in 1991 the literacy rate was 52.2 per cent – male literacy 64.1 per cent and female 39.3 per cent.

Since the acceptance of the principle of liberalization under structural adjustment, there has been an encouragement of welfare and development provision via non-governmental organizations. The best of these can be excellent, but they can be patchy in their provision and far too many are either amateurish or corrupt (or both). NGOs receive the bulk of their funding from the Government of India, not (as many people assume) from charities. Directly or indirectly, the state continues to be the major provider in this field and it is to be hoped that it will retain this role for a very long time, with the proviso that there be sufficient monitoring of the actions of civil servants.

The economy

Opinions are sharply divided as to whether increased integration into the global economy will eventually cause an economic revolution and the end of mass poverty. Advocates of the free market and deregulation claim that the medicine will take time to work, others are sceptical as to whether it works at all. India remains the World Bank's biggest borrower. Despite the fact that the New Economic Policy was ushered in as a consequence of a balance of payments crisis, India's current account balance did not improve; it moved from minus Rs 2 237 crores (see glossary) in the danger year of 1991–92 to minus Rs 13 242 crores in 1996–97. (*Statistical outline of India 1997–98*, p. 108).

There has simultaneously been a very

great increase in the volume of international trade (imports: 1991–92 – Rs 47851 crores; 1996–97 – Rs 136844 crores. Exports: 1991–92 – Rs 44041 crores; 1996–97 – Rs 117525 crores). Some believe that this increased activity should, in itself, stimulate growth; others worry about the implications for internal prices and the distribution of essential goods. Exports can almost triple in five years only if goods which were normally consumed at home are diverted to the world market, resulting in a high rate of inflation for domestic products, such as basic foodstuffs. In an article on rising prices in the popular journal *India Today* it was pointed out that, whilst consumer durables like refrigerators were getting cheaper, the food to put in them was on average rising in price by 40 per cent per annum (Chakravarti and Rekhi 1998). This small example encapsulates the impact of the liberalization of the Indian economy; for a few, life is getting a great deal better, for those with no hope of ever buying a refrigerator, food price rises of this magnitude are catastrophic.

ENDNOTE

1. I am following the Indian convention of using *state* (with a lower case 's') to apply to both the concept of organized government and the Union Government of India, also referred to as *'the centre'*; *State* (with an upper case 'S') applies to the component parts of the Union.

1

THE NEW ECONOMIC POLICY

People in India are acutely aware that in the last decade of the twentieth century there has been a mutation of their society. In this silent revolution, the nature of economic change has rapidly caused transformations in politics, social relations and culture. It has changed people's basic assumptions and expectations, the way they respond to each other, the way they earn or do not earn a living, the way they consume and communicate. Of course there are continuities, but even these continuities are changing and things people took for granted have assumed new dimensions. As always, a shift in favour of freeing the market has resulted in a movement towards a culture of individualism and competition as people are encouraged to see themselves and their relationships in strategic and investment terms. This often goes under the imprint of 'global culture' and is hyped as the aspirational lifestyle of the successful urban young.

At Independence, India's economic and social policy was grounded in broadly socialist ideology and its foreign policy in non-alignment. Partly because of America's policy of bolstering Pakistan as an integral part of its 'post-war decision to situate South Asia within its global strategy of anti-Soviet and anti-Communist containment' India was pulled closer to the USSR (Vanaik 1995, p. 23) but:

> The incomprehension of the desire and determination of newly independent third world ruling élites/classes to strengthen their own economic and political position meant that the West failed to recognise till much later that the rhetoric about 'third world socialisms' was (a) an economic rationalisation for heavy doses of state driven capitalism that was incumbent upon the larger 'late industrialisers' in the third world: and (b) a vague commitment to greater social welfarism and justice within a framework of a capitalist economy. (Vanaik 1995, p. 24)

Although there is ample evidence of remarkable improvements in life expectancy and standards of living of people in India in the decades following Independence, the country has suffered a low (though steady) 'Hindu' rate of growth and continuing high levels of deprivation. The solution was sought in the realm of a planned, relatively closed economy with a high degree of government control and a policy of widespread subsidies.

THE STATE AND THE ECONOMY

India's version of state capitalism took the form of high degrees of economic regulation through consecutive Five-Year Plans, initially concentrating on industrialization and modernization through massive capital investment, gradually concentrating more on welfare and poverty alleviation. But the private sector continued throughout to be important to the Indian economy, as Dasgupta (1995) stresses:

> The main thrust of the public sector was to set up industries in those areas where, for a variety of reasons, the private capitalists were unwilling to invest – the 'commanding heights' of the economy which influenced the course of development, and also those with long gestation periods, enormous capita and high risks. Although indigenous capitalists wanted such industries to be set up within the country, they did not wish these to be under the control of foreign enterprises; they themselves did not venture to set up these. *The public sector was not viewed by them as a threat as long as the state eliminated foreign dominance.* (Dasgupta 1995, p. 68; my emphasis)

When India attempted to raise the money for this investment from the World Bank it was refused, partly on the grounds that it was public sector driven, partly because, in the Bank's view, India's comparative advantage was in agriculture, and therefore industrial goods should be imported rather than produced at home, 'and whatever industry was needed should be set up with the help of multinational companies' (ibid., p. 69). India received the loans it needed from the USSR. However, it is important to stress that more than three-quarters of the economy remained in the private sector and by far the greater part of India's trade was with the West. Nationalization was not a major part of the project and, with a very few exceptions such as mining, only 'sick' industries were nationalized. The bulk of public ownership was in the realm of large new initiatives, many of which, like the big dams, may now appear misguided, but others, like oil exploration and refining, must be seen as well advised.

Mahalanobis was the architect of the Second Five-Year Plan (1956–61), which formulated much of the dominant policy of post-Independence India. It is his name, coupled with Nehru's, which is associated with the economic policy which presumes a virtually closed economy, import substitution, and concentration on heavy industry at the expense of consumption goods (including foodstuffs) (Patnaik 1998). Although the second plan is frequently presented as if it were the beginning of a highly regulated economy for India, this view can only be taken if one decides to forget the food rationing and restrictions on investment of the British era.

The planned economy implied a massive involvement of government employees in the regulation of trade and industry and the emergence of the notorious licence/permit/quota raj, that bureaucratic minefield of multiple permissions (and bribes) required to get anything done, from setting up a factory to getting a gas connection. Had we been looking at genuine socialism, with workers' control of production, rather than state capitalism in the surrounding context of a bourgeois small business economy, there need never have been this bureaucratic control. But, given the conditions in which Independence was achieved, and the brahmin domination of both politics and the Civil Service, this was never a serious option; bureaucratic control and corruption there was to be in plenty.

By the late 1960s, planning emphasis moved to attaining self-sufficiency in food. Favoured regions like the Punjab became dominated by capitalist farming with high investments in irrigation, fertilizers and the new 'miracle' high-yielding varieties of seed. The 'Green Revolution' delivered the absolute quantities of grain but, at the local level, it polarized large- and small-scale producers and, at the national level, it opened up huge differences between regions with capitalist and semi-subsistence based agriculture. The early Congress governments had been unable to make land reforms stick, largely because of the emerging alliance between urban élites and the old landed interests, and a distinction emerged between those regions dominated by large peasant farmers and those dominated by landlords. The former moved rapidly into market orientated production and the profits of the Green Revolution meant even further consolidation of land in the hands of large farmers, sometimes through purchase, often through renting from those who could not make a living from small plots (Parthasarthy and Murty

1997). The farmers were to become an important political force, demanding and receiving ever increasing subsidies on their inputs and high intervention prices for their product.

Jayati Ghosh (1998) has argued that India's problems of slow growth can be explained not so much by reference to the high degree of state involvement in itself, but by the government's reluctance to effect the income redistribution which would have stimulated demand for domestic production. She also points to the lack of means whereby the profits taken by the private sector could be mobilized for investment, leading to a demand for luxury goods.

In the 1980s, against this background, the electorally weak administration led by Rajiv Gandhi threw in its lot with the newly vocal business and consumerist orientated middle class. The so-called 'screwdriver industries' boomed (that is, the production of much-desired consumer white goods and motor vehicles from imported kits under licence from foreign firms). Bhaduri and Nayyar (1996) are unequivocal in their condemnation of the 1980s' attempt to expand the economy without increasing revenue from taxation.

> The fiscal crunch forced the government to finance not just the import-costs (machinery and imported inputs) which had to be paid for in foreign exchange, but also a good part of the local-costs (wages and domestic inputs) of investment which could have been paid for in rupees, from foreign inflows. What is more, external resources were also used to support consumption. (ibid. 1996, p. 26)

THE CRISIS

When the Gulf War caused a rise in oil prices and temporarily stopped valuable remittances from expatriate workers in the region, the result was a balance of payments crisis; the noose tightened and India found it impossible to borrow on the world's markets. Once this happened, non-resident Indians took fright for money they had invested in India and rapidly withdrew their Indian deposits, rendering the country even more short of foreign exchange.

> Cash margins on imports were raised from a substantial 50 per cent to a whopping 200 per cent. The government used twenty tonnes of gold confiscated from smugglers ... to raise $200 million in April 1991 from the Union Bank of Switzerland ... but this was not enough. (Bhaduri and Nayyar 1996, p. 29)

And here we have the situation in which India, who had so long struggled to build up her own independent economy, was forced to accept a structural adjustment loan from the World Bank. The conditions were not much different from those of the structural adjustment programmes imposed elsewhere.

It is important to recognize that there were many who, far from greeting structural adjustment as a humiliating defeat of India's autonomy, were delighted to welcome the New Economic Policy. Bagachi (1995), referring back to a local newspaper article he had written in 1985, asserts:

> I had known for some time that there were powerful forces in India deliberately pushing the country into a debt trap with an attendant loss of economic and political sovereignty. These forces were internationalized domestic capital, transnational corporations, economic policy makers in the government impatient with what they regarded as undue government interference in the market, large monopoly capital hoping to gobble up a huge chunk of the public sector (when the IMF–World Bank authorities enforced wide ranging privatization as part of their nostrum), and politicians hoping to gain financially and otherwise from side-payments made by the major beneficiaries. (ibid., p. 80)

Surendra (1999) reminds us that, though it is not much mentioned, India had taken its first IMF loan in 1983 and cites Carla Hills (Reagan's Trade Secretary) as saying, 'Debt is the crowbar with which we wrench open economies' (there is every indication that there were plenty of people inside willing to unbolt the door). Bagachi is convinced that the debt crisis could easily have been avoided but that it was not in the interests of controlling forces to do this. He blames the crisis on a spending spree on 'public and private extravagances' (p. 81).

The Indian economy had been gradually liberalizing since Rajiv Gandhi's regime (1984–89) and structural adjustment promised a package of market orientated policies which were enthusiastically welcomed by substantial sections of the middle classes. It was not just Bagachi's 'powerful forces' which welcomed the New Economic Policy; a whole swathe of middle India believed that it would pave the way for western lifestyles and standards of living for themselves. It is far too easy to say that 1991 marked the start of India's integration into the latest round of postcolonial globalization – like everywhere else it was in already. Indeed, it was global forces which had precipitated the crisis. However, with structural adjustment the forms and rhetoric of globalization invaded the everyday consciousness of people in India, first of the élites, gradually of a wider educated population.

Box 5 Foreign Trade

	Imports	Exports	Balance
1990–91	43 198	32 553	−10 643
1991–92	47 851	44 041	−3 810
1992–93	63 375	53 688	−9 687
1993–94	73 101	69 751	−3 350
1994–95	89 971	82 674	−7 292
1995–96	122 678	106 353	−16 325
1996–97	136 844	117 525	−19 319

Derived from: Statistical outline of India 1997–98, p. 96

As Tendulkar (1998) points out, the package of reforms launched in 1991 can be seen as comprising three major elements. First, there was the immediate problem of the fiscal and balance of payments deficits (whether or not deliberately engineered); second, there was liberalization of foreign trade; third, there was internal deregulation of markets. Everyone agreed that it was necessary to respond to the balance of payments crisis; however, left-leaning economists maintain

that if the government had acted sooner, it would have been possible for India to solve this without recourse to a World Bank loan linked to a structural adjustment programme. There is, therefore, an argument that the resolution of the balance of payments crisis was not inevitably associated with liberalizing global trade or the deregulation of the internal economy. Only ideology can make that linkage seem necessary, just as a different ideology is the basis of the rejection of that link.

STRUCTURAL ADJUSTMENT

The July 1991 budget incorporated the first stages of structural adjustment. It liberalized import and export policy and devalued the rupee to encourage exports; it cut subsidies on agricultural inputs and on prices within the Public Distribution System (ration shops); it increased purchase taxes (but cut income tax); it announced a policy of shedding public sector industrial units, together with a policy of redundancies for workers. The 1991 budget was followed by successive rises in interest rates, a reduction in the numbers of preferential loans for small businesses and agriculture, and spending cuts on welfare and poverty alleviation programmes. Michel Chossudovsky (1992) almost immediately identified a rapid downturn in the conditions of the poor, noting that there was an upsurge in sub-contracting work in the unorganized sector at the expense of unionized labour in the organized sector of the economy. With this went casualization, a depression of wages and increases in the amount of child labour. He also shows how relaxation of export controls on raw materials caused increases in the price of cotton yarn which led directly to starvation of handloom weavers in Andhra Pradesh. He further argued not only that impoverishment is increasing but also that this is reinforcing caste-based economic divisions. This view is held by a great many other socially conscious Indian economists and a further twist on the theme is offered by Roy:

> Scheduled Castes and Scheduled Tribes are likely to be adversely affected by liber-

LIBERTY, EQUALITY AND FRATERNITY IS DEMOCRACY.

....BUT LIBERALISATION, 100% FOREIGN EQUITY AND FREE TRADE IS PROSPERITY!

FIGURE I.I
Source: Lokayan Bulletin (1994)

alization. Increased reliance on the private sector suggests that employment could grow in organizations where no places are reserved for them and where caste discrimination is pervasive. (Roy 1995, p. 146)

Chalam goes further in his caste-led interpretation of the New Economic Policy. His is a view which would be difficult to understand outside an Indian context, for it relies on a concept of hierarchy which, though linked to control of wealth, assumes the existence of identifiable communities:

The brahmins having fattened their private exchequer with public money, no longer thought of the public sector as beneficial to them ... As the *bahujan* [lower castes] concept gained momentum, the upper castes thought that it would benefit them both economically and politically if the economy was privatised and linked to the international market. The *brahmin* experts in the World Bank and the *brahmin* bureaucracy in Delhi conspired and mortgaged the economy when the *bahujans* began emerging as a force to manage the [state controlled] economy and enjoy its benefits ... therefore they conspired to internationalise it ... The *bahujan* being economically poor cannot influence market forces. The *brahmin* who has already entered the private economy and is in a commanding position both at the national and international level, will be the largest gainer of the NEP. This is the *dvija* [upper castes] economic policy currently being pursued in this country. Thus caste is being used as a source of economic capital. (Chalam 1998, p. 35)

Ravi Srivastava (1995) links liberalization to the growth of new political formations and the increasing regionalization of India's politics as regions press for favours from the Union Government or compete to make themselves attractive to foreign capital. This, he believes, results in added impetus for ethnic movements and all of the attendant conflict.

Rajni Kothari, a veteran theorist of poverty who can always be relied upon for his hard-hitting analysis, ironically asserts that:

It is increasingly being felt in the board rooms of the 'new world order' ... that large chunks of the human population ... are proving an unacceptable burden on the world economy. And as these segments are incapable and unwilling to mend their ways and are proving to be parasitical, their very existence will generate pressures that will gravely endanger the health and future of the world economy and the security of the élites and 'productive classes' of the world. They must, therefore, be left to fend for themselves. To the extent that they are likely to protest and create turbulence, they should be put down ruthlessly through the development of a global strategic doctrine to which all national élites seeking entry into the world market should be made to subscribe. (Kothari 1993, p. 75)

Kothari continues to consider the implications for 'disinherited sections of society' who will find that special policies for the alleviation of their conditions will disappear under pressure from those who can (and those who think they can) benefit from the new market conditions.

One could go on piling up examples of critical responses to 'liberalization' and the rest of this volume will demonstrate that my own views are firmly in alliance with this critical perspective. However, large sections of educated India welcomed restructuring and this is reflected in the English-language press. Manmohan Singh, the Finance Minister who masterminded the implementation of the New Economic Policy, had long advocated a lowering of trade barriers and had written his Ph.D. thesis from the University of Cambridge on the subject of the benefit of international trade to India. His senior Civil Service aide, the Finance Secretary, Montek Singh Ahluwalia, had previously been seconded to the World Bank and had absorbed its values and priorities. Jagdish Bhagwati (1998), in a footnote to his summary of the economic history of post-Independence India, comments: 'Many of my non-Indian economist friends who have visited India confess to an astonishment that in India ... there are still trained economists who doubt

and even oppose, as opposed to leading, reforms' (ibid., p. 24). Here we have a clue to the nature of support for liberalization – its logic tends to appeal to those who have had long exposure to the value systems associated with global culture, rather than those who take a more local view.

Tendulkar states his absolute belief that, 'The favourable impact of economic reforms on reduction in poverty can be reasonably taken for granted once the economy shifts to a higher growth path', but goes on to admit that 'the critical question relates to the period of transition before the economy shifts to a sustainable higher growth path' (Tendulkar 1998, p. 283). Since he acknowledges that the level of rural poverty jumped by 30 per cent in 1992 it was hardly a promising start, even if part of the blame could be attributed to climatic conditions. Eswaran and Kotwal (1994) take the view that deregulation of the economy will lead to a migration of underproductive agricultural labour into industry, causing a lowering of industrial wages, which they considered to be artificially high in the organized sector as a consequence of collective bargaining. This, in a context of freer international trade, they maintain will lead to increased exports of industrial products and (ultimately) the decline in poverty. Once again, this means that incomes of workers have to go down so that the country can become wealthy.

Manmohan Singh realized that acceptance of a full-blown market system was not possible in India and that the state would be required for a long while to provide a whole range of services directly, and he coined the phrase 'liberalization with a human face' to acknowledge that welfare responsibility. But there were to be plenty of faces whose the humanity was questionable.

It was argued that, though freeing the market would cause short-term hardship for the poor, eventually this would result in economic growth which would percolate to all sections of society. However, India's poor are too poor to take even short-term hardship. Poverty means the inability to provide oneself with 2 400 calories worth of grain per day in the rural areas (2 100 in town). There is no cushion and there has never been a proper social security system. People die of starvation in the short-run; even more suffer chronic malnutrition, physical, mental and social stunting. The middling poor suffered from a withdrawal of government subsidies on farm inputs and although these were recouped by more affluent farmers in the form of increased prices for agricultural products, this was not the case for semi-subsistence producers. Small cultivators increasingly lost their land to money-lenders and more highly capitalized producers. Landless labourers, dependent on day-wages, immediately felt the consequences of the cut-back in the extent of provision of the Public Distribution System and a rise in subsidized food prices. The Integrated Rural Development Programme was severely curtailed, with massive loss of benefit to the poorest, particularly those who depended upon guaranteed work schemes in the slack season. It became evident that in squeezing public expenditure it was the benefit which gave way, rather than the employment of those who administered benefits. Surendra warns of the destabilizing effect of such uneven shouldering of the costs of economic growth:

> To think that the problems of economic growth can be handled without reference to the social system would mean that when the social system starts unravelling, it will sweep in its wake all traces of economic development. This is a problem that adjustment reform economists skirt. (Surendra 1999, p. 42)

The most often repeated argument for liberalization is that of freeing enterprise from the dead grip of the bureaucracy and the associated 'rent seeking'. There are abundant stories about the spectacular administrative and corruption costs of delivering benefits to the poor. The Public Distribution System, in particular, is a longstanding national scandal. One study calculated that an exporter needed 360 (sic) government actions in the way of forms issued, movements between functionaries, meetings, rubber-stamps, signatures, bribes, telephone calls and official fees before a large export order could be filled (Parik 1997). (Trainees at the National Academy of Administration are sometimes set exercises tracing the life history of a file in order to make them understand the need for streamlining.) The introduction of 'single window' permits for large-scale trade and industry was generally welcomed, even if its benefits largely favoured multinational corporations. Studies show that small companies still face multiple permit seeking.

INVESTMENT/ASSET STRIPPING

A major justification of liberalization was the anticipation of an inward rush of foreign capital in the form of direct investment. It was assumed that this would bring rapid growth, reduction in unemployment and rising personal incomes. This was then intended, though the percolation effect, to stimulate local demand for local products. Though significant (increasing from $68 million in 1990–91 to $1 314 million in 1994–95), foreign direct investment proved to be scarcer than expected and portfolio capital was more abundant (none permitted in 1990–91 but $3 342 million in 1994–95). Multinational corporations were more interested in local buy-outs and mergers than they were in genuinely new enterprise or export orientated industry. Their concern was predominantly to enter the Indian domestic market. Coca-Cola took over Thumbs Up – the cola drink which had been introduced to fill a market gap when George Fernandes famously banished Coke; Honda merged with Bajaj, the leading scooter manufacturer. Tarun Das, the Confederation of Indian Industry's Director General, maintained in 1996 that the new transnational firms 'were adopting a short-run, fly-by-night stance in the Indian market'. He accused them of wanting to exert 'dominance and control, with their one-way-street approach and their tendency to import outdated or obsolete technology and products' (Chandrashekhar 1996, p. 97). Foreign firms have also been permitted to set up in Export Processing Zones, where 100 per cent of production is for the export market. These are exempt from both customs duty on imported raw materials and local taxes. Between 1990–91 and 1996–97 the value of exports from Export Processing Zones rose from Rs 907 crores to Rs 2445 crores (*Statistical outline of India, 1997–98*). This may sound good until one looks down at the micro level. Rajalakshmi (1999) reports that in the NOIDA Export Processing Zone 40 per cent of workers are women (including girls of eleven) doing semi-skilled or unskilled work and being paid Rs 700–900 a month for 10-hour days.

Box 6 New foreign business collaborations		
	Number	**Investment**
	of cases	**Rs crores**
1990	666	128
1991	950	534
1992	1520	3888
1993	1476	8859
1994	1854	14187
1995	2337	32072

Derived from: Statistical outline of India 1997–98, p. 148

The rapid development of Bangalore and then Hyderabad as major centres for the production of computer software has been export driven by a mixture of international and local firms but it has also prompted a massive brain drain to the West. The software industry builds upon a defence initiative of the 1980s which fostered R&D work and trained a large reserve of young technicians (Bangalore was favoured because of its longstanding munitions and aero-space industries.) Enticed by the high salaries in the industry, legions of young men throughout India have acquired programming skills and, realizing how little they will work for in western terms, the computer companies of the West have been going 'brain shopping' in India. As Martin and Schumann point out, few of today's computer science students in the West will find the sorts of jobs they anticipated, given that temporary workers are brought in on chartered flights and so much work is assigned to India. They quote a spokesman for Swissair justifying the decision to hand reservations over to Indian sub-

contractors by explaining, 'We can hire three Indians for the price of one Swiss' (Martin and Schumann 1997, p. 100). India pays for the cost of their training in its universities and institutes of technology, and multinational firms asset strip. But the rates keep ratcheting down – already several firms are complaining that Bangalore is getting too expensive and St Petersburg beckons.

Similar international asset stripping can be seen in agriculture, where the lifting of export controls has led highly capitalized farmers to look to overseas markets for higher profits. The price of many of the foods which Indian people saw as treats, such as the fragrant Basmati rice of the Himalaya or the short season Alphonso mangoes, have entered the luxury class now that the world has become aware of them. Many farmers are switching from growing grains for local consumption to the major cash crops of cotton and tobacco, others are turning to the specialist cultivation of flowers and strawberries for newly-affluent urbanites and to be air-freighted abroad. Meanwhile, the state continues to subsidize irrigation, power, diesel and fertilizers and underwrite the prices paid for essential foodstuffs. In 1998 there was a series of food scares. The onion crop was badly affected by rain but the government neither imposed export restrictions nor gave permission for imports soon enough for this near essential vegetable to virtually disappear from the market; dealers saw to it that prices rose to exorbitant levels which more than offset the costs of the shortfall in production (Muralidharan 1998c). Rice stocks fell dangerously low in southern India and panic buying took place. Across northern India there was an outbreak of the fatal disease, dropsy, caused by adulterated mustard oil; the adulteration had been a cynical and systematic response to a fall in production and rise in price. The benefits of a free market system are sometimes rather well hidden.

Liberalizing the economy also meant that *hawala* ('laundered') money could be brought quietly back into the realm of legality as the rupee became negotiable. The intended consequence was that larger amounts of capital should become available for investment in the authorized sector. Arun Ghosh (1996) questions the propaganda element of the *Economic survey* (an annual government report) for 1996 and suggests that a large item, 'other capital flows', which was represented as probably consisting of remittances sent directly (not through the banking system) by migrant workers to their families, was in fact *hawala* money on its way back to India and not a real income line.

INFRASTRUCTURE

It is widely acknowledged that a major block to India's economic growth is an over-stretched and unmodernized infrastructure; this can only be remedied by the state, given that there can be no immediate return on investment. The docks are clogged – ships take on average five days to turn around in an Indian port because of antiquated technology, forcing up the real cost of exports and imports. The inland freight service is groaning – there are too few wagons for trains which are too slow and infrequent. Road transport is slow and lorries remain small because the roads are too narrow, pot-holed and congested to take the juggernauts. The current BJP Government has promised a grandiose modern multi-lane highway system connecting the four major cities and extending down to Kerala but no one really believes that the money will be found. Electricity supplies are insufficient and there is frequent load shedding. Regular supply of large volumes of water cannot be relied upon. The telecommunications system (this partially privatized) cannot deal with the pressure placed upon it – telephone calls are fault ridden and Internet connections slow. None of these infrastructural deficiencies can be remedied without considerable public expenditure and they certainly cannot be accomplished overnight. It is hard to see how they can be fitted into the strictures of the New Economic Policy.

DOWNTURN

Since the late 1990s, India has seen a downturn in the rate of growth: a mere 3.6 per cent for 1998–99 and a 5 per cent decline in exports (Datta-Chaudhuri 1999). Some of this can be attributed to the economic sanctions which several countries imposed on India after the nuclear tests in May 1998 and also to the collapse of East Asian demand for Indian products, but a large part can be seen as the failure of the New Economic Policy to provide any deep rooted benefits for the mass of the people of India. The consumer boom could not be sustained because it was limited to such a small section of society and even that fraction is now becoming uncertain of its future. This pessimism is frequently more vividly captured by journalists than by academic commentators and nowhere more so than in the pages of *India Today*, the glossy weekly aimed at the new middle class, which

FIGURE I.2 The highway through Madhya Pradesh to Ahmedabad

has taken a strongly pro-liberalization stance since the beginning of the 1990s. In December 1998 it faced up to what everyone already knew and ran a feature entitled 'The Great Depression' announcing the longest downturn since the early 1990s. But it is not just a consumer recession – 'the pace of economic reforms had slowed down' (Chakravarti *et al.* 1998, pp. 27–8). In May 1999 the journal was asking 'Why aren't you spending?' (Saran 1999) and drew upon a survey of people from the major cities with household incomes above Rs 3000 (generally taken as the starting point for the lower middle class) to show that people were becoming increasingly uncertain about their employment prospects and sustaining their income level. They were also worried about inflation, the rate having touched 19 per cent in January. The downturn in the value of shares in the mid years of the decade had depleted faith in investment income; a collapse in the property market had left people with negative equity; rising food prices were taking a larger proportion of income. People were worried about spending on expensive consumer durables. It had also to be recognized that many members of the 'consuming classes' had acquired a range of consumer durables in the past few years and did not yet need to replace these but the market for such goods could not be extended to a larger section of the population for the forseeable future.

Even amongst those who supported the New Economic Policy, there is a general acceptance that India is in deep recession. Ninan (1999) feels that reform has played itself out, bewailing the government's tardiness in introducing the bill to privatize (and globalize) insurance, complaining that bureaucrats are infiltrating the independent regulatory bodies, arguing that India suffers from delusions of grandeur on the world economic stage, defining 1998 as 'the worst performance in any year since ... 1979–80, barring the crisis year of 1991–92'.

As recently as 1987 the Rudolphs were able to write:

> The international environment is far less salient for explaining Indian economic or political development than is the case for other Third World countries, unless it is salient in a negative sense, as an environment to exclude or keep at bay. Its participation in the international economy has been highly selective. Its goal has been self reliance, a goal that has led it to participate in world markets less than other large Third World countries. (L. Rudolph and S. Rudolph 1987, p. 3)

Their analysis of the post-Independence political economy of India came down firmly in recognition of the state as the 'third actor' between private capital and organized labour, serving to prevent the emergence of class-based politics, but they acknowledge that 'the state in India is polymorphous, a creature of manifold forms and operations'. Reading their sensitive account makes one realize the extent of the shift in circumstances and in theoretical interpretation of economic life in India. They were researching with the assumption of the steady 'Hindu rate of growth' (3.5 per cent) in the background and the inevitability of the state as a major player in all aspects of life. Though willing to accept its utility in understanding other poor countries, they dismissed dependency theory as irrelevant to the interpretation of contemporary India because of its internal focus, its low level of international trade, the importance of the state as a player. It all seems long ago.

Box 7 Ownership of goods (ownership per 1000 households)

	Urban	Rural	Total
Refrigerator	252	20	86
TV (black & white)	456	155	240
TV (colour)	212	26	79
Cassette recorder	466	173	257
Washing machine	109	5	43
Motorcycle	56	19	29
Scooter	158	21	60
Quartz watch	680	258	377

Derived from: NCAER's *Consumer market demographics* (cited in Rao and Natarajan 1996)

2

AFFLUENT URBANITES

A LARGE AFFLUENT MINORITY?

The roads of the major Indian cities are clogged with cars; office blocks, prestige housing developments and international five star hotels are springing up; there are advertisements in the press and on TV for imported consumer goods. It is easy to believe that, post liberalization, a huge class of relatively affluent people has come into being, consuming to western standards and drawing upon a global market. Much of the English-medium press propagates the idea that there has been an explosion of consumerism and that a massive (though not mass) market is hungry for world brands. Popular wisdom has it that, whilst India as a whole is poor, its middle class is six times the population of France and, as such, constitutes a market which warrants the serious attention of the international business community. The figure suggested is a population of 300 000 000.

The actual situation is nothing like as clear-cut as this and we need to think about the nature, as well as the size, of this much vaunted middle class. The most cursory glance at people in even the major cities should demonstrate that the suggestion that nearly one third of the population is affluent is palpable nonsense. The 300 000 000 refers to people who constitute a possible market for things like radios, rather than expensive consumer durables. Western-generated notions of social class, based on employment charac-teristics in the context of industrial, market-based, national economies, do not export well to an Indian context. Class theory is, in any case, currently undergoing serious revision in the West in the light of consciousness of the new international division of labour, the decline in industrial production in many affluent countries and the corresponding shift to service-based activities. Economic transformation and awareness of globalization has encouraged theorists such as Saunders (1981) and Pahl (1984) to shift their attention to modes of consumption as a basis for understanding social differentiation at a national level, because it is no longer easy to assume that one can generalize about categories of people defined in relation to the employment category of heads of households. It can be argued that the classes and class theory generated by the processes of industrialization never had much relevance for India or other colonized countries. It is equally arguable that the class theories of the West in the era known as modern were convincing to social scientists only because of their selective ignorance of the lives of colonized people. However, even if social classes are difficult to generate, we still need to recognize the deep divisions in India's population based on unequal access to resources and life chances.

As was shown in the previous chapter, India's colonial experience did not allow for the unhampered development of a capitalist industrial economy. Although there were a small number of powerful industrialists who played a considerable role in the movement to free India of British rule and unfair industrial domination, there could be no numerically significant Indian entrepreneurial middle class before Independence. There is considerable debate about the nature of the distinction between an Indian *comprador* bourgeoisie (acting on behalf of foreign interests) and a genuine local bourgeoisie (and whether the latter really did exist) (Chatterjee 1985) but, according to Bardhan (1984), it is more useful to think in terms of three 'dominant proprietary classes', consisting of the industrial capitalist class, the rich farmers and the professionals in the public sector. Bardhan saw these three groups more often in conflict with each other than forming an alliance of capital. After Independence, since industry was nurtured under conditions of centralized planning, and protection, a considerable proportion of industry consisted of public sector units, which were administered by salaried, non-specialist civil servants who would spend relatively short sections of their careers in industry. With a few notable exceptions, one could not really talk about a *class* of industrialists or professional managers; neither was there much scope for the development of producer services and their associated professionals in banking, brokerage, insurance and consultancy. Influential positions, social status and prestige tended to be derived from government employment, rather than through entrepreneurship and corporate management. As a consequence, the relevance of models of social class based on the experience of modern western economies was limited not just because of the legacy of pre-capitalist modes of production or the debilitating experience of imperialism, but also because of the importance of the state in determining the form that modernization was to take in modern India. These considerations encourage me to focus upon consumption practices in this chapter rather than simple class position. Although there are problems inherent in this approach, I believe that it is through a consideration of consumption that we can derive the most immediate understanding of hierarchies in the upper ranges of affluence, prestige and influence. There are glaringly obvious differences of wealth in India and these are obviously associated with productive status, but they are also associated with networks of influence, naked power, cultural capital and kinship networks.

SOCIO-ECONOMIC CATEGORIES

Even the Indian Central Statistical Organisation (CSO) does not publish a class-based breakdown of the population. Whereas in the West class is taken as the primary indicator of life chances, in India, position above or below the poverty line and distinction between urban and rural are given far more emphasis. When one remembers that 38 per cent of the population of India scrapes a living below a poverty datum line which is calculated solely on minimum calorific requirements (set at 2100 calories per day in urban areas), the generation of precise social categories of those above this line might seem an unnecessary intellectual luxury. It may therefore seem strange to begin this account of contemporary India with two chapters concerned with the middle classes and above. However, where tensions between the interests of rival categories of relatively well-off people drive so much economic and political decision making, to underplay their significance would be irresponsible.

Income statistics are fairly unreliable. The great majority of the population is not eligible to pay income tax at all and, amongst the rest, tax evasion is rife. In the *Statistical abstract of India* for 1997, the CSO admits that in trying to analyse returns for taxable income it was defeated, 'due to non receipt of requisite samples from the field, which was mainly due to the fact that the samples received from the field were both scanty and non-representative' (CSO 1997, p. 524). One has to fall back on data generated by research institutes and, in trying to gauge the size of the affluent urban population, one is led by the work of the Indian National Council for Applied Economic Research (NCAER) which is usually regarded as the most reliable source of information on this subject. As shown in the Introduction, NCAER generates five income tranches, the highest of which had an annual household income of more than Rs 96 000 in 1994–95 and contained a mere 2.9 per cent of the population.

NCAER also (somewhat confusingly) gives an impressionistic view of the structure of the market, not based precisely on income, dividing society into one million households which it calls the 'Very Rich'; 30 million households it calls the 'Consuming Class'; 50 million it sees as the 'Climbers'; 50 million who are the 'Aspirants'; and 35 million who constitute the 'Destitutes'. NCAER estimates that amongst these categories only the 'Very Rich' consume at the level of middle-class Europeans and Americans (Rao and Natarajan 1996, p. 231).

By international standards, Rs 96 000 does not represent very great wealth; for a small number of people incomes reach far beyond this level. Rao and Natarajan (1996) note that NCAER included a new chapter in its 1996 publication of *Indian market demographics* to deal with the highly differentiated 'Very Rich' because:

> after the liberalization of the economy, when luxury products started entering the market there was a need to understand the market for these products in terms of their size, etc. It became necessary to extend the income distribution … (when) several MNCs and Indian manufacturers inquired from the Council whether they could provide the data. (ibid., p. 206)

They faced the problem that the higher one went up the income scale, the more difficult it became to calculate income because such a large proportion of it was was 'black' and therefore concealed. NCAER decided to assume that 50 per cent of higher-level income was undeclared and, on this basis, calculated that across India there were probably no more than 650 000 urban and 139 000 rural households with an annual income of above one million rupees. These they describe as being the only people in the market for BMW and Mercedes-Benz cars. They concluded that 'the so-called middle class is a myth' (Rao and Natarajan 1996, pp. 209).

In the second income tranche, those earning between Rs 70 001 and Rs 96 000 constitute a further 4.4 per cent of all households. These can be regarded as the upper middle class. It is these two top tranches which form the focus of this chapter. The figures quoted are not much more than guesses and little reliance should be placed on them; much wealth is concealed and its extent will probably never be known. The situation is confused by the fact that upper-middle-class households often have 'family money' as well as 'black' money, capital which can be drawn upon for special purchases.

The assumption that the total middle class is 300 000 000 or roughly a third of the population would take us somewhere down into the band Rs 22 551–45 000, which certainly does not stretch to luxury. IndiaOneStop, an organization aimed at attracting investment in India, rashly asserts that there are 40 million people in India with purchasing power parity of US$600 000, and a further 150 million people have PPP incomes of US$20 000. This figure is certainly wide of the mark.

MAKING COMPARISONS

It is difficult to make comparisons relating to standards of living between categories of people in radically different contexts; translations of rupee incomes into sterling or dollars using international money market rates indicate little in terms of their buying power in India and the concept of purchasing power parity, based on the notional international buying power of a currency, certainly seems to yield some very peculiar figures when it is applied to India. It is useful to think for a moment about the lifestyle of a household dependent on the income of a professional person, someone like a hospital doctor, a civil servant in the administrative grades or a university lecturer. A professor's salary of about Rs 8 000 a month currently, converts to about $190 or £115, a sum on which it would be virtually impossible to support a family in Europe or the US, but which will sustain an upper-middle-class lifestyle in India.

But what *is* an upper-middle-class lifestyle in India? It does not contain the

Box 8 Comparative prices – India and USA

	US price in Rs	Indian price in Rs	Days' work to buy in US	Days' work to buy in India
Colour TV	7 140	13 000	2.1 days	2.3 months
VCR	7 350	14 000	2.2 days	2.4 months
Microwave oven	3 780	9 000	1.1 day	1.6 months
PC	33 600	50 000	10.0 days	8.7 months
Mid-size car	420 000	560 000	4.2 months	8 years 1 month

Derived from: Saran 1999, p. 34

Note: Work needed is based on average middle-class income equivalents for US and India

same ingredients as that of a professor's family in America or Europe. Buying houses or apartments is something people aspire to do but there is unlikely to be home ownership amongst employed professionals until quite late in their careers, unless 'family money' in the form of dowry or inheritance has been involved. Renting remains the norm, although subsidized (virtually free) accommodation is supplied to those in government employment and some others. Until recently it would be unlikely for there to be a family car, but increased production levels and new financing schemes are putting cars within the reach of the upper middle class, though not without considerable strain on the part of the buyer. Such a household, however, will usually employ at least one full-time domestic servant; will make use of a great many personal services, such as launderers; and its children will almost invariably attend good private schools. Homes will often be sparsely furnished, but will usually contain a telephone, books, TV, a music system and, increasingly, a personal computer. Some of the differences in consumption can be regarded as deriving from local preferences (what we can loosely call 'culture') and others from different purchasing power.

Internationally branded goods are roughly the same price (or more expensive) in converted terms in India as elsewhere. To cite some of the current status signifiers (none of them a necessity), a pair of Nike trainers costs about Rs 3 000, a box of Kellogs Corn Flakes is roughly Rs 100 and a pizza in Pizza Express is about Rs 300 (remember what that professor earns in a month). If one cares about demonstrating one's prestige by consuming international products, things are phenomenally expensive. If one thinks about the use value of commodities rather than their value as a status symbol, good Indian manufactured trainers are about Rs 300 and an Indian fast-food meal in a middle-class establishment is about Rs 50. Things are still expensive, but manageable for those with a professional income. Sometimes it can seem like a topsy-turvey world when consuming in middle-class India, as many luxuries cost more than they do abroad; the prices of some near essentials are global, whilst others are local. When one shifts one's attention from goods to services, a live-in maid earns about Rs 300 a month (the same as that pizza) plus her food and accommodation, whilst a chauffeur will get about Rs 2 000 (less than the Nikes). A house in a prestigious area of Delhi can be rented for Rs 20 000 a month and a pleasant flat in a middle-class area can be obtained for about Rs 5 000, but the cheapest room at the Holiday Inn will cost Rs 12 000 a night (without breakfast or luxury taxes). Someone with a reasonable income by western standards is able to afford the international prices and clearly revels in the local ones.

SYMBOLS OF PRESTIGE

It is useful to think of urban India as having a global and a local élite, roughly represented by the 'Very Rich' and the upper middle class, but, although they have very different amounts of spending power, they often have similar family backgrounds and education. The two élite sections of urban Indian society intersect socially and are frequently related, but only the 'Very Rich' consume consistently in the global market. Imported cars and domestic appliances, international brands of clothing, cosmetics and food, Scotch whisky, French perfume are all on sale in the major cities, but one has to look for them; such goods do not cater to a mass market or even to a large niche.

Until the relaxation of import controls which accompanied the liberalization of the Indian economy, few international products were to be found on the open market. Internationally prestigious cameras, watches, fountain pens, CD players, jeans were brought back as trophies of occasional overseas trips, were given as presents by relatives living abroad or were smuggled across the border from Nepal. People working for international agencies, diplomats and high-ranking civil servants stocked up on consumer goods and even paid heavy freight charges on refrigerators and microwave ovens. Imports also carried punitive rates of customs duty. But, despite the concept of import substitution, Indian manufactured goods were not always easily available, even to those with the money to pay for them. Waiting lists to buy consumer durables, like cars, scooters, TVs, air-conditioning units and refrigerators were long (and could only be shortened through paying a premium to someone willing to sell a place high on the list, bribery of officials or special relationships). All of these commodities came to have a status-signifying value way beyond their intrinsic worth and a society which overtly emphasized frugality came to foster what traditionalists saw as 'vulgar materialism' in sections of its more affluent orders.

With the relaxation of import controls, the consumption of international products remains a device whereby the very affluent can ostentatiously distinguish themselves from the rest of the upper middle class; for such people there has been a long spending spree since the beginning of the 1990s. Price alone, not rationing, now accounts for the scarcity value of consumer goods. It hardly needs saying that in such a situation consumption in the global market has become aspirational for those outside the super-wealthy section of society. Especially amongst the ambitious young, the obsession with international brands, contemplation of exorbitant prices and what is taken for international culture has become almost pathological. Such consumer-orientated longing is actively encouraged by that section of the media which has everything to gain in advertising revenue from an increased awareness of product differentiation and branding.

Although the 'Very Rich' are numerically insignificant, they are politically and culturally very visible; as the saying goes in upper-class Delhi, 'The country may be large, but the club is small'. They act as role models for a great many young people, not only in the upper middle class, but also in the category below that, among those the NCAER dubbed the 'Consuming Class' – the lower middle class made up of educated but struggling people, whose lives will be considered in the next chapter. The tastes and consumption patterns of the super élite 'Very Rich' are monitored and communicated in magazines and lifestyle supplements of English-medium newspapers, and token elements, such as the ubiquitous Coke, are incorporated into the lives of others. The 'Very Rich' are worth considering in some detail, not only for their symbolic value, but also because it is from their ranks that many of the most influential people in contemporary India are drawn.

SOURCES OF WEALTH

Given the former degree of state control of the economy, it is undeniable that a great deal of the wealth of the very affluent sections of urban India does not bear too much close scrutiny. There was so much 'black' money washing around the system that in 1997 the government declared an amnesty on undeclared wealth, so that it could be regularized and become subject to taxation. Rs 33 000 crores were declared but this is generally assumed to be no more than 'the tip of an iceberg' (Mahalingam 1998a). It became routine for public employees in influential positions and politicians to turn their knowledge and contacts into wealth – army officers acted as brokers in arms deals (so, it is generally acknowledged, did the Prime Minister, Rajiv Gandhi); revenue officers turned a blind eye to imports in return for generous pay-offs; criminals paid protection money to the police. A whole alternative economy existed in parallel to the official one; unlicensed businesses flourished in premises constructed without building permits on land which had been grabbed illegally. Business was often conducted in cash, gold and jewellery. Wealth was laundered by means of an almost infinite number of ingenious routes before, newly whitened, it could be lodged in bank accounts. Much of the wealth stayed 'black': suitcases full of cash bought politicians and bureaucrats, or was paid in dowry to make strategically useful marriage alliances. It could also be translated into places in universities, degree grades and jobs for one's children. 'Black' money bought scarce 'black' goods and the services of the influential. It was also invested in organized crime and political campaigns.

Much of the original impetus for this black economy came from the desire to cut through the plethora of regulations and restrictions of a command economy and to seize an advantage by exploiting the gaps in a controlled system. The tragic outcome of India's brave post-Independence experiment in social justice was an exponential growth in corruption, fraud and violence, as buying and selling invaded areas of life which were supposed to be beyond the market. We will consider the outcome of this erosion of civic responsibility for ordinary citizens in later chapters but here I am concerned with the affluent section of society, the people who were best able to manipulate the system. Accumulation of wealth could be through accepting bribes whilst occupying a strategic post in the bureaucracy or politics; it might be the result of successful business deals, pulled off because the way had been cleared by bribed officials; it could be straightforwardly illegal (smuggling, drug dealing, extortion, money laundering, kidnapping, etc.) with police or

political protection; or it could be the absolutely legal fees levied by the lawyers of any of the above who were caught out. (The daughter of a successful lawyer recounted that her father used to say, only half-jokingly, 'Don't worry, so long as there are *dacoits* in the hills, we'll be all right'.)

Of course, there was also legitimate wealth in the form of old money tracing back to colonial and pre-colonial systems of ownership of land and other property. Similarly, there were well-established industrial concerns, flourishing trade and active liberal professions, but, with restricted opportunities for untainted investment, there were few legal ways in which large-scale growth and accumulation of wealth could take place. Wealth taxes, urban and rural land ceilings (limits on the amount of land which could be held by an individual) and the public ownership of large corporations were intended to pave the way towards a more egalitarian society, but, perhaps inevitably, more concentrated effort went into subverting the socialist intentions of the system than maintaining it. It is well known that a great deal of wealth is still 'black'. One cannot attend a lavish wedding without hearing guests gossiping in a rather unspecific way about black money being the likely source of the hospitality; residences in prestigious housing developments and expensive imported cars are assumed to be at least partly paid for in cash but nobody has a clue just how big the black economy has been or still is.

Liberalization has provided legitimate outlets for the investment of accumulated wealth, whatever its original source. It has also provided legitimate means of obtaining very large incomes in a range of private entrepreneurial schemes, consultancies and senior management posts in multinational corporations. It is no longer the case that the only people who can legally earn global salaries are the fortunate few who can gain employment in international agencies. Liberalization has allowed wealth to come out from its hiding places into the public realm and it has simultaneously provided new ways of spending it. The old forms of wealth – gold, jewellery and houses – are not likely to go out of fashion, but the enthusiasm for more transient expressions of wealth such as luxury holidays, interior design, imported clothing, dining out, personal computers and family cars is catching on fast and discrepancies of wealth are more keenly felt by the finely differentiated strata of the relatively affluent.

CONSUMPTION OF SERVICES

Although the consumption of luxury goods is important as a status signifier, one of the major ways in which the élite differs from all those below it is in terms of its consumption of services. It is able to avoid consuming with the mass. Members of the upper middle class have good health insurance cover which allows them to visit the best private clinics and hospitals equipped to international standards (the very rich go abroad for major surgery). They avoid the routine fear of crime by living in gated and guarded colonies. They send their children to private schools in private school buses and they move about town, insulated from atrocious levels of pollution, in air-conditioned cars. They do not feel the effects of power or water rationing because they have their own private back-up supplies. When they travel long distances they will usually use public transport because road travel is slow, dangerous and tiring, but they will fly or travel air-conditioned on Indian Railways. Tourism is a relatively recent phenomenon amongst Indian people, who have tended to use their holidays visiting relatives in different parts of the country or abroad (there is however a long tradition of pilgrimage). Younger members of the élite, often to the disapproval of their elders who regard it as a waste of money, have begun to enjoy tourism at home and abroad. The relaxation of currency controls has meant that foreign holidays are possible and luxury vacations in exotic destinations like the Seychelles and the Alps seem high on the list of desires of the most well-off. Inside India, luxurious resorts and heritage hotels (converted palaces) no longer aim exclusively at the overseas tourist. There is a way of gliding through life in India without being exposed to any of the routine inconvenience, dirt and violence, and the people who take this route are as insulated from the hardships of the great mass of society as anyone from the equivalent class in the West.

COSMOPOLITANISM

Since the colonial era, the upper levels of metropolitan Indian society have been conscious of the importance of operating on an international scale as a means of preserving their impermeability to the classes below. Education has long been an important aspect of this and during the British raj many upper-class families strove to educate their sons expensively in the most exclusive British boarding schools and universities. The trend has continued and even expanded, though today, as Appadurai (1996, p. 2) points out, the hegemonic United States is a greater lure than declining Britain and the emphasis is on university education, rather than schooling abroad. In 1998, 33 818 people left India for places at American universities; 4 500 went to the United Kingdom and 4 100 to Australia (Chowdhury 1999). The outflow of funds for education is beginning to concern the Human Resources Development Ministry (Singh 1999) but it should also be worried about the cultural implications of the super-élite no longer obtaining an Indian higher education but becoming increasingly remote from the mass of the people.

There are many, connected, motives at work in the outlay of large sums of money in the overseas education of the children of the super élite. The first of these is the one already alluded to, whereby an unbridgeable gulf between the Very Rich and the merely well-off is constructed. An annual expenditure on one child at college in America is higher than the lifetime's earnings of a member of the lower middle class. Chowdhury (1999) cites a total expenditure of about Rs 20 lakh (see glossary) for a year spent obtaining an MBA in the United States. This expenditure results in qualifications which are internationally recognized and open up employment opportunities on a global scale; but such qualifications also put a candidate in a very strong position when competing for

FIGURE 2.1 Planning for an overseas education

senior positions in national and international corporations in India. Given the relatively poor facilities in many Indian universities, an overseas education is often, but not invariably, intrinsically superior to its Indian counterpart, but practically all of the several hundred young people I talked to at education fairs in four major Indian cities in 1998 said that they were interested in the international prestige of an overseas education rather than its inherent quality. They were also virtually all inclined towards professional training, particularly in Business Studies, rather than in a liberal education. The overseas education was desirable *because* it was expensive and because it was overseas. It is self-evident that for something to be regarded as exclusive, the majority must be denied access to it. The prestige accorded an overseas education itself devalues the reputation of an Indian education, but it also results in the super élite having little concern to raise the standard of local provision. It has a vested interest in ensuring that the gap is as wide as possible.

Overseas education is not just a matter of the content of the courses followed, it also socializes young people in what are taken for 'western' ways. The reason for my inverted commas is that what is both desired and derived is an exposure to globalized commodity culture, rather than the culture of organic communities in western settings. It is a culture for export which is recognized in those settings throughout the world which

can be regarded as international – offices, hotels, shopping malls, but also diplomacy, the conference circuit and the larger aid agencies. Its main value in an Indian context is that it establishes a rupture with the *deshi* culture of Indian-educated students and young people. A recent media example of this, played out from the point of view of affluent young people caught between two sets of cultural practices, is the film *Hyderabad Blues* (1998, Director: Nagesh Kukunoor), where a young man returns on holiday from America to find himself despising his home culture, but still loving his family and friends. The interest in this film is that the contrast is being made not between the 'authentic' American experience and Indian rural life or urban poverty but with 'westernized' urban people who have not lived abroad. The dialogue is in English since the film is aimed at the educated young across India and beyond. It is only a story – the protagonist ends up reassuring local sympathies by opting to realign himself with his roots – but when I saw the film in an affluent suburb of Delhi, it was obvious that many of the young men in the audience thought that his choice verged on lunacy and that he should have returned to America without qualms. They openly jeered at what they saw as a sop to those who would never have a real chance of getting away (had they been watching it in Europe or the United States they may have been more nostalgically sympathetic).

The ideal educational career of a very

wealthy young Indian man from a major city consists of nursery schooling at an exclusive, English-speaking establishment, followed by expensive primary education at an English-medium day school. At eleven he will probably go to one of the most renowned boarding schools, perhaps the former princely Mayo College in Ajmer or Doon School in Dehra Dun (Sanjay Srivastava (1998) provides an excellent account of the way in which Doon School socializes élite boys). After that, a place at one of the best colleges of the major metropolitan universities, such as St Stephen's, Delhi University or Presidency, Calcutta; then comes the move to an overseas university. The Indian schooling and college facilitate the establishment of good personal networks in the country, but the move overseas is seen as infinitely preferable to further Indian qualifications. Of course, only the very tiniest minority even of the élite achieves this ideal, but one does keep running into such people in important positions and their successes act as a further inducement to emulation. At an education fair in Hyderabad in 1998, a senior Andhra Pradesh politician stated quite categorically that families were willing to make huge sacrifices to educate their sons overseas, saying, 'Mothers will sell their jewellery to pay for it.' Of course the mothers had to have the jewellery in the first place. In this State, which is staking a great deal on building itself up as a centre of excellence in high-tech industries, and the knowledge business in general, it is interesting to see that the government line is to encourage overseas higher education as a means of establishing credibility.

PRIVATE EDUCATION

Private schooling in English is seen an essential requirement of the affluent middle classes and above and, as a consequence, school fees have a prior claim on household income over consumer goods. Although the media likes to report the material over-indulgence of middle-class children, the reality is that the big expenditure on children of both sexes is in terms of their education, rather than their leisure pursuits or possessions. A good day-school in a major city has fees of about Rs 8 000 a year; a place at one of the top boarding schools is about Rs 80 000.

The education of children of the élite is relentlessly directed towards achievement; even very young children are given punitive amounts of homework and anxious parents employ tutors after hours to keep them up to scratch in their weaker subjects. In addition there will be instruction in various accomplishments such as music and drawing. The children are taught a great deal but education all too often takes the form of rote learning and pouring information into them, rather than encouraging their own abilities. They are made competitive and taught to win because their families know that places in the super élite are scarce. The idea of the unbridgeable gulf between élite and non-élite education is internalized very early in life and children learn to see themselves as absolutely and essentially different from those in social groups below them. This was brought home clearly when an eleven-year-old child of an affluent family asked me about the British education system and I told him that the basic school leaving age was sixteen. He was incredulous, asserting that this was impossible in India where *everyone* had to go on being educated until after their Master's degree. When I challenged this, reminding him that lots of people in India never went to school at all, he looked scornful at my naïvety and sniffed, 'That is an altogether different matter!' So, *everyone* receives a long and expensive education in order to separate him or her absolutely from the ranks of *no one*.

India spends a scandalously small proportion of its education budget on schools and a remarkably large amount on higher education. The poor provision of free schooling means that a disproportionate number of unreserved places at the highly subsidized universities are won by those who have received a private schooling – a good reason for those who can afford it to invest in the school days of their children, but also a good reason for them not to be concerned to raise standards in government schools. The class of professionals and bureaucrats reproduces itself through its appropriation of higher education of a high standard. But a degree is no guarantee of career success; it needs to be reinforced by connections and lifestyle.

FAMILIES

There is probably no area of Indian life that is more idealized than that of the family: one's base, one's moral and financial support. The huge and loving Indian extended family is a familiar cliché, but families are stuck together with social glue, not just blood magic, and when societies change, families change too. From what I have been saying about education, it is obvious that the family makes considerable investment in its replacement generations and acts consciously to reproduce and improve its social and economic standing. Formal education, however, is only one part of this process.

Every social anthropologist knows that 'family' is a portmanteau word – you can put an awful lot of different meanings into it. For a great many people, the 'ideal' Indian family is the type often referred to as the 'extended family', but technically known as the 'paternal joint family'. It typically consists of a senior couple plus their married sons, the sons' wives and children, and any unmarried sons and daughters; there might also be the widowed mother of the senior man. Today this family type is most often associated with land ownership but it is also found amongst members of the traditional affluent urban population, particularly traders and contractors. (Menon and Shweder [1998] offer an interesting present-day account of extended family amongst wealthy traders in Bhubaneshwar.) This kind of family depends on there being family property as a source of livelihood (land or a business) and this being owned and administered by a senior man, with his sons as his helpers. In Indian legal terms, it is known as the 'Hindu Undivided Family' and is recognized as a single taxable unit, where the family is assessed as a whole rather than as a collection of individuals. Apart from unmarried daughters, the women in such a family are not related to each other or the men,

except through marriage. When relationships between the members of an extended family are amicable, this is a most rewarding way of conducting family life; both men and women have others with whom to share their work, their worries and their leisure; old people are guaranteed the support of the next generation and continue to be useful to their children; children grow up amongst grandparents, uncles and aunts, and have cousins who are so close that they are referred to as brothers and sisters. When there are tensions, this kind of family is quite famously almost intolerable especially for the younger married women.

The paternal joint family is by no means as common as is often supposed. Amongst modern affluent people, the usual residential unit is the nuclear family, sometimes with extensions – an elderly parent or a married son or daughter (but rarely more than one) with their small children. The nuclear family is becoming normal, not just in the statistical sense but also as the preferred type. The

FIGURE 2.2 Patriarch and grandson in Bharwani, a *mofussil* town

extensions I referred to are coming to be regarded as expedient, established in order to support a frail parent who was having difficulty alone, or to help a married daughter maintain her career after her children were born. It is hardly surprising that the nuclear family is the preferred form amongst élite sections of urban society; now that incomes are derived from professional or managerial positions in large corporations rather than from land or family firms, the joint family is rarely a producing group with a shared income. Given that young people can earn individual incomes, it would be unusual were they to be willing to pool these into a large joint family housekeeping unit. Instead, affluent young married couples seek to set up homes on their own and to cultivate a lifestyle rather different from that of the previous generation. Brides have always found it difficult to adjust to moving into their husbands' households and have traditionally found relationships with their mothers-in-law strained; today they not only prefer to have their own households, but increasing numbers have the means to obtain them. The new apartment blocks targeted at wealthy urban society are designed for nuclear, not joint families.

However, just because more people live in nuclear family-based households, we should not assume that society is necessarily becoming more atomized. The death of the Indian extended family has been much exaggerated. Here I am not referring to the paternal joint family, which is by definition a residential unit, but to all of the ways in which a range of relatives interact and support each other. The joint family made it difficult for a married woman to interact with her own relatives; she was supposed to transfer her loyalty to her husband's family (that is to say her husband's father's family, for her mother-in-law would have experienced the same separation). To some extent, one can say that young women belonged to traditional families in the same way as possessions belong, rather than as members. The rupture of the joint family allows for other family links to be continued and for women to maintain relations with their parents and married sisters and brothers and their children in a co-operation between households. The web of effective kinship links is becoming more extensive at the same time as the intensive and exclusive paternal joint family is going out of favour.

MARRIAGE

Nowhere is the extent of kinship more apparent than at a wedding. During auspicious seasons for marriage it has always been difficult to get a booking at short notice on a long-distance train in India; now the same phenomenon relates to international flights, as far-flung extended families re-unite. Generally speaking, weddings are the most elaborate where marriage is a structurally significant institution; if there should ever be a decline in the importance of the web of bilateral kinship for élite groups in India, then we shall probably see a movement towards more modest wedding celebrations focusing on close family and friends – but that is likely to be far into the future. As it is, the majority of weddings are large, elaborate and very expensive.

Middle-class families save and invest for their daughters' marriages and LIC (Life Insurance Corporation) hoardings seek to attract these huge savings into the national insurance system by playing on fears that a family may have to go into debt in order to marry their daughter 'well'. A lavish wedding in a metropolitan city in India can seem like a carnival and, sitting in a marriage hall decked with thousands of flowers, carpeted with costly rugs, fountains playing, huge mechanical peacocks turning and spreading their tails, bands playing, tables groaning with food and drink, liveried waiters bearing trays of delicacies to thousands of guests, it is hard to remember that the bill is being met privately. In addition to the cost of hospitality and entertainment, the bride's family will also have given expensive presents to honoured guests: silk sarees, silverware and so on. The wedding of Jayalalita's adopted son in Madras shocked even those accustomed to incredible levels of expenditure; obscene displays of wealth and power were paraded before the people – mounted police and soldiers in special feudal costume escorted the wedding party, the streets were decorated, mountains of expensive gifts were distributed, dazzling clothes and jewels were worn – everything was orchestrated to signify that the Chief Minister of Tamil Nadu was above and beyond the law. It was certainly not a normal wedding (to start with, it was arranged by the groom's family) but it was the extreme culmination of a practice which is generally understood – that a wedding is used to make a public statement of the standing of a family in its socially significant milieu. Lavish weddings are illegal and there is a limit to the size of a wedding party – not that anyone cares to do anything about it.

DOWRY

Weddings are not the only expense of a marriage; in most cases they are not even the major expense. Structurally far more important than the display of affluence is the transfer of wealth between families in the form of marriage settlements. These take the form of dowries paid by the bride's family and will be examined in more detail in Chapter Nine. The payment of dowry is a much maligned practice because perverted forms of dowry can cause much suffering – but dowry only becomes corrupt when social and gender relations are themselves corrupted. Dowry is the means whereby when a woman marries she takes wealth from the family she comes from into the family she marries. Remembering that the traditional joint family was an economic unit, it was reasonable for a woman entering it to bring her contribution to its working capital, taking her share of the inheritance she would otherwise have been due. Dowry was intended to give a degree of dignity to a young married woman, but Chapter Nine will look at the many problems which can arise in a consumerist society.

I referred earlier to women selling their jewellery to finance their sons' education. Most of that jewellery would have been part of her dowry. It should be hers and she should be able to decide how to dispose of it. An upper-middle-class girl will be given several sets (three seems to be regarded as the minimum decently acceptable) of heavy gold jewellery, usually encrusted with precious stones. Most of the time it is kept safely in a bank vault, but it will be taken out to be worn on special occasions. It will also be refashioned periodically by a trusted family jeweller and it will be added to in the form of gifts from one's husband or mother and perhaps a small inheritance from one's maternal grandmother. Women think strategically about their jewellery and its value; they are reluctant to sell it other than to make an investment – such as the deposit on an apartment – since it gives them independence within their marriage and it forms the core of their own daughters' dowries. They are reluctant to allow their husbands and affines (in-laws) to have any control of their jewellery, and therein lies the source of the problems we will look at later.

Apart from jewellery, a middle-class dowry will contain a large number of silk sarees, which should, in theory, keep the bride respectably dressed for the rest of her life; it can consist of cash, a car or scooter, consumer durables, a house or apartment, shares, help with setting up a business or professional practice. All of these are less obviously the exclusive property of the bride; traditionally this sort of wealth would have merged into the holdings of the groom's joint family but today it is increasingly the means whereby a young couple establishes itself independently. I am trying to make it clear that dowry, when it has not been perverted by unscrupulous people, is the generous endowing of a young couple by the concerned parents of the bride. Why only the bride's family? Because the groom's family will have invested in the groom himself – his education, career and contacts – and will also provide him with an inheritance which, as Indian feminists (Sen 1995) are at pains to point out, usually exceeds the amount paid to their sisters in dowry.

Even amongst families which consider the payment of dowry to be ideologically unacceptable, one finds the generous giving of gifts to daughters when they marry. In a society where men are still seen as the main providers for their families and have considerable control over their wives, it would be difficult to imagine parents who could afford it denying their daughters some personal security in marriage.

In the sections of society we are concerned with in this chapter, 'self-arranged' or 'love' marriages are becoming common, but they are still outnumbered by parentally-arranged marriages. When a family is looking for a suitable partner for its son or daughter, it will be concerned with social, economic and personal criteria, in much the same way as an individual is when contemplating marriage, but without the dubious benefits of romantic haze. It should not surprise us to find that self-arranged and parentally-arranged marriages are generally indistinguishable in social terms, but for some reason the popular assumption is that 'love' marriages fly in the face of social divisions and conventions, transcending class and caste in defiance of parental wishes. The reality is that, in a society where family is so important, people usually fall in love with someone their parents approve of – someone they met at college or at work – perhaps not *exactly* the person their parents would have chosen, but rarely someone who is totally unacceptable. To cut oneself off from one's family in a marriage which it rejects is an almost certain recipe for unhappiness in any society, but particularly so in one in which kinship networks count for so much. Patricia Uberoi (1998) refers to this practice as the 'arranged love marriage'.

Many westerners have great difficulty with the idea of arranged marriage and are surprised to find it persisting amongst those sections of Indian society which are educated, affluent and cosmopolitan. Probably the most important thing is to forget about compulsion and to think about encouragement and facilitation. Families conspire amongst their contacts to present young people with the best possible marriage opportunities (though of course not everyone invariably trusts parental tastes in these matters). What family anywhere in the world does not think affluent is better than impoverished, secure career is better than casual employment, educated is better than uneducated, healthy is better than sickly, well connected is better than marginalized, beautiful is better than ugly? But families, like individuals, have to make compromises when putting together the bundle of attributes in an acceptable partner. Dowry can make quite a difference in tipping the scales when the characteristics of a boy and girl are being weighed up and a girl's family will often stretch itself as far as it can to make a good match for its daughter.

Although the matrimonial advertisements in the national newspapers are a very visible sign of the first stages of the arrangement of marriages, for the sections of society we are considering they represent the breakdown of the system, since, ideally, a suitable match should be possible by using one's own network of contacts. Advertising or responding to an advertisement is a statement of one's inability to make the right contacts otherwise; it probably indicates that one is upwardly socially mobile, has 'new' (perhaps suspect) money. It is also resorted to by people who experience difficulty in making a match for their children who have some form of disadvantage or disability and will be willing to lower their sights socially.

Arranging a marriage is always a delicate matter; obviously the happiness of the young couple is important, but it goes well beyond this. Kinship networks are extended every time a marriage takes place – a girl obtains a husband, parents-in-law, brothers and sisters-in-law, grandparents-in-law and so on, but her parents, brothers and sisters also get a whole range of affines (in-laws). The relationships between brothers-in-law and co-sons-in-law (the husbands of a group of sisters) are often very important in affluent urban society as they constitute a peer group made up of family members – people one ought to be able to trust above mere friends. Extended kin are an important means whereby support can be recruited, information is gathered, further contacts are made, favours are solicited, jobs and contracts secured. All this means that, when a marriage is being arranged, the reputations of one's prospective spouse's kin are carefully considered, as are the contacts they can provide. Too many divorces, mental breakdowns, political scandals or criminal cases on either the boy's or girl's side will lower the family's, and thus the individual's, social standing. The previous marriages that have been made by the family with whom an alliance is sought are very important – if a girl has married well, her younger brother's network of contacts improves, his marriage-ability is increased and, along with it, the amount of dowry he can command in a wife. With his marriage into a wealthy family of good standing, his younger relatives become even more attractive to families looking for partners.

I have deliberately avoided mentioning caste, not because it is unimportant in understanding social stratification in India, but because people brought up in the West all too often make an exact equation between caste and class. However, when considering marriages it is never possible to keep caste out of the conversation for long. One of the major requirements of a 'good' marriage continues to be that both families belong to the same *jati* and ideally the boy's family should be of superior status (within the *jati*) to the girl's. It should be obvious from what I have been saying about the strategic considerations involved in making an élite marriage that the preference for caste endogamy (marrying inside the group) is a vital way of strengthening the internal networks of *jati* and of keeping influence and wealth within relatively closed boundaries. Marriage is the means whereby the politics and economics of kinship are transacted and is a major reason why I did not want to overemphasize productive position as the basis of hierarchy in affluent urban India.

THE NEW SERVICE CLASS

It is in the major cities (Delhi, Mumbai, Calcutta and Chennai) and new growth poles (such as Bangalore, Hyderabad, Pune and Kochi) that we find a new Indian service class coming into being. This new middle class invariably builds on the prior existence of a traditional urban middle class (whether administrative, professional or commercial) and a local history of prestigious higher education and research institutes. This section of society straddles the categories 'Very Rich', upper and lower middle classes, with the upper middle predominating, but the 'Very Rich' acting as influential role models (Mitra 1999). The new service class consists of people who in the past would almost certainly have made their careers in government service; they are the people who, in Bourdieu's terms, have 'cultural capital', that is, they live off their superior education. Again, we cannot avoid thinking about caste, since *brahmins* have controlled knowledge since time immemorial. *Brahmins* constitute the (supposed) pinnacle of both systems of caste; caste as *varna* (ancient religious categories) and caste as *jati* (endogamous social groups associated with traditional occupations). Traditionally the *Brahmins* specialized in religious activities, and many are still priests, but, with British rule, many transferred their knowledge base from Sanskrit to English in order to specialize in clerical work, the liberal professions, science, administration and academia. They virtually took over the government service at Independence.

As the New Economic Policy gains ground in India and more remunerative employment is to be found in the private sector than in the state bureaucracy, the new generation of *brahmins* is attracted into the cutting edge professions – management, finance, corporate and international law and the high-tech industries. They are also massively involved in the globalization process both in India and as diaspora. Young, highly-educated *brahmins* are seeking and training for a global career, mainly because much higher professional incomes are available abroad but also because of political shifts away from *brahminic* hegemony in favour of the 'backward' sections of society. Mandalization means that *brahmins* believe they are now discriminated against in the allocation of university places and government jobs, because close to 50 per cent of places are reserved for people coming from 'Scheduled Castes, Scheduled Tribes and Other Backward Classes' (all official terms). Given that *brahmins* constitute rather less than 10 per cent of the population, it is hard to sympathize very much with their complaints, but this well-established élite feels beleaguered and is fast adopting coping strategies.

Research in progress on the software

industry in Bangalore (Asser 1998) shows that *brahmins* virtually monopolize the industry in management, research and development, whether we are looking at small local firms or the Indian branches of multinationals. When questioned, managers denied any positive discrimination or caste nepotism in the recruitment of staff and, given that there is a sellers' market for the good programmers, Asser is inclined to agree that the industry is *brahmin* dominated because it is the *brahmins* India-wide who have so conscientiously specialized in information technology. She shows that when they reach their mid to late twenties they seek employment in the United States, where their high-level skills are much in demand, but that currently significant numbers return in their early forties to take on managerial positions, make sure that their children get a good private secondary education and settle down to an affluent lifestyle financed out of their expatriate savings.

The advertising pitch made by property developers in Bangalore certainly bears out Asser's findings, as new residential complexes seek to emulate an affluent American lifestyle, with guarded compounds providing club facilities and swimming pools. Bangalore, long famous for its weapons industry, has become the high-tech capital of India; like other new service-class dominated towns it has rapidly developed a plethora of secondary services catering to the cosmopolitan aspirations of the young affluent – restaurants serving 'continental' cuisine, the full range of international fast-food outlets, pubs and clubs, 'designer' clothing, hairdressers, florists, interior design consultants (*Inside Outside*, India's first and leading glossy interior design magazine, quite typically is based in Bangalore and the advertisements it carries demonstrate a local abundance of high quality providers).

The software industry is not exclusively male. Girls from middle-class *brahmin* families have long received a higher education (though often not as expensively as their brothers) and over the past decade have increasingly seen the advantage of moving into information technology rather than the more traditionally 'feminine' subjects which lead to less remarkable career paths. Delayed age of marriage and dual career families are becoming the norm.

INDUSTRIAL AND COMMERCIAL ÉLITES

Along with the new service class, it is the industrial and commercial élites who have profited the most from liberalization and there have been obvious and radical increases in their ability to make and spend money. A number of the smaller cities have suddenly boomed as investment opportunities have emerged. The Gujarat 'industrial corridor', focusing on Ahmedabad and Surat, has the dubious reputation of having allowed its investors to grow rich by adopting a notoriously lax attitude to pollution but the already industrial region has seen dramatic growth, thanks to accumulated local capital and investments on the part of the huge Gujarati diaspora. Other notable growth cities have been the port and steel town of Visakhapatnam, the textiles centre of Coimbatore and the port of Kochi. In all of these centres there have been property booms and the rapid enrichment of local builders and contractors.

This particular class fraction has many political similarities to its counterparts elsewhere in the world; it manifests the right-wing tendency towards glorification of the market and opposes government expenditure other than on infrastructure and defence. In caste terms, this class tends to draw upon *jati* generally classified as *vaishya*, traditionally associated with trade, jewellery and money-lending, and is characterized by others as inward looking and rigidly community conscious. Although properly the term applies to shopkeepers, the name *baniya* is applied, often derisively, by members of other communities, implying an obsession with making profits. In return, this section of society claims that its accumulation of wealth is justified by arguing that it is only through the 'trickle-down' effects of its own enrichment and increased efficiency that the poor of India will ever rise above levels of destitution. Vanaik (1990), referring to what he sees as the Thatcherization of the Indian middle classes in the 1980s, asserts that the trickle-down thesis simply 'legitimizes the growing unconcern in an increasingly hedonistic middle class and the Americanized upper élite about "the other India"'' (p. 56).

'Increasingly hedonistic' and 'Americanized' are intended pejoratively and to mark the shift of this class, which was so important in the Independence movement and the years following Independence, from any pretence of social conscience and one nationhood. We are considering a section of society which prefers to look West for its symbols of status and which seems to be able to plug into the most crass forms of consumerism.

I shall end this section with a vignette based on a news story which much exercised the 'chattering classes' in Delhi, and elsewhere, in January 1999. A group of young men who had been to a night-club set off in the early hours of the morning in a very expensive, imported BMW. The driver, the son of a licensed arms dealer and the grandson of a retired admiral, was home on vacation from his American university where he was following a course in business administration. All of the men, including the driver, were very drunk. The car swerved into a group of five policemen, killing them all. They did not stop, but took the car to Delhi's most affluent suburb to be washed and concealed, dragging the body of one of the policemen several miles.

It is a grisly tale by any standards, but it contains all of the ingredients I have been referring to – overindulged and irresponsible young men; a 'westernized' pattern of consumption (night-club, drinking); an overpowered foreign car; an American education; a wealthy father, whom many criticized for using his intimate family network of senior army and navy officers to his advantage in the arms trade; the callous attitude of the seriously affluent to the lower middle classes; the assumption that the rich can get away with their crimes. The story rapidly became an allegory for the state of the urban élite. The press went to town and the story rolled on for several weeks – the press variously used the

event to criticize westernization, parental neglect, the breakdown of the family, the irresponsibility of the young; but some commentators asked whether the accident would have received so much attention had it been a bus or a rickshaw that killed the policemen, implying that the affluent were being picked upon unfairly. Some later reports said that the young man was contrite, had refused special privileges in prison and had started to give lessons to his fellow inmates; others latched onto the fact that his father had offered immediate payment to the bereaved families and interpreted this as an attempt to buy them off, though the alternative interpretation was that he was making an *ex gratia* payment to alleviate suffering; some suggested that the accused would be bailed and never really have to face his responsibilities, given the slowness of Indian justice. The event frightened affluent parents; they expressed fears that their children could not handle the rapid changes, had no moral basis to work from, and were often concerned as to how they could give their offspring the advantages of wealth without seeing them corrupted by it. The case became a focus for almost every possible position on the social outcomes of the liberalization of the Indian economy, but the most strongly held view was that the extreme wealth of a tiny minority held no benefits for anyone else (Thapar and Ramani 1999). When the Jessica Lal murder story broke a few months later (see Chapter Seven) the whole debate opened once again.

SOCIAL CONSCIOUSNESS

So far I have written as if the whole of the affluent urban élite is obsessed with increasing its income and its social prestige, manipulating personal networks and flaunting its wealth. It is easy to fall into the trap of representing this category of society as selfish and superficial because much of the time this is exactly how it represents itself in the media and literature. It is here that we have a contradiction: the media, literature and academia are dominated by people from the same educational and social backgrounds as those who are going into corporate finance. It is quite difficult in India to find right-wing social theorists (though right-wing economists proliferate) and even pro-liberalization publications like *India Today* regularly carry scathing critiques of the lifestyles of the most affluent.

India has a free press which should be the envy of the world. Although it permits the import of foreign publications, it remains the law that Indian newspapers cannot have international owners – despite his best efforts Rupert Murdoch has not been able to take control of the prestigious English-print media in India. Although Ajit Bhattacharjea, the Chairman of the Press Institute of India, deplores what he sees as the post-liberalization trivialization of the news (personal communication), most outsiders are impressed not only by the seriousness and depth of coverage and the quality of writing but also the obvious freedom of journalists from excessive control. But the free press is not just a matter of large circulation newspapers: there are hundreds of good quality small journals, local publishing houses for monographs and experimental literature; there are also political pamphleteers, video makers and theatre groups – many of which are linked to social movements or specific causes and issues.

A significant section of the Indian educated élite is dedicated to socialist or Gandhian principles and to social causes. There is a thriving feminist movement; there are anti-corruption campaigns; there is support for health, welfare and education programmes for poor people in urban and rural areas; there is a considerable concern for the environment and a growing anti-nuclear movement; there is agitation on human rights issues and opposition to communalist tendencies. Some of this is intensely political – a great deal takes the form of consciousness raising and communication – but much is directed towards nothing more than sponsorship of crafts and fund-raising charities. Virtually all, for better or worse, is masterminded by people who are part of the educated élite and can be seen as the inheritors of the anti-imperialist legacy of the Independence

FIGURE 2.3 Affluent liberals are the patrons at craft fairs

struggle. This section of the élite is full of contradictions: it is often as internationally orientated as any other strand of the upper middle class, travelling to conventions and conferences, keeping itself abreast of international intellectual trends and making extensive use of global communications, including the Internet (there is a list of websites in the bibliography of this book to take you into a sample of the concerns of this fraction of Indian society).

Characteristically, members of this section of society are employed in the liberal professions, academia, the arts and media, some elements of the administrative service, or they work for international agencies or local non-governmental agencies (NGOs). Although it abhors ostentation, its members are often acutely aesthetically aware and design conscious, marrying their tastes with their ethical concerns to emphasize traditional craft work and natural products in a style which was dubbed 'ethnic chic' in India long before the term migrated west. This is the market for classical music and dance, theatre and the serious cinema and yet it finds itself ideologically opposed to the narrow nationalism of neo-*swadeshi*.

Practically all of the Indian references in this book are written by people who come from this section of the educated upper middle class, people who are urbane, intellectual and socially aware. They are still a privileged élite but they are acutely aware of it. The one area in which few people have any hesitation or guilt about conforming to their class position is in the education of their own children, and these attend the same exclusive schools as the market orientated section of the middle class, perpetuating their families' privileged positions. Given the poor standard of government schools, this is entirely understandable and even commendable for those who value knowledge and the ability to communicate their views.

3

THE MIDDLE MASS

The poorest section of the urban middle class, with a household income of around three to five thousand rupees a month, is potentially the most dangerous section of Indian society. Like squeezed lower middle classes everywhere and throughout modern history, it has considerable potential for revolution or extreme right-wing reaction.

As Ashis Nandy (1998a) so eloquently points out, members of the urban lower middle class live in fear of the slum, the fear that a precarious security will be shattered, that a hard-won respectability will be stripped away. Only a slim margin divides the lower middle classes from the poor. The people I am referring to in this chapter are the around 10 million households of clerical workers, typists, social workers, telephone operators, ticket inspectors, policemen, non-commissioned officers in the armed services, junior school teachers and so on. In the past this class was almost entirely in government or quasi-governmental service, and a fair proportion of it still is, but although (once a post has been landed) government employment is as safe as anything can be, there are constant worries about the erosion of real income, impoverished retirement and, more than anything, the job prospects of one's children. This class finds that reproducing itself over generations is a continuous battle against the aspirations of those in the classes below. For those people who are not in government employment, job security is poor and the competition for employment daunt-

ing. Praful Bidwai (1997) gives a poignant example of a young freelance journalist who had not found work in months turning in anger and despair on his wife and being so close to starvation that he died when she returned his blows. Malnutrition does not just affect those without an education in a society where there is no unemployment pay. Bidwai (1995, 1997) is adamant that the post-1991 New Economic Policy is radically impoverishing the poor and the lower middle classes, as workers, including clerical workers, are squeezed out of employment when public sector industrial units are privatized. Even those in work are impoverished by the deliberate curtailment of the Public Distribution System (fair price ration shops run by the government).

HOUSEHOLDS

Households which are categorized as lower middle class will rarely have working wives and mothers, although an extra income would make a difference. The reason for this is that, since families of this section of society are more likely to invest in their daughters' marriages than in their education, its women have domestic skills rather than those which would fit them for the kind of employment their families would regard as respectable. In the past, households in this sector of society would have a high probability of having some paternal joint element; young women moving into their husbands' parents' households on marriage and living at close quarters to their mothers-in-law, even though younger families would often seek to strike out on their own before a fully-fledged paternal joint family was established. Today one finds that the nuclear family (perhaps with the addition of a widowed elderly parent or a young relative) is the norm. The care of children becomes almost the sole responsibility of mothers in nuclear families.

It is a truism of Indian sociology that as families' fortunes improve, they demonstrate their new economic and social status by withdrawing their womenfolk from work in the public domain; this applies as much in urban as rural areas (although much of the foundational work on the subject was on farming families) (Epstein 1962; Das 1976; Srinivas 1977). Hilary Standing's (1991) study of women's employment in Calcutta demonstrates that it is the poor and the college-educated women of the upper middle classes who are most likely to be in paid employment. Notions of respectability and family duty keep most lower-middle-class women from being willing to be seen to need to take up paid work, although, as Standing points out (p. 52), there is considerable disguised employment in the form of home-working, which usually brings in only a pittance.

MARRIAGE

Marriage is clearly an important institution for this section of society with its reverence for domesticity and family virtues. Virtually all marriages are arranged by family; the upper-class 'love' marriages are regarded as scandalous because they imply immodest behaviour on the part of the young. Girls in particular tend to marry young, in their teens and very early twenties, and boys in their mid twenties. Most marriages will begin in the home of the husband's family and, given the small size of apartments, there is little privacy for the young couple. Unlike a traditional rural paternal joint family, there will not be a range of younger women to befriend the bride; she is on her own with her mother-in-law, who can scarcely help being resentful of the young intruder.

Although dowries are by no means as lavish as those paid by the more affluent sections of society, the dowry is crucial to making a 'good' marriage – that is, one to a boy with a reliable source of income and preferably a family with property. The same ideas about the network of affinal and kinship ties applies for the lower middle classes as for the classes above – a 'good' alliance improves the marriage chances of one's younger siblings and the standing of one's family as a whole. The chain of dowry payments is virtually unbreakable by any individual; a boy cannot easily marry without taking dowry (in a love match) because in doing so he will jeopardize his sisters' opportunity of marrying well (or at all), since much of the dowry a boy's bride brings in will be transferred out as dowry for his sisters or will pay off old debts incurred with the marriages of sisters who married before him. Incoming dowry can be used to settle other debts, like those incurred for the boy's education, or it can meet household expenses. Dowry may be jewellery or cash, but it can also be consumer durables for the joint household. Here we can see that the idea of dowry as a woman's own property giving her security inside her marriage has virtually disappeared.

What I am about to describe is very much an extreme and minority occurrence, but it serves to demonstrate the structural tensions inherent in the system of dowry-taking in modern circumstances of wage labour. Indian feminists have highlighted the phenomenon of 'dowry murders', whereby rather too many young women die as a consequence of their in-laws deciding that insufficient dowry has been paid. The usual practice is for mothers-in-law to fake kitchen accidents with kerosene stoves. A widowed boy can remarry and take a second dowry. Far more young women find themselves the brunt of systematic ill-treatment and humiliation with the suggestion that their families have cheated by paying less than they promised or that the bride was less valuable than she had been represented as being; this is designed to persuade the women to try to extort more wealth from their own families. It must be stressed that, though these cases get a great deal of publicity, they are far from being the norm; most girls experience no more than routine friction with their in-laws and most mothers-in-law are neither murderesses nor torturers. The pain and violence consequent upon pathological situations emerge from routine desperation about survival.

A bride is supposed to bear sons. Sons support their families and bring in dowry whereas daughters leave the home and take wealth with them. Daughters are valued as individuals and it is also considered sad if a man does not have a sister, but a family with more girls than boys has problems with raising the dowry that will allow them to marry. Despite the fact that men determine the sex of children, it is the wife who will be blamed if boys are not born – this can be another element in the issue of persecution and 'dowry murders'.

FIGURE 3.1 Shopping for brassware

STANDARD OF LIVING

What sort of standard of living are we considering for the people we are thinking about? In a large city, some could be living in slum accommodation – in the sense of overcrowded tenements with shared facilities – but only in the most deprived of circumstances would we find people we could classify as middle class living in the *bustees*. Here life for women is a continuous struggle against dirt and what they regard as disreputable influences as they strive to make a decent home. People in government employment often have highly subsidized (virtually free) accommodation provided as part of their conditions of service, living in railway, police, etc. 'colonies' consisting of small two- or three-roomed apartments. Those employed in the private sector will aim to provide a similar standard for themselves by renting. The accommodation will usually be modestly furnished, and generally at least one person sleeps in the main living space. Such households are beginning to constitute a market for consumer durables, often purchased through credit schemes, though saved up for by the more frugal. It is no

longer surprising to find a refrigerator in a lower middle class home – though they are still regarded as luxuries – but tape recorders and televisions are almost ubiquitous.

This category of people buys few imported goods, as is obvious when one considers the Indian prices for 'global' products I quoted in the previous chapter. They constitute the major market for the expanding Indian consumer goods industries and for faked 'brands'. The nature of their employment is such that they must retain a smart appearance and their notions of respectability require the same of their families.

In terms of foodstuffs, they also draw upon the local market. In 1998 the insecure coalition government became very rattled when a combination of failed harvest and market manipulation caused the price of onions to rocket out of the price range of all but the wealthy (onions are a near necessity in northern Indian cuisine and widely used elsewhere). The shortfall had not been anticipated in time for import controls on the vegetable to be lifted before the crisis hit. The press became full of stories of possible shortages of other essential foodstuffs, like rice, highlighting the extreme sensitivity of the poor and middle classes to the price of food which is by far the biggest element of household expenditure, with little margin to absorb price rises. This class of people bears the brunt of local price inflation, being acutely responsive to increases in the cost of foodstuffs, kerosene, bus fares, whilst they struggle to set aside savings against misfortune, dowries, retirement and to educate their children.

Convenience foods are not particularly common in India (and by convenience foods I mean foodstuffs which are taken for granted in most western households like packaged flour, instant coffee, ground spices and ready made bread – I am not referring to frozen TV dinners). In wealthy households servants take on the drudgery associated with food preparation; in lower-middle-class households a great deal of a woman's day will be taken up with picking over lentils and grains to remove the inevitable debris of sticks and grit, grinding and chopping, making heaps of *chapattis*. Such women will probably make their own pickles, preserves and cordials from fruits and vegetables when they are in season and they will dry mint etc. They will learn to become frugal shoppers and household managers in order to provide within their means and, even if the family is not vegetarian for caste or ideological reasons, one will find little meat eaten other than on special occasions. Beyond this, housewives will usually cultivate other skills which add to the standard of living of their family, repairing and making clothes for their children (and sometimes husbands), knitting winter garments, making those household goods which help to enhance the respectability of the family and the comfort of the home – chair-covers, embroideries, and the like.

The nature of food preparation leads us into some circular arguments about women's roles; a 'good' wife and mother provides directly for her family and this level of care is seen to be forgone if she is out in paid employment all day – hence only in a struggling lower-middle-class family will a woman work outside the home. A woman working at home can considerably reduce the housekeeping bills and her contribution to the household is in economizing rather than earning. Then again, one can also argue that the laborious work is only economically viable because of the perceived lack of value of women's time. Certainly any woman of this class who takes paid employment finishes up with a very heavy double workload.

TRANSPORT

Low-cost decent housing is hard to find in the larger cities and workers often have long journeys to their place of employment, usually by bus or train or, if close enough, bicycle. In the major cities, local public transport is very poor – irregular, massively overcrowded, dirty and in a poor state of repair. All commuters complain vociferously about it for it exhausts and demoralizes them as well as adding to the length of their working day. Taxis and auto-rickshaws are far too expensive to be used on a regular basis, so it is little wonder that a major aspiration is the purchase of a motor scooter. With easier credit facilities and increased levels of production, the past decade has seen an explosion in the volume of motorized traffic on the roads of the major cities as the ownership of scooters has proliferated among the lower middle class. (As Chapter Eleven will show, there are considerable environmental consequences of this.)

SERVICES

Where the lower middle class feels particularly deprived in relation to the wealthier classes above is in the realm of services, including education. Supply of services in the public sector is erratic and generally of poor quality. In most large towns there is 'load shedding' of electricity – this is a euphemism for not providing a continuous electricity supply because of lack of capacity. Affluent people routinely install electricity generators or inverters (which store power in large batteries) in their homes to cut in when the power from the grid fails. These are

FIGURE 3.2 A modest private hospital in Gwalior

expensive to buy and, in the case of the generators, expensive to run. The piped water supply is rationed too in many cities; this does not affect wealthy people who have their own storage tanks (even in apartment blocks) to even out the supply and circumvent the rationing. The poorer people have to make do with a few buckets.

More worrying is the provision of health care. Ill health in the family can cause serious suffering to people in the lower middle classes as they try to afford private medicine. This becomes particularly acute if hospital treatment is required. Many plan for this by taking out health insurance policies. There are no significant welfare payments for people who become chronically sick and cannot work; people try to save against this and hope they can rely on family reciprocal care.

EDUCATION

This is an educated class of people, frequently with qualifications much higher than one would expect for their standard of living and type of employment in a western context. Many have university degrees and virtually all men have completed 12 years of schooling. This category of society is literate, informed and politically aware. It exercises a considerable demand for newspapers and periodicals. For all this, it is not invariably intellectual in its tastes.

As the previous chapter suggested, the divide between the comfortable élites and the rest of society rests in large part on the nature, as well as length, of formal education and the point of differentiation is at school rather than college level. State education is widely regarded as a scandal, with poor standards of provision and high incidence of teacher absenteeism. The curriculum is pedestrian and uninspiring and levels of achievement are low. The medium of instruction in government schools is predominantly Hindi or a State language, although English may also be taught to older children as a second language. Though there are plenty of good reasons for not using English as a medium for education in terms of not undervaluing local languages and not discouraging the mass of children from attending school, it cannot be denied that it puts children educated in this system at a considerable disadvantage in the market for the jobs which would allow them to partake of the benefits of the newly liberalized economy. As a consequence, middle-class families do everything they can to educate their sons (in particular) in the many small private, profit-making, English-medium schools, often not of very high standard and with underqualified teachers.

Box 9 A middle–middle class school

Having sent my son to what was supposed to be one of the better (and slightly more expensive) of these schools for a short while, I feel more qualified than most to comment on the quality of this sort of education, where computer science was taught without the benefit of a computer (and the textbook implied that floppy disks really were still floppy), the sciences managed without a lab and even PE was taught from a book rather than in the playground. I decided he'd be better off reading at home the day that his English teacher had marked as 'wrong' his reasoned answer to the question 'Do you like this poem?' (The 'correct' answer was 'Yes, I like this poem.') The school cost Rs 3 000 a year, plus uniform and books, a struggle for a lower middle class family. But at least the teachers did attend and the lessons proceeded regularly.

INSECURITY

I hope I am conveying the fact that, for the large lower middle class, life is a continuous struggle against real impoverishment and loss of the few advantages they have. In the post-liberalization era, these people are acutely aware of the gulf which is widening between themselves and the more privileged. They are becoming absolutely and relatively poorer in a world where new wealth and new and blatant forms of consumption are characterizing cosmopolitan India. This insecurity is translated into political and cultural tactics intended to reaffirm the worth of this section of society – and this is what I meant at the outset of this chapter about the middle mass being potentially very dangerous.

Satyamurthy states that:

> The rigours of the new economic policy, the sharp edge of which will be felt more intensely by the lower rungs of society, point in the direction of greater and more anomic urban violence, on the one hand, and ruthless and systematic upper and middle class violence against lower castes, on the other. (1996, pp. 20–21)

It is the lower middle class which is at the shatter point in this structural conflict. A few will see their life chances improve by landing jobs in the growing high-technology and communications sector and a tiny number will even charm their way into bursaries for overseas higher education, but the majority of this class sees itself as being sucked down into mass poverty.

Sometimes it is literature, rather than sociology, which brings social situations home most immediately; Kiran Desai's (1998) bestseller, *Hullabaloo in the guava orchard*, uses the techniques of magic realism to explore the beleaguered position of the lower middle

FIGURE 3.3 Investment opportunities

class. That the resolution of the story is an impossibility further enhances one's sense of the class's untenable status.

CASTE ISSUES

Much of the lower middle class has traditionally had a similar caste identity to the classes above it, that is to say, it is predominantly made up of the so-called 'forward' castes, which fall into the categories *brahmin, kshatriya, vaishya*, with *brahmins* and *kayastha* (*kshatriya* who had served as accountants and revenue collectors) in the majority. The British raj had hardened out existing caste categories by recruiting its own functionaries by caste and the urban lower middle class is very much a legacy of British imperialism. After Independence, the Government of India extended the British policy of reserving a small proportion of government posts for members of the Scheduled Castes and Scheduled Tribes and a minority of members of those communities were able to attain relatively high class. However, in the early years the principle of reservation was often satisfied by filling low-status government posts, such as sweeper and messenger, and the majority of clerks and so on were recruited from the ranks of the higher castes.

As a consequence of increasing *dalit bahujan* political mobilization, it is now required that most grades and types of work in the government service apply positive discrimination quotas. The Mandal Commission has already been mentioned in the previous chapter in connection with *brahmin* employment in the private sector; since the application of its recommendations in 1990, the 'backward classes' too have employment quotas in government. When this was introduced, many lower-middle-class students from the 'forward castes' demonstrated on the streets and wore black arm-bands in mourning for what they regarded as the erosion of their career prospects. There were hunger strikes and public burnings of the Mandal Commission Report. A few young men even burned themselves to death in protest and despair.

THE RIGHT

Mandalization and liberalization (which threatened to reduce the size of the state bureaucracy) hit the traditional members of

FIGURE 3.4 A better socialism?
Source: Lokayan Bulletin (1994)

the lower middle class at exactly the same time. One consequence was a rapid swing of many middle-class people belonging to the forward castes to the political Right and to *Hindutva* (Hindu cultural and political chauvinism). As Chatterjee (1997) reminds us, drawing upon Gramsci on the subject of 'modern Caesarism':

> in those States where the bourgeoisie faced an organic crisis of authority, the ruling party sought to create cadres from among unemployed petty bourgeois youth and backward sections of the working class. These were precisely the sections ... which could make use of illegal means to strike at the cadres of organized opposition, while the state itself could maintain its facade of legality. (pp. 51–2)

Although Chatterjee originally wrote this in 1975, when Indira Gandhi's Congress Government was inching towards the Emergency, it has once again become relevant. There is a growing interest in the right-wing organization, the RSS, and its associated societies and the class has shown an increased tendency to vote for the BJP, the political wing of the RSS. Such organizations as the *Bajrang Dal* are growing. This is the militant RSS group which has been associated with murderous attacks on Christians in various States. It is predominantly made up of disillusioned sections of the urban lower middle class and impoverished members of the rural upper castes. (The *Sangh Parivar*, a combination of right-wing Hindu groups, will be dealt with in more detail in Chapter Eight.)

THE MEDIA

The lower middle class is a major consumer of media products; the Hindi- and State-language print media is largely aimed at this section of society, as is much of the film output and national television. The core virtues of this class – thriftiness, piety and family loyalty – form much of the new media mythology, but so do their frustrations – the sense that they are unfairly excluded from privilege and liable to be stricken down by powerful people or by inexplicable blows of

fate. Ashis Nandy's consideration of the role of the Indian cinema sees film working to make social change thinkable in traditional terms:

> The middle classes in India have often successfully processed, that is, creatively endogenised or ritually neutralised on behalf of the society, disturbing inputs from the modern West and simultaneously helped update or renew the society's traditions. In other words, these classes have often provided the baseline for a critique of modernity as well as of tradition. (Nandy 1995a, p. 197)

Whilst Nandy's monolithic views on culture (whether 'traditional' or 'modern') are not to my theoretical taste, his understanding of empirical situations is sensitive and nuanced as he shows the ways in which a mass culture is emerging which not only draws upon global culture but also introduces a pan-Indianist culture, 'which may self-consciously use regional or ethnic differences but [these] are perfectly commensu-

FIGURE 3.5 The Picture Palace in Mussoorie

rable, as far as mutual understanding and the common grid goes' (ibid., p. 201).

Kazmi builds upon Nandy's ideas about a traditionalized modernity articulating the present condition of the lower middle class by examining a relatively recent phenomenon in the Indian cinema, that of the violent anti-hero, best portrayed by Amitabh Bachchan, whom he sees emerging in the 1970s when

> [Government policy] only aggravated the social crisis, sharpening class and other social conflicts, polarizing different classes and intensifying the economic and social misery of large sections of the masses, especially the lower-middle classes. Unemployment and inflation were on the rise and the standard of living was falling. (Kazmi 1998, p. 139)

The 'Angry Young Man' was one who 'though he belongs to a subordinate class, rises to equal his exploiters. His image is of one who can give justice to his class when the police cannot. He protects them from official tyrannies' (ibid., p. 139). The point is that though seeming to be rebellious, the anti-hero acts within the conventions of tradition. The individual avenger, not social action, is offered as the fantasy palliative to worsening conditions. Kazmi maintains that the charismatic man of violence is a dangerous figure who paves the way for the politics of the extreme Right, a view which is endorsed by Sardar (1995). The genre continues to this day and we find it being augmented on television by that of the child's superhero, notably the controversial *Shaktiman*, who has a considerable following. It is not too much of an exaggeration to make the jump from *Shaktiman* to the 'heroes' of the *Bajrang Dal*.

Veena Das (1995b) considers the role of soap operas in lower-middle-class consciousness. The form was late to arrive in India because it had to wait until the 1980s when television became common in middle-class households. Das shows how the programme *Hum Log* ('We people') shifted from being a vehicle for propagating the message of family planning into a conventional family-based soap, in which typical domestic tensions and concerns could be aired. It and its imitators became the basis for a flow of correspondence from viewers to producers, whereby the audience interacted with the developing story-lines. Das shows that it was young members of the lower middle class who wrote in in the greatest numbers, revealing their new aspirations and their frustrations with their position in society.

FUNDAMENTALISM

The contradiction of the lower middle class in the contemporary world is that it no longer forms a continuum with the upper middle class, as it arguably did after Independence, but it shies away from recognizing

FIGURE 3.6 'Educated Unemployed' betel shop in Ranchi

that its solidarity should be with the classes below it. Its younger members in particular seek to emulate the upper middle classes who do benefit from policies of liberalization and globalization, but the structures are such that, though fortunate individuals may be socially mobile, the class as a whole cannot be.

The problems arising from their status encourage a tendency towards looking back to imagined 'golden ages' seen as existing before the onslaught of 'corrupting' foreign influences – whether these be identified as the Moghul Empire, the British Raj, American cultural hegemony, international Islam or Christianity. It dissipates its anger in actions designed to restore a Hindu purity to the nation. Examples of this can be seen in painting over offending images on film posters; picketing Kentucky Fried Chicken in Delhi in 1996; the demonstrations against the Miss World contest in Bangalore in 1997; hijacking lorries of Pepsi in Gujarat in 1998; the compulsory reconvertions of Christians and the destruction of churches from 1998; digging up cricket pitches to try to prevent Pakistan playing in 1999.

Most of all, it meant the demolition of the Babri Masjid in Ayodhya in 1992, the subsequent Hindu/Muslim riots all over India and the continuing militant Hindu pretence that Indian Muslims are quasi-foreigners. It escalates into the jubilation at the testing of a 'Hindu' bomb, which people foolishly believe will defend them against their enemies. It is for this reason that I claimed at the start of this chapter that the modest people who make up the urban lower middle class are potentially dangerous.

4

THE URBAN POOR AND MARGINALIZED PEOPLE

The urban poor live in the cracks of Indian society and, though they are both visible and numerous, they count for little when others are making decisions. Kothari (1993) refers to 'the increasing alienation of and from the poor, a sense that they do not matter, both in their eyes and in our eyes' (p. 90). Mander (1997, p. 115) quotes Dandekar and Rath's observation that 'The urban poor are only an outflow of the rural poor into the urban areas', and Asthana (1993, p. 506) maintains that 'Despite the scale of urban poverty, much of the literature on health and development has focused on rural problems ... the plight of the urban poor received very little attention.' Pendse, trying to describe conditions for the poor in Bombay, refers to the way in which everything one tries to say is likely to be highly caste- or class-specific and that generalization is almost impossible, especially since 'The most prevalent [images] represent the self-perception of the city's élite. They do not represent the realities and perceptions of the majority of the population of the city' (Pendse 1995, p. 4). Although a certain genre of western writing lingers voyeuristically on pavement dwellers and slums, never more so than in Lappierre's *City of joy*, there is remarkably little serious understanding of the urban poor either in academic literature or the media. Perhaps this is because of the middle-class fear of being sucked down into the slum which was referred to in the previous chapter.

India calculates its poverty line on the basis of ability to provide 2100 calories per day for an adult in an urban area; this is a parsimonious definition of poverty and I intend to use the term rather more loosely to mean those who have to struggle to get by. I mean the people living in the slums and on the pavements, doing work in the unorganized (and therefore unprotected) section of the economy. In an essay on the impact of the New Economic Policy on the urban poor, Kundu chillingly notes that 'people in rural and urban areas are too poor to afford unemployment' (Kundu 1996, p. 225). Unemployment is a miserable thing not to be able to afford; what he means is that when people are destitute they will work for whatever pittance their labour value is driven down to and they also experience what he calls 'poverty-induced employment', that is, the employment, for whatever return, of children, the very elderly and women who would normally be at home full-time.

India's urban areas are growing at a rate of about 3.5 per cent per annum; about half of this growth is natural increase, the other half is rural-to-urban migration. Some of the fastest growth is in the smaller towns in the wealthier agricultural areas, such as the Punjab and western Uttar Pradesh. This is particularly noticeable for those *mofussil* towns which are within easy reach of the major metropolitan areas, for example Muzaffarnagar, Ghaziabad and Meerut, where new industries have sprung up to take advantage of a combination of agricultural capital, feudal

FIGURE 4.1 Heavy work in Mussoorie

political and employment structure, and relaxed health and safety and pollution controls. These towns are growing rapidly because they can specialize in the sub-contracting work which is a characteristic of the increasingly deregulated industrial production. They are frequently dominated by local bourgeois families who can ensure that land-use law is applied in ways which are advantageous to them and that unionization of labour is made difficult. Khilnani (1997) describes such towns as having 'fostered new and distinct kinds of social relations, neither modern nor traditional. Ties of kin and caste remain strong, but operate here on a more expansive terrain than in the village, and have acquired a thinner, more instrumental form' (ibid., p. 146). These are places where the new 'bullock capitalists' from the intermediate castes can translate agricultural wealth into industrial wealth, whilst building upon the old relationships of debt, bondage and caste-based power. Employers, landlords, *dadas*, politicians overlap to control the poor as sources of labour, rent, illicit power and political support.

The *mofussil* towns had little in the way of infrastructural provision and, when large numbers of rural poor migrated to them, housing, sanitation and water facilities were stretched almost to breaking point. It is not only the large cities like Mumbai, Calcutta and Delhi which are ringed by and infilled

with congested and often insanitary slums with little formal civic provision.

LACK OF AMENITIES

India now has 23 cities with a population of more than a million and for these cities it is estimated that about a third of the population lives in slums and squatter settlements; Pathak (1993) estimates that in 1990 this came to about 51 million people. Slums can be divided into those which are recognized by the municipality and those which are not – the former will receive piped water, legal electricity connections, sanitation, though often shared. The latter will have none of these things. According to Pathak, only 44 per cent of the urban population classified as poor have access to tap water (that does not mean that they have a tap in their dwelling place). For the others it is hand pumps, tanker deliveries and a variety of unsafe sources of water. Regarding sewerage, things are even worse; 60 per cent have no access to a latrine of any kind – open spaces and gutters are used and Swaminathan (1995) reports that in the interests of modesty, when women have to defecate in the open they leave their homes under cover of darkness in the very early morning. However, people do make homes in these conditions; they keep these clean and neat and clean the spaces around

FIGURE 4.2 Sharing water in Delhi

their huts; notions of personal cleanliness are not sacrificed to the overcrowded and difficult conditions. Kundu (1991, p. 2167) argues that the poorest people in the Indian cities are 'more vulnerable to the problems of ecological degradation and environmental pollution than others', and those who argue that rapid economic growth is more important than environmental protection lose sight of the fact that those who benefit from the growth and those who experience the degradation are not the same people.

The slums of India's cities are not uniform; in some, dwellings are constructed from brick and have proper windows and doors and tiled or corrugated iron roofs; in others, they are shacks made from whatever materials come to hand. In the settlements of the rag-pickers, the hutments merge into the piled-up refuse for recycling and into the tips themselves. The close proximity of dwellings and the presence of inflammable materials makes the *bustees* dangerous fire risks. Annually there are reports of widespread fires in the slums and high death tolls. With narrow lanes and lack of proper water supplies, fire fighting is difficult.

The combination of poverty of diet, overcrowding, unclean water, lack of sewerage and often also industrial pollution, means that the people of the slums are prey to disease. Mosquitoes breed in fetid water and spread malaria; cholera, hepatitis and typhoid break out periodically; diarrhoea is endemic and a major cause of infant mortality (Swaminathan 1995). Tuberculosis is common. It is only when the slums are seen as a source of epidemics in the wider community that any of this becomes an outrage, as in the case of the outbreak of plague in Surat in 1994. Shah (1997) shows how the endemic ill

FIGURE 4.3 A slum in Pune

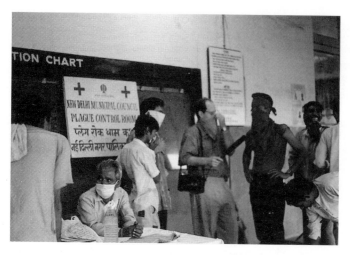

FIGURE 4.4 Panic in Delhi about the Surat plague

health of the slums of Surat was not regarded as being newsworthy, but that the relatively small number of plague cases were given massive publicity which galvanized the municipal authorities into programmes of clearance.

Many of the inhabitants of the slums are Gadgil and Guha's (1995) 'ecological refugees', those people forced from the land by 'development' or environmental degradation. Arundhati Roy (1999) cites the estimate by N.C. Saxena (Secretary to the Planning Commission) that there are 50 million people in India who have been displaced from their homes by 'development' projects. Given that there is a shortage of cultivable land for 'oustees', a significant but unknown proportion of these come as destitutes to the urban centres with few relevant skills and only their labour to sell, refugees in their own country.

Everything that is consumed in the towns has to be paid for – there is no subsistence sector; every scrap of land for a shack has a rent attached; there is no space to cultivate, no wild products or common grazing, no source of free fuel. Even water may be charged for. Often men who come to the towns in search of a cash income will try to leave their dependants in the rural areas in order to cut living costs, but also to protect them from the conditions of the towns. The very poorest families, however, will need to mobilize the labour of all their members who may well work as a unit, for example on construction sites. There are also the chil-

dren who have run away from home, been orphaned or deserted who live by their own wits.

Urban poverty is intimately connected with rural poverty. As a consequence, so long as there is greater economic growth in the towns than in the villages, economic growth will not lead to increased wages for urban workers. Urban poverty declines only when there is a growth in regulated labour intensive industries, but, as Mitra (1992) shows, the tendency has been towards investment in high productivity, capital intensive industry with ancillary outsourcing of labour intensive production in the informal sector, where wages are driven down by the excess of available unskilled and semi-skilled labour.

ILLEGALITY

As Saxena (1997) points out, 'Urban migrants pushed to the city because of abject rural poverty and unemployment have no legal access to house-sites or to establish temporary petty business activities. *They are therefore criminalised by the very process of survival.*' This initial illegal residence leads to further offences – people without legal title to land cannot get water or electricity connections; they may well steal these, taking terrible risks of injury or even death. 'Because most of them are forced to be encroachers, they get caught up in a vicious cycle of degraded living conditions without minimal facilities, because of this unrealistic legal requirement' (ibid., p. 68). Gill (1998) refers to the ways in which the theft of electricity is blatant – tangles of wires attached to distribution lines in full view of the electricity board inspectors who take a bribe not to notice them. Obviously, people who live in illegal 'colonies' have no access to municipal street cleaning, public lighting, road repairs, or to the protection of the public health department. Vermin abound, not only spreading disease but also destroying possessions. Policing is more orientated towards raiding and controlling than protecting the slum residents themselves.

It is easy to demonize the residents of the slums, but it should be emphasized that they are 'criminals of want'. The perception is that crime rates are rising in Indian towns and cities, but the published statistics do not support this; this is likely to be because many victims of crime feel that involving the police will only add to their miseries. The total number of reported crimes in India rose from 1 385 757 in 1981 to 1 695 696 in 1995 (*Statistical abstract of India 1997*). This is not just wide of the mark, it bears no relation to the experience of crime. (Given that the population grew from 683 million to 846 million between the 1981 and 1991 censuses, it would actually suggest a considerable drop in crime.) We are left with subjective views and descriptive accounts, which are of the opinion that the young underemployed men are increasingly drawn into both organized and petty crime, that burglary and violence are increasing. It is hardly surprising that the recruiting ground for the next generation of criminals is in the colonies of the urban poor, when images of affluence are displayed daily to those who have no hope of achieving wealth legally.

The residents of affluent and middle-class areas are becoming increasingly afraid of the proximity of the urban poor and are sealing themselves off in gated communities with considerable amounts of surveillance and guarding. Sometimes these gates are themselves illegal. So, for example, on 24 June 1998 *The Hindu* reported that:

> Residents of Pocket B in Siddharth Colony in Sriniwaspuri area are angry over the allegedly arbitrary manner in which the Municipal Corporation of Delhi employees removed a gate which separated the colony from adjoining slum clusters last afternoon. The gate, put up more than a decade ago, had been locked in an effort to stop a spate of robberies.

Manor's (1993) study of an incident of widespread illegal alcohol poisoning in a Bangalore slum (in which about 300 people died and others lost their sight) gives a meticulous account of the complex of poverty around the illegal trade, the networks of corruption which maintain it, the alienation of the poor from the medical and welfare institutions which should support them, and the conspiracy of indifference of the middle classes. The case study captures the symbolic distances which exist between suburbs and unofficial slums.

CASTE

Even amongst the poor there are social divisions, none more significant than caste, and one finds that *bustees* are likely to be dominated by one, or a restricted range of close caste-based communities. They will also be differentiated by region of origin, so settlements will often have a clear identity emerging from the fact that rural networks are transferred into urban areas to form a basis for mutual support. One should not make the mistake of thinking that all slum dwellers are members of the most oppressed castes – the people in Figure 4.5 are *brahmins* and even in their poverty remain aloof from those they consider to be less pure than themselves. The caste-based nature of the *bustees* leads to their becoming mobilized as vote-banks. Politicians descend upon them at election time to hand out small favours like sweets and alcohol in order to win blocks of support. (In a 1999 by-election in South Delhi, mass food-poisoning in one of the slums was caused when this happened – the donors claimed that the sweets had been tampered with by their opponents, who themselves insisted that cheap supplies had been used.)

However, given the poverty of *dalits* in rural areas and their precarious relationship

FIGURE 4.5 Keeping clean in a slum (Pune)

FIGURE 4.6 'For a dream of four mud walls'

to rural land, it is they who are most likely to become unskilled urban migrants, looking for labouring jobs. *Dalits* and 'Other Backward Classes', therefore, do predominate. Looked at the other way around, one can say that the vast majority of *dalits* in urban centres are poor and locked into casual employment, in the same way as this is their lot in the villages.

Some of the most evocative writing on the lot of *dalits* in urban areas comes from the *Dalit* Literature Movement associated with the *Dalit* Panthers of Mumbai. In a poem called 'Mother', Jyoti Lanjewar celebrates the pride, dedication and relentless poverty of *dalit* women in towns:

I have never seen you
wearing one of those gold bordered saris
with a gold necklace
with gold bangles
with fancy sandals.
Mother! I have seen you
burning the soles of your feet in the harsh
  summer sun

hanging your little ones in a cradle on an
  acacia tree,
carrying barrels of tar
working on a road construction crew ...

I have seen you
for a dream of four mud walls
stepping carefully, pregnant,
on the scaffolding of a sky scraper
carrying a hod of wet cement on your
  head ...
I have seen you
washing clothes and cleaning pots
in different households
rejecting the scraps of food offered to you
with pride
covering yourself with a sari
that had been mended so many times
saying, 'Don't you have a mother or a
sister?'
To anyone who looked at you with lust in
his eyes ...
(Lanjewar 1992, p. 100)

This poem catches the nuances of the lives of millions of poor women, struggling to retain their self respect, wishing that their children's lives could improve in circumstances where there is little hope. It is a poem written by someone classified by the upper castes as an 'untouchable' about his mother and all mothers and it is an object lesson to anyone who believes that people who live in poor conditions and are stigmatized somehow become immune to suffering.

DIMINISHING OPPORTUNITIES

A study of child labour revealed the normal monthly budget of a family of two adults and three children earning their living rolling *bidis* at the rate of Rs 51 for 1 000. They would receive between them 'at most' Rs 1 575, from which Rs 300 went on rent for their hut, leaving them with nine rupees a day each for food, fuel and everything else (Ghosh 1999).

In the past there were government schemes, such as Urban Basic Services or the Integrated Development of Small and Medium Towns, for 'uplift' of urban members of Scheduled Castes. These extended loans to set up the means of self-employment, for example the purchase of a rickshaw. Unfortunately many of these schemes have fallen victim to the processes of structural adjustment and the rolling back of the state. Although they were an entitlement, such soft loans were generally arranged with the connivance of a *dada* ('godfather', in the criminal sense) as an intermediary; with the increasing retreat of the state the *dada* himself becomes almost the only source of loans and work, with the inevitable crippling debt relationships.

SLUM CLEARANCE AND URBAN IMPROVEMENT

The New Economic Policy triggered a building boom in the cities of India, although this hit recession in the late 1990s. Labourers on the building sites are recruited from the slums, often to work in almost entirely unregulated conditions and considerable danger ('pregnant on the scaffolding of a sky

scraper'). But the building spree has forced increasing numbers of slum settlements to be cleared to make way for up-market developments ('a dream of four mud walls'). These slum clearances may look like the beautification of the cities, but, though they make way for wider streets and lower densities of population, they simply force the poor further afield into more and more marginal sites, removed from urban facilities. The slum clearances are rarely carried out for the benefit of slum dwellers who have no rights to their dwellings or to compensation when these are cleared.

Progressive administrators are campaigning for the extension of land rights to the urban poor, arguing that the granting of *pattas* (deeds of entitlement, though not ownership) to slum dwellers would not only give them a measure of residential protection, it would also allow them to free themselves from slumlords, improve their dwellings and act corporately in relation to municipal authorities. This policy has been followed in relatively small experimental schemes such as the one launched by the Mumbai Metropolitan Region Development Agency for the upgradation of slums (Panwalkar 1995). Mander, a senior officer in the Madya Pradesh administration, claims that:

> For too long have government, urban administrators and planners neglected the problems of the urban poor, leading to the choking of all cities with vast sub-human uninhabitable slums. A many pronged approach with vast political and administrative will, which guarantees planned and accessible shelter for the large masses of urban poor is urgently required. (Mander 1997, p. 117)

He lays down a simple programme of recommendations for urban authorities which assumes the legalization of the status of squatters, the provision of basic facilities like water and sanitation, but also primary schools and health care. He sees that the local authority provision of temporary shelters for new migrants is essential if they are not to fall into the hands of unscrupulous property agents. Intrinsic to the programme is the involvement of planners in the improvement of the slums, whereas the current attitude of planners to slum settlements is to see them as illegal encroachments. As Mander maintains, 'the slum dweller is a victim of a system that has failed to provide livelihood and dwelling space to the urban poor. Slums are not a problem but a solution, even if an imperfect one, organised by the people in their struggle for survival' (ibid., p. 118).

Das (1995) argues that it is important that any scheme for slum improvement should be based upon the notion of the rights of the slum dweller, rather than ideas about charity and favours. As a housing activist he is sceptical about the role played by many NGOs in the housing field, since he claims that a major role of NGOs is to fulfil the World Bank requirement that the responsibility for housing provision should move firmly into the private sector, minimizing the role of the state. When Das was writing, the Urban Land Ceiling Act was still in place and his preoccupation was with the fact that it was not being zealously applied. This Act provided limits to the amount of urban land which could be owned by an individual or company and was intended to give fairer access to land, eventually to stop the excesses of urban landlordism. The Act was repealed in 1999 as a very deliberate concession to the forces of liberalism, the freeing up of the market in land. The repeal does not just mean that large tracts of land can now be purchased by landlords, it also means that property developers, who are bound to seek the largest rate of return on their investments, are looking towards provision for the affluent, providing one more turn of the screw against the poor seeking modestly priced accommodation.

All too often, initiatives for improving housing for the urban poor fail to reach the people targeted, but are taken advantage of by the middle classes. So, a new housing loan scheme introduced in 1999 requires too large a deposit for the really poor to be able to avail themselves of it. Similarly, the privatization of the state-owned Life Insurance Corporation, which has long invested in low-cost housing, means that loans for the poor (which are expensive to administer) are not an attractive prospect for the new private insurance companies, particularly those which are transnationals. The World Bank's preference for market-driven provision of resources has left the very poor with little hope of housing improvement. The slums have always been market driven and that has been their problem; there is no incentive for slumlords to act in the interests of their tenants.

GENDER

Sex ratios are skewed in favour of men in poor urban settlements. This makes the lives of women and girls difficult. Women from the most oppressed communities are regarded as easy game by the men of the (so-called) higher-caste communities and fight a constant battle for their own dignity. Attacks upon women are frequent. Many urban middle-class households depend upon the services of young women domestic workers. These are often recruited direct from a village by means of long-standing semi-feudal networks between servant and employer families. The family she works for will undertake her protection in town and her material standard of living may be relatively high, living in the servant's room of a middle-class apartment or sleeping in the kitchen. However, the situation in major cities is such that a young woman alone can have little personal freedom, being afraid to leave the premises. Single, poor, lower-caste women are accorded little respect or safety on the city streets and there are few places of recreation where they can go.

Whenever there is an excess of males over females there is prostitution – this is particularly the case when poor women have few sources of income. Every Indian city has its red-light district with women, often bonded, frequently very young, soliciting from caged balconies. Some of the prostitutes come from castes of traditional sex-workers and it seems that their networks of support are rather better than for the women who are forced into the trade by circumstances, since they have functioning non-marital families. The chances of escaping from prostitution into other work or into marriage are slight and older women rely on the earnings of their daughters. AIDS is becoming a very real problem amongst sex-workers in the cities of India, though the women claim that health authorities are more worried about clients than they are about the women. Drug dealing and potentially lethal illicit alcohol are closely related to prostitution and other minor crime.

CHILDREN

The children of the poor work for their living. As will be shown in Chapter Six, there is an indication that liberalization will actually increase the numbers of child workers in cities. The children working at tea stalls, selling newspapers, scavenging and begging are the obvious child workers, but behind these are many more in industrial workshops. Education is a luxury that few can afford, even though it is free. The majority are members of families and return home at night, the remainder are the runaways and orphans of the street.

Many of the female street children graduate into prostitution in their early teens, just as the boys find it difficult to live without turning to crime. This is what one means by a reserve army of labour; what exists below the level of casual employment in outsourced production. The few slum schools and outreach programmes aimed at destitute children barely scratch the surface of this large and growing problem.

THE POOREST OF THE POOR

Gandhi asked us always to remember when we thought about any project we were planning to contemplate its likely impact upon the poorest of the poor. This is a sobering injunction, partly because many of us never

FIGURE 4.7 The trickle down effect
Source: Lokayan Bulletin (1994)

encounter those he was referring to, the people even the poor think are deprived. Whereas in village communities it was possible to integrate people with physical and mental disabilities, in the cities such people are marginalized into beggary, often rejected even by those who are closest to them. Leprosy patients are often banished from their villages because the disease is seen as a sign of ritual impurity (and is also assumed to be much more contagious than it really is). They make their way to the towns where they can beg – deriving their scant living from being paid to go away, descending to the lowest levels of abjection.

Then there are the hidden margins. There are the patients who are incarcerated in very poor conditions in mental institutions, sometimes stripped naked for the convenience of those who have to keep them clean. Inmates are often people who are amenable to treatment but who will only receive control. In January 1999 I visited a suspiciously clean mental hospital which was trying to live down an earlier damning media report; the occasion was an inspection from representatives of the Human Rights Commission and the staff was on its best behaviour. The first tell-tale sign that we were witnessing a whitewash was that there was no evidence of anything for patients to do – no work, no recreation, no posessions; the second was that people crowded around beseeching to

be released, all except those who looked, dazed, into the middle distance. A few probing questions to the staff began to reveal the likelihood that even these deserted people were being exploited, cheated of their rations and of the drugs which would effect an improvement.

A marginalized group which people forget is that known as the 'undertrials'; these are the people who have been accused of a criminal offence but not brought to trial. Whereas the politicians, extortionists and sons of the influential who find themselves in this position generally manage to get released on bail, the poor rot in prison. If there is no one to stand bail or to bribe the police or to pay for the case to reach the courts, people can wait for years on trivial charges, often for much longer than the maximum sentence for their alleged crime. Those who are mentally defective are liable to serve decades in gaols or the secure wings of mental hospitals, forgotten for decades (Mander and Rao 1996; Malik and Chakravarty 1998).

It is impossible to do more than hint at the struggle of daily life of poor people in the cities of India, where there is no organized system of relief and no prospect of any in the future. Optimists believe that liberalization and globalization will create vast numbers of new jobs which will take the marginalized poor into the ranks of the solid working class; others think that the *Lokayan* cartoons are nearer the mark.

5

RURAL LIFE

Whereas many developing countries have seen rapid and unmanageable rates of urbanization, India still has an unusually high proportion of its population living in the rural areas. At the 1991 census (the most recent) only 25.7 per cent of India's population was urban and there are no indications that the proportion has changed much since then. This stability is because, although the towns and cities are growing and there is a considerable amount of migration, the rate of natural increase in the rural areas is high and there is also return migration (Racine 1997).

It is tempting to think of India's rural areas as timeless and unchanging and to assume that all of the transformations consequent upon liberalization and globalization are concentrated in the urban centres, where the bustle of traffic, the imported consumer goods and the high-rise buildings loudly announce radical modernity. However, some of the most far-reaching (and often unintended) consequences of the liberalization of the Indian economy are felt in what look like traditional villages.

As the Introduction has emphasized, there is considerable regional diversity in India, partially reflected in the relative autonomy of the States which make up the Union. This geographical diversity is particularly felt in the rural areas, where climatic and topographical differences impact upon the everyday economic and social life of rural producers. In addition, regional variations such as local social structures, indigenous

FIGURE 5.1 The 'timeless' rural

cultural preferences, local political configuration, transport systems and market conditions seem to be felt more acutely in the countryside than the cities.

POVERTY

A superficial glance at the Indian countryside, perhaps from a train window, can give one the impression of great beauty and tranquillity – villages with thatched or tiled huts the same colour as the surrounding land, a man driving a pair of oxen ploughing a field, saree-clad women bent weeding the crops. There will be girls drawing water from wells and gracefully walking home, balancing brass vessels on their heads. If one enters the villages there will be generosity and hospitality, a charpoy will be pulled out to sit on, there will be smoke rising from kitchen fires and the wonderful reek of smouldering cowdung. It is seductive and somehow poverty is always photogenic. The truth is that many people living in the rural areas are grindingly poor and the sadness is that they need not be. The rural poverty line is based on a minimum calorific requirement of 2 400 per adult. In money terms this is taken to be a household income of Rs 6 400 per anum, or its subsistence equivalent (Department of Rural Development 1991a, p. 3). A household is taken to comprise 5.52 people but, of course, the composition of households varies considerably. The poverty line in India represents destitution, not just deprivation.

Gandhi's dream of an independent India based on 'village republics', where the wealth of the nation was built up through the co-operative work of small peasants, was never to come about. Gandhians continue to toil to encourage local self-sufficiency in food and craft goods, but in a modern India not even the seemingly remote villages are unconnected to the global economy. Selling crops to buy polyester clothing is more economic, if only in the short run, than hand spinning and weaving.

One should also not be misled into assuming that the social and political structures of rural populations are less complex or hierarchical than those of the towns. As well as the supportive solidarities of kinship and neighbourhood, there are deep social and economic divisions, systematic exploitation, cheating and even homicidal violence to be found behind the apparent calm. Arvind Das's (1996) *Changel: the autobiography of a village* is a semi-fictionalized account of a village in northern Bihar which catches these interwoven strands of village life.

TRIBAL PEOPLES

An important division of India's rural population is between tribal and non-tribal populations. There is little justification for the common assumption that tribal people are racially distinctive from surrounding non-tribal populations and there is certainly no reason to subscribe to the often expressed view that tribal people are in some way more 'primitive' or 'simple' than others. Tribal people have a different social structure from the mass of the Hindu population and both tribal and Hindu society like to assume that this difference is based on the tribal peoples being uniquely the remnants of autochthonous populations prior to Hindu/Aryan invasion. However, the similarities between tribal and non-tribal people living in the same region are such that it is more realistic to assume that the different social groups and cultural practices crystallized out of different modes of livelihood, rather than vice versa. The term used collectively for tribal peoples is *adivasi*, which literally means 'original people', but most of the non-*adivasi* are equally 'original' and not the descendants of invader populations at all. (It is usual in India to refer to people with a tribal identity as 'tribals', but I find the term offensively essentializing and avoid it. 'Tribal' is an adjective, not a noun.) Tribal peoples are those who have resisted being pulled into the lowest levels of the Hindu caste hierarchies, even though others may elect to think of them as if they were on a par with the *dalits*.

The British recognized tribal people as different from the mainstream and firstly reflected and then reified this difference by scheduling the tribes of the various States. Each District Gazetteer dutifully recorded the population and characteristics of the various tribes. The independent Indian Government perpetuated the principle of scheduling and the Ethnographic Survey of India has continued this tradition with its exhaustive enumeration of the tribes of India.

People classified as belonging to tribes constitute only 8.08 per cent of the population of India (this excludes Jammu and Kashmir which has a large tribal population, but where the last census could not be carried out due to political instability). This average contains within it the North East States where around 60 per cent of the population is classified as tribal. Excluding the North East,

the States with the highest proportion of the population tribal are Madhya Pradesh (23.27 per cent) and Orissa (22.21 per cent) but one also thinks of southern Bihar as having very significant tribal populations (even though the State as a whole is below the national average) and also parts of Rajasthan. Tribal peoples live in pockets throughout India, though the remarkably low figure for Uttar Pradesh (0.21) and the non-existence of tribal peoples in the Punjab, both of which have high proportions of Scheduled Caste people, reinforces the argument that tribal people are different from others socially and ethnically rather than racially.

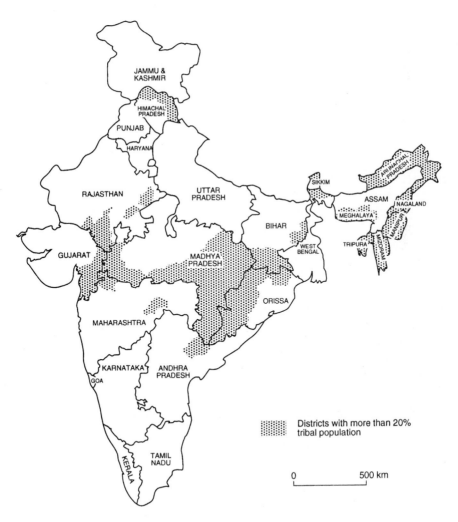

FIGURE 5.2 Scheduled Tribes

In order to generalize about the status of tribal people it is sensible to set aside the North East, where people classified as tribal form the majority and where there are political movements around the nationalist aspirations of distinctive ethnic groups (this will be considered in Chapter Nine). Elsewhere, we can think of tribal peoples as occupying marginal lands and economic niches in the rural areas. They typically have semi-subsistence economies with a high degree of dependence on wild produce and a low incidence of capitalized agricultural production. They have a low degree of division of labour and live in more or less egalitarian communities of their own beyond the confines of the hierarchically organized Hindu villages. But people of tribal origin are not completely outside the cash economy and, when necessary, they take paid employment with large farmers, trade their surplus products at *haats* (weekly markets) or migrate to towns as labourers.

All generalizations are invidious, but tribal groups in India tend to have certain basic commonalities, such as lineage and

Figure 5.3 Making cups from *sal* leaves

clan-based (rather than hierarchical) social organization; communal ownership of land is a major characteristic of tribal society; and there is relative gender equality in comparison with other populations. Tribal people may follow the Hindu religion, but most have religions based around local deities associated with the land, often referred to as 'sacred grove' cults because of the practice of protecting small tracts of woodland as symbolic of the primacy of nature. Some have converted to Christianity in the last century. Arguably, much of the current violent opposition to Christianity in rural India can be re-read as the tension between tribal and non-tribal peoples.

Because of their marginal status and minority languages, the tribal peoples of India find themselves some of the most victimized of all populations. It is illegal for any individual to buy tribal land (tribal land is by definition inalienable) and yet the land of tribal communities is constantly being encroached upon not only by unscrupulous money-lenders but by large mining corporations, as in southern Bihar, and by the various State governments themselves, as in the case of the flooding of vast areas of the Narmada Valley in Madhya Pradesh and Gujarat for the sake of the hydro-electric power for the industrial centres and irrigation for the cash croppers of Gujarat.

In reaction to this victimization, there has been considerable resistance among tribal peoples, partly because their social structures and egalitarian ethics are fertile ground for the formation of social movements and activism. (I am uneasy about the 'new' that conventionally qualifies ecological and similar 'social movements' because there is a long history of tribal resistance to government, whether one thinks of the brigandage of the Bhils during the British raj or the long struggle of the Jarkhand Movement for an autonomous State.)

Undoubtedly the most empathic and clear-eyed study of tribal exploitation and resistance I have encountered is Amita Baviskar's (1997) book, *In the belly of the river*. Baviskar's work is free of the romanticizing which besets so many views of tribal life. She sees urban-based environmentalists senti-

Figure5.4 Women of the Munda Tribe

mentalizing a presumed embeddedness of tribal peoples into nature and resents their annexation of them as primaeval ecologists. She accuses anti-development theorists of dragooning tribal resistance into their own ideological struggles and suggests that, well-meaning as these may be, they are just the latest round of exploitation of tribal peoples for the agendas of others. Baviskar, who was not only an ethnographer but also worked for the *Narmada Bachao Andolan* (Save Narmada Movement) and as a teacher, is adamant that the Bhilala people she worked with have a pragmatic attitude to the environment and are not ideologically opposed to development, merely to 'development' which impoverishes and disempowers them. As I make my final revisions to this text in July 1999, this takes on an added poignance, since the world's press is unhelpfully polarizing its accounts of Narmada activism into pro-tribal and pro-development camps.

Because of their geographical and economic marginalization, tribal peoples have poor access to formal health services and education. Their educational chances are further hampered by the fact that many people of tribal origin do not speak the official State languages, which are the media of instruction in government schools. The official reason for 'scheduling' tribes is not for ethnographic purposes, it is directed towards the 'uplift' of tribal peoples, even though this is more honoured in the breach than the observance. Like members of Scheduled Castes, Scheduled Tribes should benefit from reservation of quotas of State and central government employment, places in schools and at university, with grants to back these up.

STRATIFICATION

It is rare to find examples of the old landowning élites living in the rural areas; their palaces and hunting lodges lie in ruins or are used only for occasional visits. Until shortly after Independence the *zamindari* system prevailed, whereby the British had endowed what it took to be the local aristocracy with large grants of land in return for their collecting the revenue for the government. These landlords operated a form of feudalism, whereby subordinate cultivator and artisan families were virtually tied to the land and family of their lord.

After Independence there were various attempts at land reform, designed to allocate 'land to the tiller' and to impose ceilings on land ownership – though these were far from universally successful. However, far more important than land reform in driving the élites from the rural areas were the counter-attractions of urban life and, particularly, the realization that in future their children needed to be educated for the professions

Figure 5.5 Village youths, Madhya Pradesh

and administration rather than for feudal lordship. Mendelsohn and Vicziani (1998) show that, for example, the West Bengal *Estates Acquisitions Act* of 1953 found the landlords willing to surrender their lands willingly 'in order to buy peace' (p. 154). Das (1996) shows how in Bihar they distributed it to relatives and to *yadava* (a cattle-rearing and milk-vending caste) clients, whom they thought they could trust.

Associated with the principle of landowning and dominant castes was the *jajmani* system. Although its universality has come into question (Fuller 1989), functionalist theorists of the 1950s and 1960s assumed that this system of division of labour was the basis and justification for elaborate local caste hierarchies (Srinivas 1952; Bailey 1957; Mayer 1960). To simplify, the *jajmani* system consisted of landowners (the *jajman*), who were generally members of warrior castes who had been given grants of land by their princes, entering into agreements with families from castes whom they needed to work for them. These would have been 'untouchables' and members of *jati* classified as *shudra*, who did the agricultural labour; in addition there were village servants, agricultural craftsmen such as carpenters and blacksmiths, potters, washermen, barbers; again, all of these *jati* were classified as *shudra*. Finally there were the *brahmin* priests, all of whom were paid a share of the harvest, which they could consume or trade. A village

was, ideally, an organic whole made up of the interdependent specialist castes, with access to towns and visits from traders for sales and special purchases.

Within the villages, divisions of labour were underwritten by finely differentiated hierarchies of purity and pollution; everyone knew their place, literally as well as metaphorically, since the caste divisions were reflected in the sections of villages, with 'untouchables' living outside village walls or on one side of a dividing path. They were also marked by access to water – wells being shared only by approximate equals, since water was perceived as being subject to ritual pollution.

McKim Marriott (1955) is usually credited with introducing western sociologists to the significance of the practice of accepting or refusing cooked food as a means of demarcating caste hierarchy (unfortunately, like so many functionalist theorists, he implied that ethnographic observations were based on structures set in stone, rather than snapshots at a particular point in time). The notion of food as a pollutant was such that people would accept cooked food only from those they considered to be their equals and those superior to them, whilst the only food they would accept from those below them in the ritual hierarchy was the raw material for cooking. Similarly, they would eat only alongside their equals. (The point is that cooked food represents social solidarity. A wedding was almost an experiment in social structure as the distribution and consumption of food would demonstrate clearly the local hierarchy.) Adrian Mayer's (1960) *Caste and kinship in central India* gives a detailed account of this system in practice. Elements of this system certainly still prevail. Many people are still very status conscious about accepting cooked food and particularly about access to wells.

Although it is obvious that the *jajmani* system revolved around the economic and political power of the landowners, most western social scientists have until recently subscribed to the view, propagated by *brahmin* scholars, that caste hierarchies are predominantly based on religious criteria and take as their reference point the supposedly dominant 'moral' position of the *brahmins*.

In contemporary India this kind of immediate control of local communities through landownership is virtually extinct and the lord living off the direct labour of his clients is a phenomenon of the past. In much of India, small landowning peasants are the norm, leading semi-subsistence livelihoods, the members of a family being both producing and consuming unit. Elsewhere larger farmers employ labourers (who may themselves be entirely landless) to work for wages in cash and in kind. As demonstrated by Varshney (1995) there has been a continuous growth in the political power of the farming lobby from the mid 1960s, with demands for higher food prices and increased subsidies for fuel, fertilizer and seeds.

DEBT

The largest single cause of rural poverty is indebtedness. Cash incomes are small. In 1994, according to a study carried out by the National Council for Applied Economic Research, 58.9 per cent of rural households in India had an income below Rs 20000 per annum; this leaves little cushion for crises, especially since a great many households receive nowhere near the Rs 20000 which is the ceiling for 'low' income. If ploughing oxen die and need replacing, if a daughter marries, if sickness strikes a household,

people are driven into the hands of money-lenders who demand such usurious rates of interest that relatively small sums quickly become impossible to repay. Land mortgaged against such loans is lost for a pittance and, although bonded labour is strictly illegal, people, including children, are taken in bondage against loans too. The cycle of deprivation is then virtually complete; there are few resources available which will enable an indebted landless labourer to escape lifetime poverty and the debts will be inherited by his children. No one knows how much of the wealth of the rural areas is syphoned off by money-lenders and it would be impossible to find out.

The accounts in *Everybody loves a good drought*, Sainath's (1996) collected journalism on rural poverty, almost invariably turn on stories of people who have become indebted or have been swindled out of their land in some other way. So who are the money-lenders? They can be local traders who extend small loans, first against the jewellery that brides bring as dowry, then against land and labour itself. Quite often they are the distillers and sellers of liquor, who prey upon the weakness of poor men and turn alcohol dependence into debt. Sometimes they are local landowners with surplus cash. Olsen (1996) demonstrates the possibility of competition between lenders driving interest rates down and easing the conditions of loans in rural areas in Andhra Pradesh where lenders have learned that foreclosing on mortgaged land is not always economically viable and where they have reason to be afraid of anti-usury laws – however, this is far from the norm.

In general, one can see private lending taking place in grossly unfair conditions, but there have been counter movements. Particularly in southern India, women, often originally motivated by their successes in literacy campaigns, have spectacularly banded together in anti-*arrack* movements to force out liquor traders and to shame men into taking a pledge against alcohol. It may seem puritanical and draconian, but the women are motivated not only by fear of the family destitution which so often follows the arrival of manipulative liquor traders, but also of the too frequent fatalities from consuming illicit alcohol. Successful anti-*arrack* movements have sometimes grown into women's co-operatives and rotating credit associations (Narasimhan and Sattiah 1997). Like many others, I am convinced that the answer to the problem of breaking rural destitution lies in small savings and credit unions. If there are means of borrowing at reasonable rates, where the interest goes back into the commu-nal 'pot' of borrowable money, not only are family crises weatherable, but small capital sums for investment in new sources of liveli-hood become available. The inspiration for this comes from the *Grameen Banking* in Bangladesh and, if it catches on, it could transform the rural areas of India by beating the usurers in the same way as the friendly societies transformed urban working-class security in Britain. A major source of lending for capital ventures (though not family crises) is the government, sometimes in con-junction with the banks, through its many poverty alleviation schemes.

Government poverty alleviation schemes

There is no shortage of good ideas for improving the standard of living in India's rural areas; there is also a veritable army of people supposedly involved in the 'uplift' of

the poor and government expenditure on agricultural and rural development is cer-tainly not insignificant. In 1996–97 the Union government alone spent Rs 94 190 000 000 on rural development (this does not include the rural share of national expenditures on other development and welfare matters, including Rs 8 110 000 000 specifically for Scheduled Castes and Tribes welfare). Although this does not work out at a great deal in per capita terms, it is still a significant potential investment. Cynics are fond of quoting Rajiv Gandhi's off-the-cuff remark that only 15 paise in every rupee of development money came anywhere near to the people who were intended to benefit from it. (They usually add that this shows what a protected life he must have led if he thought it was anywhere near to being this high.) Certainly a great deal of development money is syphoned off in various corrupt practices by officials, politicians and contractors, as the next chap-ter will show.

There are many government-backed liveli-hood promotion schemes aimed at the poor-est of the rural people. Whereas the first three Five-Year Development Plans after Independ-ence had concentrated on capital invest-ment, with the assumption that the benefits would eventually permeate the whole of society, the Fourth Five-Year Development Plan, covering the period 1969–74, placed the emphasis on poverty alleviation, with partic-ular concern for rural poverty, and an

FIGURE 5.6 Guaranteed labour under JRY, Madhya Pradesh

emphasis on food for work. The motivation for this was several near famines in the late 1960s. It is, however, the sixth planning period (1980–85) which has the most significance for contemporary conditions, since it was directed towards the redistribution of rural wealth in favour of deprived people, through the National Rural Employment Programme.

To pull a number of initiatives together, the Sixth Plan introduced the Integrated Rural Development Programme (IRDP), major elements of which were Small Farmers' Development Agency, Community Area Development and the Drought Prone Area Programme. IRDP also spawned Development of Women and Children in Rural Areas (DWCRA), Training of Rural Youth for Self Employment (TRYSEM) and the Rural Landless Employment Guarantee Programme (Department of Rural Development 1991a).

The Seventh Plan (covering the period 1985–90) put its emphasis on the stimulation of rural employment, not just agriculture but also rural industry and trade; the lynchpin of this initiative was the guaranteed work scheme known as *Jawahar Rozgar Yojana* (JRY), named after Jawaharlal Nehru (Department of Rural Development 1991b). In all of these schemes, the prior claim of members of Scheduled Castes and Scheduled Tribes is endorsed along with released bonded labourers, women, disabled people, cured leprosy patients, and ex-convicts.

The various schemes which come within the remit of IRDP place their main emphasis on establishing sustainable sources of non-agricultural income for landless people. Beneficiaries have to be identified by the *panchayats* and by district administrators as being amongst the most needy and receive government soft loans extended through the rural banks. The regulations for IRDP contain lengthy lists of examples of the sorts of schemes that can be considered – they range from animal husbandry, through fish farming, bee keeping and sericulture, to handicrafts and small industries. DWCRA projects require women to form co-operatives for self employment; these have been some of the most successful ventures under IRDP. TRYSEM caters for people under the age of 35 and is intended to impart economically valuable skills for use in the rural areas. It is a mixture of short (up to six months) residential courses at technical institutes and apprenticeships with master craftsmen.

There have been notorious scandals under IRDP, none more publicized than the Bihar 'fodder scam', when hundreds of public servants and politicians collaborated in a huge scheme involving purchasing the same (sometimes fictitious) cattle several times over, supplying them with inordinate amounts of free veterinary care, and subsidized fodder requiring large amounts of transport. The whole enterprise was a complicated bureaucratic exercise, involving trumped-up firms and creative accounting. If the money syphoned off from development schemes were really invested, one would see a rapid increase in rural productivity.

JRY not only guarantees minimum incomes, paid in both grain and cash, it is also intended to provide amenities for the whole community. Contractors are expressly excluded from JRY projects, which are supposed to be managed through bodies set up by the *panchayats* co-operating with voluntary organizations and government employees. Typical JRY activities include road building and repair, constructing tanks and minor irrigation, social forestry, building schools. However, contractors and middlemen do creep into JRY, using state-funded labourers on their own projects. Minor officials underpay workers and pocket the difference, relying on the illiteracy of most poor people who have no way of checking what is due to them and the timidity of those who think that if they make trouble they will be excluded altogether. It is only when transparency of information, combined with effective *panchayati raj*, can be established that the abuses of rural development will be avoided.

EDUCATION

With notable exceptions, such as the State of Kerala where the literacy rate is 89.9 per cent and virtually all children of primary school age are in education, rural education is the subject of major concern in contemporary

FIGURE **5.7** A well-attended
school, Madhya Pradesh

India. Primary education for all is well within India's capabilities but many children in rural India work for their living. Dreze and Sen (1995) demonstrate that in 1987–88 only 40 per cent of rural girls and 52 per cent of rural boys in the age group 5 to 9 were enrolled in school. However, they emphasize that when one adds the caste dimension, the lack of schooling becomes even more marked – among rural Scheduled-Caste women, the literacy rate was only 19 per cent; for rural Scheduled-Caste men it was 46 per cent across India.

The low rate of literacy is not simply due to lack of uptake amongst children; a survey of rural education in Uttar Pradesh conducted by Dreze and Gazdar (1996) revealed that there was no teacher in attendance in two-thirds of the schools which were visited unannounced. They further found that when teachers were there they did little more than child-mind and levels of learning were low. In Uttar Pradesh only 8 per cent of Scheduled-Caste rural women and 39 per cent of men are literate.

Without literacy it is difficult for people to pursue their rights and one finds that, where it is made easier for people to learn, they come forward. The Total Literacy campaigns are an example of this, as are children's night-schools such as those co-ordinated by the Barefoot College at Tilonia. When free school lunches are provided parents are more willing to spare their children from work.

WEALTHY FARMERS

The farmers' lobby is politically important in India. In the general election of 1996, farmers became the biggest single occupational group in the *Lok Sabha* and they had long been a force to be reckoned with at State level. These are the people who have been able to benefit from India's Green Revolution, based on irrigation, improved crop strains, chemical fertilizers and pesticides. Those who could thus benefit were the already relatively substantial *raiyats* (roughly the equivalent of *kulaks*) many of whom had enlarged their holdings with the demise of the *zamindari* system.

The transformations of Indian agriculture have not just been in terms of improved yields and the country's ability to meet its food needs, they have also had far-reaching effects in terms of flows of people, social structures and political movements. This change has further polarized landed and landless rural people, changed employment relations and rural political configurations. At a State and national level, farmers throughout India have been able to campaign successfully for massive subsidies on seeds, fertilizers and pesticides. They have obtained irrigation at little cost and in some States even the electricity they use is free (invariably, like their diesel, it is subsidized). Measures that were intended to benefit a peasantry and offer better life chances to the landless have, in many regions, resulted in the capitalization of agriculture and the growth of agribusinesses which force out small semi-subsistence units.

We can particularly associate the Punjab with capitalist agriculture, where its effects have been longest established. Agricultural profits have not only resulted in higher standards of living, including impressive residences and consumer durables, they have also been invested locally in building cold-storage plants which allow farmers and traders to take advantage of price fluctuations, and in setting up factories and shops; they have paid for higher education and they have sponsored overseas migration. It has also prompted some farmers to diversify out of staples such as wheat into high-risk, high-profit crops such as mushrooms and strawberries, for which a new demand has been stimulated by both the globalized tastes of the Delhi élite and the opportunity to airfreight perishable fruits to the supermarkets of the West (Vinayak 1998b). The Punjab today is relatively affluent but contains discrepancies of wealth and opportunity. It imports cheap, seasonal, indentured labour from other poorer parts of India, particularly Rajasthan and Bihar. In the rural areas of Bihar after the wheat harvests, one sees lorries arriving from the Punjab, piled high with grain, the workers sitting on top of their season's payment in kind.

It was a success story for many, but there were costs. The benefits of the Green Revolution have not been capable of sustained growth; division of property and lack of investment in non-farm activities have meant the impoverishment of smaller farmers, who look to the emigration of their sons to improve their family fortunes. Partly encouraged by expatriate Sikhs, partly by less affluent strata of Sikh society at home, there has been an escalation of Sikh/Hindu tension (which has no historical justification) corresponding with a growth of fundamentalism and separatist tendencies.

But it is not the Punjab alone that has seen the rise of capitalist farmers. Parts of the neighbouring state of Uttar Pradesh have seen a movement from mixed peasant farming to virtual monoculture of sugar, the rise of a relatively affluent class of sugar farmers and a class of landless wage labourers (Corbridge 1997; Jeffrey 1997). There are large tea, coffee and rubber estate owners who have succeeded British planters in the North East, Kerala and Karnataka (Shivalingappa 1997) and in much of Central India there are large farmers of sugar and cotton.

There are substantial profits to be made in agriculture, but the most secure farmers are those who can diversify into other activities and, particularly, those who are not undercapitalized. In 1997 and 1998 considerable publicity was given to a spate of suicides of farmers particularly in Madhya Pradesh and Andhra Pradesh (Sridar 1998). These were men who were seeking to break into the ranks of the affluent by moving from the cultivation of food crops to the production of cotton. They had overborrowed to buy pesticides, often borrowing from the same unscrupulous dealers who had diluted the pesticides to such an extent that they were ineffective, requiring more to be bought. When the crops failed and they could not repay their loans, destitution threatened.

OBC

Most of the people we can think of as farmers (as opposed to labourers or landlords) come into a category of society which has become politically very significant, that of the Other Backward Classes. These are people who under *brahminical* notions of *varna* come way down the social hierarchy, people whose *jati* were associated with manual work and the category of *shudra*. In the latter part of the twentieth century there has been a remarkable upsurge in the political aspirations of this section of society. The implementation of the recommendations of the Mandal Commission in 1992 was very much a response to the increasing political clout of these communities in the rural areas and the need for 'backward' politicians to be seen to be able to deliver favours to their constituents. Under the farmers' leader, Bansi Lal, farmers have become a highly organized pressure group.

The northern, Hindi-speaking, States have

in particular become associated with OBC rural politics, most spectacularly with the dramatic rise to power of the *yadavas*. Shortly after Independence, the *Janata Dal* became associated with the OBCs in Bihar, whereas the Congress Party was locally associated with landowning. Party politics became suffused with caste issues and the narrow economic advantage that flows from personal power. *Yadava* power became synonymous with the charismatic figure of Laloo Prashad Yadav, Chief Minister of Bihar, until charges of corruption forced him to step down in favour of his wife. The press does not find it difficult to find reasons to trivialize Laloo Prashad Yadav and Rabri Devi or to heap accusations of corruption upon them, but it is undeniable that their rise has represented a political trend away from the old ruling classes which is probably irreversible. This, rather than Laloo's deliberate buffoonery, populist gestures, and many 'scams', is the real basis of the constant establishment criticism.

VIOLENCE

Under feudal systems, systematic violence underwrote the oppressive relations between caste groups and the memory is recent enough for true stories still to be told and fictious ones to suffuse the products of the film industry. Landlords claimed power of life and death and *droit de seigneur* without fear of repercussion since they were the local representatives of government.

In the poorest States, community-based (in the sense of caste-based) violence is endemic. I am reluctant to see this as a remnant of past systems, even though a resentment of loss of power is certainly an element, because present situations are always best explained by reference to present causes. Bihar is always the State first associated with rural caste-based violence but Uttar Pradesh, Madhya Pradesh, Orissa, Andhra Pradesh and Tamil Nadu all have more than their fair share (and nowhere is exempt). When the Union Government

sought to impose President's Rule in Bihar in 1998 (and fleetingly succeeded in 1999) on the grounds of breakdown of law and order, the Chief Minister, Rabri Devi, disarmingly protested that Bihar was no worse than a list of other States which the government seemed unwilling to pick upon.

No one would deny that conditions in Bihar are bad. It is the State with by far the largest proportion of its population below the parsimonious poverty line – 58.21 per cent in 1994 (Tata Services 1997). It has long been associated with the lawlessness of private armies (known as *senas*), recruited by and from landowner castes, tyrannizing subordinate castes and the counter violence of Naxalite groups (Banerjee 1980; Ray 1988; Singh 1995).

Arvind Das (1992) is realistic about the way in which the rule of law has broken down in Bihar to such an extent that it almost seems naïve to question the efficacy of an alternative system. 'The long-evolved public works systems involving substantial expenditure from the government's coffers sustained a relatively stable economy where contractors flourished, engineers battened and some employment was generated' (p. 135). It seems almost churlish to mention that these contractors mostly thought that actually completing the public works (such as irrigation schemes and road maintenance) was a drain on this 'relatively stable economy'. He concludes that illegal 'Privatization became a reality in Bihar well before it became a slogan of the New Economists. But, if Bihar should gladden the hearts of dyed-in-the wool rightist ideologues, it should also thrill utopian leftists for, in privatized Bihar, the state too has withered away' (p. 135). But, joking apart, Das recognizes the deadly nature of the now institutionalized lawlessness of Bihar and I can do no better than to recommend his book to you.

Trying to get any public works completed is a frustrating business, as contractors, who are unwilling to do the work they are paid for, employ thugs to frighten villagers when they try to take matters into their own hands and organize their own irrigation and

FIGURE 5.8 Pastoral idyll (or child labour?), Rajasthan

other schemes. Organizing people into such schemes as water harvesting becomes a risky political activity and though the reports of activists such as the *Pani Chetna Manj* (Water Awareness Group) in Pallamau may seem to be straightforward accounts of development work, they conceal within them considerable personal courage. Although charges are occasionally brought for corruption and violence, the rot has spread through virtually all parts of the system. The so-called politician – bureaucrat – contractor nexus, with its connections into the private armies, makes for an alternative structure which only the most optimistic can see being effectively challenged in the foreseeable future.

Another form of rural violence surrounds the poaching and forest mafia. There are large sums to be gained from poaching tigers and elephants in particular, and the poachers obtain the silence of villagers by implementing a reign of terror. The sandalwood smuggler, Veerappan, has dominated the rural areas of Karnataka and Tamil Nadu throughout this decade; his gang seems virtually invincible, kidnapping tourists and foresters, and he has certainly become something of a folk hero (Sharma 1997).

THE FUTURE

India is fortunate that it still has so large a rural population and that much of the rural-to-urban migration is not permanent (Mahadev and Racine 1997). As Racine insists, 'the town is part of a strategy that lays stress on peasant moorings' (Racine 1997, p. 358). But this means that an increased emphasis should be placed on developing not only employment opportunities, but also amenities in the rural areas. Initiatives often fail because of poor transport and marketing; human resources are wasted by the chronic illiteracy and lack of modern skills.

In a situation as poor as exists in India's rural areas, only the state can provide the investment needed and yet policies of liberalization require increasingly market driven approaches. The market will not bring about the application of land reform which is so desperately needed, neither will it ensure that persons displaced by development schemes get adequate land in compensation. There is every indication that the emphasis on cash crops will cause greater landlessness, increased indebtedness and also competition for water.

6

WOMEN AND MEN; OLD AND YOUNG

This chapter is about the ascribed characteristics of gender and age which, though they are based on biological givens, are socially determined. Because the categories generated are universally deemed to be natural, we find that in all societies the predominant behaviours and statuses associated with age and gender are taken to be self-evidently right and, therefore, hedged about with ideas of morality. India is no exception to this principle, but neither is it uniquely unyielding in its practical interpretation of notions of sex and age. To say anything of a general nature on this subject is immediately to lay oneself open to the accusation of essentializing; I want to stress that people are obviously individuals, personal relationships are all slightly different, and families are not clones of each other but, that said, I shall perhaps seem at times to generalize in a rather heavy-handed fashion.

PATRIARCHY

India is a predominantly patriarchal society. This is not surprising since we can assume patriarchy in those situations where there are landowning peasants, where there is a landed aristocracy and where there are family firms. Peasantry and family firms flourish and though the landed aristocracy has gone, its memory lingers. The paternal joint family, governed by a property-holding patriarch,

FIGURE 6.1 Working together on newly-irrigated land, Bihar

has long been the favoured household form, ensuring the concentration of related men and the dispersal of women into families of marriage. In a paternal joint family, the men are all related to each other by kinship but the women have only affinal ties to each other and to the men until they become mothers and, even then, they know that their daughters are transitory members of the group. It is no wonder that the tie between women and their sons is so especially powerful in a traditional Indian context.

There are certain characteristics of patriarchy that we can expect to find, regardless of its context – a preference for boy children, curtailment of women's property rights, notions of modesty which involve excessive concern for the sexual reputations of women, restriction of women's behaviour in public, sexual jealousy on the part of men, control of women's movements. None of these is absent in India, but they are not universal either. The form that patriarchy takes is highly dependent upon the economic, social and political situation of a family; one cannot usefully construct a stereotype which cuts across caste, class, religion, region, but there is some degree of commonality of structure and behaviour. Though patriarchy is a concept with its roots in kinship it extends into gendered relationships well beyond families and households into notions of what men and women are and can be in totality. It extends into views of women, often internalized by themselves, that they are inferior, incomplete, polluted and polluting to others – restricted from serving food or entering temples when menstruating, dangerous after giving birth or being widowed (Hershman 1974). Such views are disappearing fast among educated women, but they lurk deep within the culture.

The ideology of *Hindutva* which underwrites the politics of the *Sangh Parivar* is unambiguous in its interpretation of the place of women in society, stressing their role as mothers and wives. In a newspaper article, Karat (1998), criticizing the use of the scriptures to reinforce the Laws of Manu, quotes (from an unspecified RSS journal) 'the main function of a woman is to impart noble *samskaras* to the young generation – her prime

responsibility is caring for the family … most women are kind, soft and shy, whilst most men are strong, firm and brave … in our tradition women look after the house and men outside.' She continues to point out that for the Hindu Right, 'women's struggles for justice in the economic, political and social spheres are westernized concepts which should be rejected'. However, one finds that the Hindu Right has contradictory attitudes and is willing to encourage women out of the home in the greater cause of militant *Hindutva* (Banerjee 1995). One of the main planks of the RSS policy is the introduction of a common civil code which will impose Hindu-based family law on non-Hindus (not that Islamic personal law is an improvement). Much of the Hindu Right virulence against Islam and Christianity is conducted using the rhetoric of rape and the need to protect Hindu women from alien men (Kannabiran 1996).

As the previous chapters have shown, the divide between domestic and public life corresponds closely to social status. Women of the lower castes and classes have always worked hard outside the home, in fields, factories and quarries, on the roads and building sites. They work for very low wages, often less than 10 rupees a day, and they take their small children with them. At the other end of the scale, educated upper middle-class women have careers, if they wish. Women running businesses, lecturing in universities, piloting planes, practising as lawyers, doctors or architects are not unusual and, though there is a certain amount of juggling of roles to be done, servants make the life of a working wife and mother much simpler than it is in more affluent countries. Between these two, middle-class respectability is indicated by the domestication of women, who, if they work for money at all, do so within the confines of their homes. It is the women in the middle who are most obviously subject to the pressures of patriarchal systems and also it is they who are most likely to concur in the maintenance of patriarchy, despising as inferior the labouring women and disapproving of the 'selfishness' and lack of modesty of the upper classes.

The Miss World contest in Bangalore in

FIGURE 6.2 Women planting seedlings, Bihar

FIGURE 6.3 The leader of a village water committee, Bihar

1996 was an opportunity for many ideological positions to be expressed on the subject of 'ideal' womanhood, for it was opposed by both feminists and conservatives, championed only by a tiny fraction of women. Some women of the far Right threatened

to self-immolate, and demonstrations and obstructions were organized and met with considerable force (Menon 1996)

WOMEN IN GOVERNMENT

When India gained its Independence there was immediate universal suffrage; women had participated fully in the Independence struggle and there was no question of excluding them from the electorate or from government, and yet, as in the rest of the world, women have come through into positions of political leadership in relatively small numbers at all levels of governance. However, women are more visible in active politics in India than either Britain or the United States.

It is important to note that India is the only country to have incorporated positive discrimination in favour of women into its Constitution; the 73rd Amendment, which introduced the system of local government known as *panchayati raj*, required that at least one third of each category of seat (for the open list and the reserved lists for Scheduled Castes, Scheduled Tribes and Other Backward Classes) on *panchayats* (local councils) should be filled by women. Additionally, a third of all *sarpanches* (heads of *panchayats*) in a district should be women. When *panchayati raj* is fully implemented it will revolutionize the way in which rural areas in particular are administered. Many States have delayed setting up a full *panchayati raj* structure and there are accusations that powerful men try to place their wives in reserved seats to echo their interests, but there is no denying that women are taking their place in rural local government and are learning to speak out. Even placed women realize that they have a voice of their own. NGOs, such as the Rural Litigation and Entitlement Kendra in northern Uttar Pradesh, are organizing training for women representatives, drawing upon volunteer senior government officers to demystify administrative processes. There are already a few *gram panchayats*, notably in the State of Maharashtra, where all of the representatives are women as a consequence of their fighting and winning unreserved seats. These have come into being where determined women have demonstrated their willingness to act effectively on local issues and captured not just women's votes but also those of the younger men, who are themselves victims of patriarchal structures (personal communication, Maiah Wankhede, *Sarpanch* Medikhela). Less idealistically, we can observe that all women *panchayats* tend to be in the villages where a majority of the men have left as labour migrants.

In 1998 a bill to reserve one third of seats in the *Lok Sabah* for women was defeated by an alliance of parties representing the Other Backward Classes who claimed that men from the weaker sections of society would be excluded in favour of modern, educated, articulate women from the upper castes and classes (pejoratively described as 'the ones with cut hair'). They argued that such women have their own agendas and do not necessarily have the interests of the mass of women at heart. They also worried that such reservation would work to the advantage of the parties dominated by upper castes. Few women or progressive men can see the logic in holding up women's reservation in the name of caste considerations; even fewer are able to condone the scenes of physical fighting which broke out in the house over this issue.

THE WOMEN'S MOVEMENT

India has an active and effective women's movement which permeates all strata of society. The Gandhian legacy has been considerable. After Independence small numbers of politically aware women throughout India took to village work, where their developmental goals were orientated towards local needs rather than modernizing and market imperatives. In the first generation there were people like Gandhi's close associate, Mira Bhen, pioneering the organized ecological awareness in the Garwal Himalaya which was later to flourish as the *Chipko Andolan* (Shiva 1989).

Throughout the post-Independence era élite women have joined neighbourhood clubs orientated towards domestic skills, formed charitable organizations and groups devoted to the arts and general interest talks. They have also belonged to international bodies such as the Federation of Business and Professional Women's Clubs (Caplan 1985). These may not be revolutionary movements, but in bringing women together outside their homes they provided seed beds for Indian feminism.

After Indira Gandhi's State of Emergency (1975–77), there was a sudden regeneration of activism in all aspects of Indian social life as people seized back the freedom of association and expression which had been denied to them. Internationally, the 1970s was a time when women's movements were establishing themselves and challenging social agendas; it was not surprising that feminism flourished in the context of post-Emergency India. Though this was initially a concern of educated middle-class women railing against their personal and professional lack of freedom, a consciousness of women's issues in a wider sense soon took hold. The Committee on the Status of Women in India, an *ad hoc* group which reported on a range of women's concerns in the late 1970s, achieved an important coup when it persuaded the government to make a categorical statement of intent by focusing upon women in the Sixth Five-Year Plan (1980–85). The Planning Commission was required to turn its attention specifically to women in their own right, not just as submerged members of male-headed household units. Research on women was funded and female academics and activists were drafted into think-tanks. The intention was to see women as economic actors, not just marginal contributors. Women were to become major beneficiaries under poverty alleviation programmes; to be encouraged to acquire skills and set up their own businesses; importantly, they were to be entitled to apply in their own name for government grants of land and also to joint title to land with their husbands. Additionally, childcare facilities were to be incorporated into the Minimum Needs Programme and a government department for women and child welfare came into being (Agnihotri and Mazumdar 1995). There is still a pronounced orientation towards women in government poverty alleviation schemes and the same approach has been followed by the many development orientated NGOs.

SELF-HELP

There are self-help women's groups throughout India, though these are rarely established without some opposition from established forces. Educated activists have frequently taken a role in initiating organization; not only do they have the necessary skills, they also have knowledge of successful movements in India and elsewhere. Importantly, their class and caste background is such that they are likely to be less intimidated by government or banking officials and more able to gain access to people with influence. This said, social movements are successful only when they are owned and run by their members in their own way, according to their own, rather than middle-class, priorities and values (Kabir 1995).

Probably the best known of the women's movements in India is the Self-Employed Women's Association (SEWA). This emerged from the textile workers' trade union in Uttar Pradesh when it was realized that the interests of marginalized women workers, at home or in the informal sector, could not be addressed by formal union politics directed towards confrontation with employers. There was the fur-

ther caste-based consideration that, whereas the majority of women casual workers were *dalits*, the union was dominated by anti-*dalit* elements. From a concern with the piece rates and flow of work of textile workers, SEWA expanded to take account of the plight of all women in the unorganized sector, including market traders, casual labourers and rag-pickers, amongst others. Although the term 'self-employed women' in a western context may conjure up ladylike membership of the business community, it does not have the same meaning in the context of SEWA and was adopted because the women targeted did not have contractual relations with an employer. SEWA has given its members a sense of solidarity in a fragmented sector of the economy; this means a degree of independence from middlemen and a consequent rise in remuneration. SEWA has also extended to establish its own bank on *Grameen* principles to finance women's income-generating projects and tide them over the emergencies which would drive them to use money-lenders. As an organized force it has been able to tackle social issues relating to violence against women, dowry and the like. Since it is generally acknowledged that one of the most serious outcomes of liberalization and globalization in India is increased pressure on the informal sector, associations such as SEWA gain an enhanced significance as organized bodies which can provide an interface with the market, financial institutions and the suppliers of raw materials. In the absence of such associations, the millions of women who work for piece rates sewing garments, embroidering, leather stitching and so on can only find themselves unable to negotiate successfully in the global marketplace. The other side of the coin is that SEWA is itself an embryonic firm orientated towards the profit motive; the embroidered garments it is most associated with are sold abroad and through SEWA outlets in the affluent suburbs of the mega-cities, where only the wealthy can afford them.

Another important but quite different movement is the Women's Development Programme which grew up in Rajasthan, a State which is notorious for its women's rights record. Many of the women of rural Rajasthan, particularly members of Rajput and Gujar families, are still kept secluded from public life; they have little freedom of movement or control of property. Though these are landowning and governing castes this by no means implies that all of their households are wealthy, or even in possession of land, as the State as a whole is poor, even by Indian standards, and much of the land desert or scrub. Rajasthan scores low on all development indicators and has the lowest female literacy rate (20.4 per cent) in India. Upper-caste Rajasthani families have long practised female infanticide, there is a preference for child marriage, and still occasional instances of *sati*. There are many affectionate and supportive marriages and it would be unfair to suggest otherwise; however, the social structure is weighted heavily in favour of men's interests. Domestic violence is common and dominant-caste men sometimes use organized gang rape as a way of demonstrating their superior power over the lower castes. For all its touristic appeal and its vibrant folk culture, there is much concealed misery in Rajasthan (Sangari and Vaid 1996).

WDP was a government initiative aimed at rupturing the cycle of women's deprivation, and as such it is an example of the way in which the organized state can successfully intervene. The basis of the programme was to enlist rural women as volunteers to raise women's consciousness about a range of development issues and to act as a bridge between women and government schemes. These were known as *sathins* (friends) and given a small stipend and basic training. They were frequently recruited from the ranks of traditional midwives. WDP emphasized adult literacy, women's health, participation in income generating schemes and knowledge of women's legal rights, but it also encouraged the formation of community-based groups which could act corporately over injustices to individual women and to campaign against the use of alcohol. Given the social environment in which they were working, the *sathins* had to be remarkably strong women and they came constantly under moral and physical attack from conservative male elements. Several *sathins* have suffered 'punishment' rapes to remind them of women's inferior position (Mander undated).

Box 10 A sathin's story

Ramkaran Gujar was determined to marry off his infant daughter who was less than one year old. Sathin Bhanvari tried to reason with him, but he refused ... finally the police were sent by the District administration and they stopped the marriage, but the marriage took place clandestinely the next morning and no subsequent police action was taken against the family. But the Gujars were convinced that Bhanvari was responsible for calling the police into the village.

Therefore the Gujar community resolved that Bhanvari should be punished. Retribution first came in the form of a social boycott .... Threats were issued and her husband assaulted at home. For the sake of Bhanvari's security he stopped plying his cycle rickshaw in Jaipur. The family fell into acute economic distress.

Five men assaulted Mohan .... Two men restrained him and one held down Bhanvanri while two took turns to rape her .... They grappled with hostility, suspicion and humiliation in the *thana* (police station) ... even the women constables taunted her...

Finally the Rajasthan High Court confirmed that it was 'a case of gang rape which was committed out of vengeance because Smt. Bhanvari Devi made efforts to check child marriage of the minor daughter of the accused Ramkaran.'

Source: extracts from Harsh Mander's (undated) account, *One woman's battle*

Chapter Five mentioned women's anti-*arrack* movements in the context of rural development. These are particularly associated with the southern States of Tamil Nadu and Andhra Pradesh and have often become successful rallying points for other women's development issues such as co-operative formation and credit associations.

The anti-*arrack* movements go back as far as the Independence struggle. They involve women banding together to drive liquor dealers out of their villages and to shame and punish excessive drinkers. The form that alcohol consumption takes is always culturally determined and traditionally in India only *kshatriyas, shudras* and *dalits* should drink (others do it clandestinely) and it is almost exclusively limited to men. Traditionally, when *jati* made a bid to improve their social status, teetotalism and vegetarianism were used as conventional signs of their upward mobility (Srinivas 1962). Men drink in order to get drunk and forget, and this encourages desperate, melancholic and pathological drinking; poor men vent their frustrations in violence towards their wives. The anti-*arrack* movements are not about stopping men from enjoying themselves, they are about keeping families safe. Liquor dealers often double up as money-lenders and have a double reason for encouraging men to drink rather than save and invest. When men default on usurious loans, they are liable to lose any land they may have, surrender their families' ration books and ultimately give their children in bondage; the anti-*arrack* movements are about women seizing power (Sainath 1996). They have sometimes influenced State governments to introduce total or partial prohibition, though this is rarely the answer since prohibition encourages the distillation of quicker-fermenting, more dangerous potions with sometimes lethal chemical additives. Successful anti-*arrack* movements have frequently progressed to form *mahila mandals* (women's institutes) for social and developmental purposes, co-operatives and night schools.

SURVIVING

Few countries have such explicit governmental recognition of the importance of women and yet women in India are disadvantaged at every turn. Just staying alive is a struggle for many, as is revealed by the population statistics which show a deficit of women in all age tranches. Dreze and Sen (1989) estimate the number of India's 'missing women' for 1986 to be 36.9 million (or 9.5 per cent of the female population); they calculate this by comparing India's female-to-male ratio not with the affluent West but with sub-Saharan Africa. Only Pakistan has a greater proportion of its women 'missing' than India. Dreze and Sen (1995) show that this imbalance has been deteriorating throughout the century and that, whereas in the past it was the higher castes and the north-western States which demonstrated the greatest female shortfall, by 1991 caste and regional variations were becoming less pronounced as the sexual imbalance widened in the lower castes and in the South. When we remember that at all ages, given equal opportunities, females normally have a higher survival rate than males, we have to recognize that not only is something seriously wrong, but that it is getting worse as India 'modernizes'.

Selective feeding and medical care amongst poor people mean that men and boys survive better than women and girls. Malnourished women are prone to difficult childbirths and have high perinatal mortality rates. The World Bank reports that 80 per cent of women in India give birth at home and that only half receive even one perinatal medical check-up. Certainly there are traditional alternative forms of care and not everyone is a supporter of medicalized childbirth, but the study reveals that Indian women are an appalling '200 times more vulnerable to maternity related deaths than their counterparts in the developed world' (World Bank 1997, p. 24). In 1997 India's maternal mortality ratio was 570 per 100 000 live births with post-partum haemorrhage by far the greatest cause (Athreya and Chunkath 1998).

Poor women work substantially longer hours each day than men, characteristically rising before dawn to begin their domestic tasks. Rural women then spend long daytime hours cultivating, collecting fuel and fodder, fetching water; urban women may work on construction sites or as servants, etc.; both have to prepare food for an evening meal after their other work. Women are often starving and exhausted as they provide the best they can for their children, husbands and the older generation; 60 per cent of them are anaemic (Athreya and Sen 1998, p. 24). It is no surprise that they fall prey to illness.

WILLINGNESS TO CHANGE

It is these same women who have been the most receptive to initiatives to improve conditions. Though women are often accused of being conservative, it is clear in India that young and middle-aged women have a clear awareness that there is plenty of room for improvement and are receptive to relevant change. Time after time when visiting projects where people are getting on and seizing the initiative to improve yields through water harvesting, setting up rural health networks, running literacy classes, one realizes that the most ardent enthusiasts are women. It is generally acknowledged that women's anti-*arrak* movements and rotating credit unions have the power to break rural indebtedness and bonded labour, that women's co-operatives are the most likely to be genuinely productive and that women are the keenest environmentalists. Total literacy campaigns find that it is women who are most likely to grasp the chance of learning to read and write, even though they have less personal spare time than men.

The women who are active in a whole range of development activities are not just any slice taken across the whole of society; they are, characteristically, members of the most deprived sections and this implies a predominance of Scheduled Castes and Tribes. Guru (1997) points out there is a long tradition of *dalit bahujan* women's activism, particularly in Maharashtra. These sections could never afford to forgo the labour of women or require their seclusion from public life. There has always been greater equality of the sexes in tribal communities (some of which are matrilineal) where land is held communally, not by individual male-headed families, and where women contribute in full as producers of food and craft goods. In *dalit* communities, too, there has long been a considerable degree of equality of poverty, husband and wife co-operating in a landless partnership (Ilaiah 1996). There is no reason to idealize this into a perfect harmonious relationship – it can be marked by considerable brutality – but women of this section of society are reared to be tough and assertive

and to be capable of taking responsibility for their children.

MARRIAGE

There are diametrically opposed views on the subject of the family-arranged marriages which predominate across the social spectrum in India. Where extended families are the norm, it is clear that a marriage is a matter of concern for more than just the bride and groom – families must be matched rather than individuals. In all classes the most usual view is that 'love marriages' (now fashionably referred to as 'self-arranged marriages') are more likely to flounder in divorce than those which are family arranged. The term 'love marriage' is an unfortunate one, since it implies that arranged marriages are loveless and this is certainly not intended to be the case, as millions of couples of all ages demonstrate in their considerate and affectionate behaviour towards one another. Whilst arranging a marriage the elders are trying to do their best by their children and the whole family – compatibility and sexual attraction are part of the equation. India's stories and poems through the ages glorify the ideal of romantic love within marriage. Anees Jung, herself brought up in *purdah*, gives a touching description of the love demonstrated by an elderly washerman for his blind wife in her book *Unveiling India* which reminds me of many couples of all classes I have encountered in India (Jung 1987).

However, the trend towards individualism in the educated upper classes means that many people no longer see family-arranged marriages as appropriate, given that modern marriages are based upon individual rather than social characteristics. Seymour (1999), however, warns against assuming that modernization always implies a change in family structure. Rights of veto over parental suggestions are no longer always seen as providing a sufficient element of choice amongst people who have the opportunity to meet potential partners at college, at work, through friends or in political movements. But the best 'self-arranged' marriages are

DOWRY CALCULATIONS

Amongst the poor where women contribute to a household's income, they are commonly valued more than in those castes and classes in which they are not economically productive. There is a proverb which brutally reflects the economic status of daughters of middle India: 'When you rear a daughter you are watering another man's plant.' Circumstances will determine how well that 'plant' is watered. An ideal family unit will contain daughters and the bond between brother and sister is usually an affectionate one. In the middle classes and above, daughters are often treated indulgently, particularly by their fathers, and they will be educated in a range of domestic accomplishments which will make them desirable wives to 'good' families. As was indicated in Chapters Two and Three, dowry is routinely paid in the higher castes but the practice of giving dowry is now extending down through the social hierarchy. As well as being a pre-mortem inheritance by a girl when she leaves her natal family, a part of the dowry given represents the assumption that wife takers are superior to wife givers, and that, within a *jati*, a woman should marry upwards in social status. When a family attempts to make the 'best' match possible for its daughter, it is bridging a status gap between the bride and the family into which she marries. A large dowry helps to make a bride more acceptable. Kishwar (1994) argues that a woman would be more secure in a marriage if it were her inheritance prospects which were taken into account, rather than a dowry. She also believes that women would obtain a larger share of family property under this system since, for all the fuss about dowry, sons generally inherit a greater share than daughters receive in dowry.

If a family has an excess of daughters over sons, arranging marriages for its girls can impose a terrible financial burden unless it is exceedingly wealthy (Menski 1998). Families start thinking about a girl's dowry as soon as she is born, setting aside the cash and accumulating the jewellery which will help her to marry 'well' (Wadley 1994). In a balanced

FIGURE 6.4 Young married women, Madhya Pradesh

those of which families can approve, given that alliances which fly in the face of social expectations often encounter more strains than they can bear. Even when she arranges her own marriage, a woman needs to give some thought to the matter of her relationship with her mother-in-law.

The self-arranged marriage tends to be a phenomenon associated with the urban 'westernized' élite; it is uncommon in rural communities, where marriage of girls tends to be very early, and amongst the urban lower middle classes, where notions of family respectability are pronounced and where dowry considerations loom large.

One should be cautious about invariably championing changes in the structure of marriage and its associated rights. Kishwar (1995) argues that a system of joint matrimonial property, whereby half of a man's wealth could be assigned to a woman on divorce, would be inappropriate in India because a divorcing woman would dispossess her husband's other dependants such as elderly parents.

family, dowry received for sons will, in part, offset that expended for daughters, but where there are 'too many' girls there is an absolute outflow of wealth. Many families see having no son at all as a disaster (Nabar 1995).

The patriarchal landed castes, particularly those groups from North India known as the 'martial castes', were always the predominant dowry givers. Traditionally, women of these groups maintained *purdah* and, because of the presence of lower-caste servants, did little domestic work; they could be seen as contributing to the wealth of their families of marriage only by bringing dowry and by producing sons. Although *purdah* is hardly found today, the practice of dowry-giving is extending geographically and in caste terms; it is also subject to massive inflation. There are good grounds for seeing the current practice of dowry-giving as a vibrant modern phenomenon, rather than a continuation of tradition. It has become consumer driven and investment orientated in the context of the free market economy. By no means all

Figure 6.5 Young mothers, Madhya Pradesh

brides' families offer, or groom's families demand, kilos of gold, cars, a range of consumer durables and that the young man be set up in business, but there are abundant cases of those who do. In Chapter Two we saw that, ideally, dowry was intended to give women security within their marriages. However, the practice has notoriously become perverted into a form of blackmail – the parents of a girl being afraid that she will not marry at all if she is not endowed.

Demanding and offering dowry was made illegal by the Dowry Prohibition Act of 1961 but there can be no law which was more honoured in the breach than the observance. Women's groups in the major cities have campaigned for the implementation of the act, seeing dowry as the source of much maltreatment of young brides and, ever since the Independence struggle, socially-conscious young men have been willing to marry without dowry; most observers however see little chance of the practice disappearing.

The worst cases

It is in the context of dowry that we find the most spectacular cases of abuses against women, though it needs to be considered whether the routine neglect and maltreatment of women are really any less deplorable than the extreme practices I am about to describe. The women's movement of the 1970s lifted the veil which had been drawn over dowry-related murders whereby a husband, or more commonly a mother-in-law, faked the accidental death or suicide of a bride whose family had disappointed in their dowry payments. This allowed the young widower to remarry, again with dowry. Police had been reluctant to investigate suspicious deaths because the families concerned were predominantly 'respectable' middle class.

No one knows whether the increase in the number of cases of 'bride burning' reflects greater awareness of the phenomenon or whether it reflects an increased incidence; it is quite likely that it is a mixture of both but whereas, India-wide, 1912 dowry-related murders were reported in 1987, a mere seven years later in 1994 there were 5199. This represents only those deaths which appeared in the statistics of the National Crimes Bureau and is widely assumed to be the tip of an iceberg. Uttar Pradesh (16), Punjab (15), Delhi (15) and Harayana (12) have the highest concentration of notified dowry deaths per million population (for all-India the figure is seven per million with the predominantly non-Hindu north-eastern States recording none) (Thakur 1998). It needs to be remembered when thinking in per million terms, however, that dowry murders tend to be concentrated in the middle classes and upper castes; there are no figures which reflect the incidence for the most-at-risk categories, but it is chilling to contemplate 132 women burned in 1994 in the suburbs of Delhi or 1977 among the affluent farming communities of Uttar Pradesh. The numbers are far fewer than for women dying in childbirth or from pernicious anaemia – they make little contribution to the 'missing millions' – but they need to be taken seriously as the extreme cases indicate the far more widespread practice of routine maltreatment of young women with the aim of extorting more wealth from their families. A survey conducted by a Chandigarh NGO, the Institute of Development and Communication, showed that there is underreporting of dowry extortion, its research revealing 17 649 cases of dowry harassment in the Punjab in 1995. It estimated that for every dowry death reported, a further 299 are not (though this is probably a guess) (Vinayak 1997). Vinayak refers to the rapid growth of affluence and the commodity culture in the rural Punjab and the unrealistic aspirations of the middle classes, leading to what he refers to as 'Maruti marriages' (Maruti being a popular make of car).

In anticipation of dowry problems, some of the higher castes in certain States, most notoriously Rajasthan, have long practised female infanticide. It is easier to conceal the murder of a baby than a grown woman and there is a high infant mortality rate in any case, but substantial numbers of girl babies die from poisoning, suffocation or starvation. The girls are simply excess to requirements. The most typical situations in which these murders take place are those in which poor families belonging to high castes know that they will not be able to afford to marry more than one daughter. Failure to marry one's daughters rebounds upon the honour of the family and therefore the attractiveness of sons in marriage.

What really affects the sex ratio in the middle and upper classes is selective abortion (often referred to by its opponents as 'foeticide' in order to link it to infanticide). The development first of amniocentesis and then ultra-sound scanning to determine the sex of an unborn child has allowed those who can afford it to detect and abort unwanted female babies, and thousands do. It is illegal to use these techniques for the purpose of selection of the sex of a child, but it is virtually impossible to prove in any particular instance that this has happened. The most respectable medical institutions do not perform scans for purposes of sex determination, but plenty of others do, in particular in the affluent Punjab and Delhi.

These patriarchal practices have until recently been seen as virtually the exclusive preserve of the upper castes who have been

FIGURE 6.6 An abortionist's clinic

the major property holders. With the increase in consumer desires, not only dowry but also the related devaluing of women is extending to other sections of society, especially amongst those families which are upwardly mobile. Srinivas (1977) noticed this beginning to occur in the late 1970s but it is becoming increasingly prevalent.

WIDOWHOOD

The plight of a widow is never easy in a patriarchal society because women without husbands lack an effective kinship role but widow remarriage blurs family boundaries. Amongst the higher castes, widow remarriage has been virtually impossible and widows regarded as inauspicious. The practice of *sati* (whereby widows were burned with their husbands on the funeral pyre) was made illegal in 1827 but occasional instances continued to occur and *satis* to be revered as holy. Following the much publicized *sati* (suicide? murder?) of Roop Kanwar, an eighteen-year-old woman in rural Rajasthan in 1987, the issue of the treatment of widows as well as the narrower issue of *sati* came onto the agenda. Nandy (1995) reports that a *Times of India* survey found that 63 per cent of its respondents supported Roop Kanwar's *sati* (*The Times of India* is the country's most prominent English-medium newspaper). Nandy himself questions the right of educated élites to criticize the glorification of *sati*, which culminated in the 1987 Commission of Sati (Prevention) Act; this not only outlawed the already illegal and exceedingly rare practice, but also banned the reverence accorded to *sati*. Many think that Nandy is carrying respect for tradition too far and that this reverence for the sites of *sati* is enshrined in a notion of wifely devotion which denies a widow any dignity or respect. Joseph and Sharma (1994) give a chilling account of the salacious newspaper reporting of Roop Kanwar's burning and the revival of enthusiasm for the ritual.

Roop Kanwar's was an exceptional case but, if she was not forced, she was probably driven not just by grief at the death of her young husband but also her knowledge of the role that was mapped out for the rest of her life – no children, banned from attending weddings and other joyful occasions, banned from wearing bright colours, a drag on both her parents and her affines. In traditional upper-caste rural communities such as she came from, widows have their heads shaved in mourning, they may not wear any adornments and they are often accused of having the evil eye. This applies even to virgin widows – those small girl children who are married quite illegally for the honour of their families and whose lives can effectively be obliterated by the death of a boy they do not even know.

However, most widows are not young. They have completed all their wifely and motherly duties and must take a back seat in the household of a son, where their daughter-in-law reigns over domestic matters. A mother-in-law is only powerful so long as her husband is alive. No one who has seen Satyajit Ray's film *Distant Thunder* can forget the pathos of a dependent old female relative. Susan Seymour (1999) explains that many older women compensate by withdrawing into spirituality and contemplation.

Women's groups have organized training for widows so that they can work and support themselves; they have also encouraged these women to fly in the face of convention, to wear bright clothes and glass bangles rather than to try to efface themselves.

PUBLIC VIOLENCE

The patriarchal principle that women should not assume a public role runs deep and is liable to provoke sexual attack. College girls run a gauntlet of cat-calling and mauling by young men at bus-stops. The practice is trivialized by calling it 'Eve-teasing' (Eve standing for all womanhood) and very easily degenerates into sexual abuse; they are felt to be fair game because of their 'brazen' behaviour. Women supporters of the Uttarakhand Movement on their way by bus to demonstrate in Delhi were raped when the bus was ambushed by opponents (Ramakrishnan (1994b and c); Catholic nuns have come in the front line of attacks against Christians.

When young women researchers complained about sexual harassment from a senior professor, Delhi's Health Minister rebuked them for bringing themselves into disrepute by complaining. Women members of *panchayats* commonly find that they become the target of slanderous accusations about their loose morals (Mayaram and Pal 1997). Rape of *sathins* has already been mentioned. When women dare to bring complaints to the police there is a strong chance that they will not be treated sympathetically, as the offence of 'custodial rape' indicates. All of these incidents underline the principle that women with a public role undermine patriarchy.

Sexual attacks on the women (often just children) of the lower castes are common in the most feudal States like Bihar, Rajasthan and Uttar Pradesh. This is seen as a way of asserting the dominance of the upper castes over the men of the lower castes whose honour is despoiled. Rape is political.

PROSTITUTION

Patriarchal systems are underwritten by prostitution and rape – these are the means whereby inflated notions of virility can co-exist with extreme control of the modesty of one's 'own' women. Prostitution thrives in contemporary India and, as with many other practices, though it harks back to tradition has mutated to fit modern conditions.

A film like *Pakeeza* (Director: Kamal Amrohi) contemplates the status of the prostitute in feudal society, marginal and stigmatized, but with a degree of freedom not accorded to many women. It draws upon the way in which matrilineages of dancer-courtesans are groomed within particular *jati*, such as the Bedias of Madhya Pradesh, sometimes to operate independently, sometimes to be incorporated into the retinues of landowning men. Such prostitute *jati* still exist with complex conventions governing the way in which working women support their children, mothers and brothers. They frequently act as entertainers – singing and dancing at celebrations. The best they can hope for, as in the past, is to become the mistress of one long-term client, but the majority have multi-

ple clients and are badly treated. They, and their children, carry a terrible social stigma. Children are often excluded from schools and it becomes difficult for girls to break the cycle of recruitment into the profession. They operate in the small towns where they have their own districts and a degree of autonomy, pimping being within the *jati*. In the town of Shivpuri in northern Madhya Pradesh, when local movements campaigned for their removal the consequence was that the younger women migrated to Mumbai. There they discovered a far more lucrative market and realized that the wealth of the Gulf was just a short plane journey away, with visas that declared them to be members of troupes of traditional dancers (Mander and Rao 1996). (Mander also generously allowed me to participate in interviews with people from the Bedia *jati* working for the release of women from traditional prostitution in Shivpuri in 1999).

In contrast to this caste-based prostitution is the far more common and infinitely more exploitative prostitution of young bonded or kidnapped rural girls, the street children of both sexes and the abused wives and widows who are sold into brothels. There is nothing glamorous about the red-light districts of large Indian cities where the trade is as overt as it is for any other commodity. The painted girls calling down from barred balconies are rarely free to quit, bound to the trade by debts and by the violence of pimps. As the women say, the only reason that other people are concerned that prostitutes are ready victims to AIDS is that 'respectable' society fears the directness of the link from the brothels to the smart suburbs. The long-distance lorry drivers' overnight stops are almost invariably served by prostitutes – in a survey conducted by *India Today*, virtually all lorry drivers said that they used the wayside brothels.

Young men often leave their wives behind in their villages when they seek work in towns. There is a pronounced predominance of men of the lower classes in urban areas which encourages prostitution, but so too does the impersonal and commodified nature of more affluent urban communities.

Similar to the situation of prostitutes is the practice of giving girls as *devdasis* to temples in payment of a family supernatural debt. Here the girls officially become the brides of the deity; but they are under the authority of the temple and their plight can be as pitiful as that of any secular prostitute controlled by a pimp.

WOMEN'S EDUCATION

Education and all professions have long been open to women and yet at the 1991 census only 39.3 per cent of women had even bare literacy (by comparison with 64.1 per cent of men). As we might expect, the literacy rate varies considerably by caste, class and State and between urban and rural residents.

Amartya Sen (1992) has argued that literacy should be seen as one of the basic capabilities which is constitutive of human well-being, that is, it is not merely an indicator of social and economic condition but also the means whereby a degree of freedom can be exerted over one's own life. It is for this reason that so many voluntary schemes attempt to impart literacy. For example, the Women's Development Programme taught women labourers on employment creation schemes to read enough to understand when contractors were trying to trick them into signing against payments of 11 rupees a day when they were giving them only three and four rupees (Kabir 1995).

The State of Kerala is always quoted as the best example of the linkage between education and other indicators of well-being with 86.2 per cent of its female population literate in 1991. In Kerala it is annually reported that the girls' schools obtain the highest scores in secondary school certificate examinations, sometimes with spectacularly high scores (as in 1998 when the pupils at Cotton Hill Government Girls' High School in Thiruvananthapuram achieved average marks of 93 per cent) (*The Hindu* 26 May 1998). In Kerala we find that although cash incomes are not amongst the highest in India, the male/female ratio is in favour of women, life expectancy is 70 years (as opposed to 57 years for all-India) and the infant mortality

rate is lower (Sen 1992, pp. 126–7). Some of us may prefer to take the argument back a little further to enquire why education is virtually universal in Kerala and to remember its upper-caste matrilineal heritage, the influence of Christian missionaries on the former untouchables and, perhaps most of all, its history of Communist governments.

WITCHES

It is just short step from the metaphorical demonization of women to their literal demonization. Accusations of witchcraft are a well-established way of explaining misfortunes whilst attributing blame to the unpopular members of society. Not just amongst tribal peoples, in-marrying women can find themselves blamed for the sicknesses, deaths and lack of prosperity of their affines. In 1998 a group consisting of members of several different NGOs in Gujarat was protesting at a tribal *mela* (fair) against the practice of witch-hunting and beating out evil spirits from women. The group lodged a protest with the Governor of Gujarat that they had been harassed by an armed mob of members of the VHP, a right-wing Hindu organization, who accused them of being foreign-funded Christian agitators against traditional practices (*Veham Andhshraddha Virodhi Manch* 1998).

CHILDHOOD

As with everything else in India, how childhood is experienced very much depends upon one's social situation. Children of the upper middle classes and above are cosseted and, some may say, kept artificially naïve for too many years. They are indulged but have few freedoms to act in their own right or to move about unchaperoned. In a world of servants, children of the upper classes work only at their studies. Their lives tend to be interior based, hanging about their own or friends' houses, reading comics, watching TV and playing computer games (even though their parents like to project healthy images of their playing cricket and tennis). In the lower middle classes, boys' lives are a mixture of school work and play, but girls will take on household chores and generally leave education sooner than their brothers.

Child workers

This bears no relation whatsoever to the experience of the children of the poor who start to work as soon as they can walk. Tiny children can be seen on building sites 'playing' at sieving sand for their mothers or by road sides grading the chippings whilst their mothers carry head-loads of stones. Small girls take on the care of their smaller siblings, fetch water and do housework. Children also work in their own right, tending animals or working in the fields of richer farmers. They work in the factories and workshops of the unorganized sector of the economy and in the restaurants and hotels. They work because they have to, many entirely missing the education which might allow them one day to escape from the lowest paid and most unreliable labour. Of the 105 million children in the age range six to ten years, 33 million do not attend school and of these about 18 million take on paid labour – the rest will work at home, including agricultural production (World Bank 1997).

Neera Burra's (1995) overview of child labour makes harrowing reading as it reveals lives blighted by some of the cruelest exploitation. She shows how for the very

poor a child is an economic asset, not a source of expenditure and that much child labour is beyond surveillance since it takes place in the home, with children helping their mothers with piece-rate work. That might sound like a happy domestic scene, until one contemplates five-year-olds working nine hours a day rolling *agarbattis* for a daily income of about three rupees. Some industries quite systematically recruit children because of their docility and willingness to work without interruption; the dangerous match and firework industry is notorious for this (Burra cites a study carried out by Kothari in the early 1980s which found the youngest worker in a match factory to be only three-and-a-half years old). Other industries which rely heavily on child labour are carpet weaving, silver jewellery making, *bidi* making and glass making. Virtually every motor repair shop and spray-painter has at least one child worker. There are children doing decorative brass work, handling chemical dyes, and sorting refuse. They also work long hours and sleep on kitchen floors in middle-class households. Sometimes one hears children's work explained away as a kind of informal apprenticeship in the craft industries, or an alternative education for working-class children; the poor conditions, dangerous work, long hours and miserable payment would refute this as an explanation. Given that it is illegal to employ children

FIGURE 6.7 Apprentices (or slaves?)

FIGURE 6.8 Working with her family on a government scheme, Gwalior

under the age of 14, it is obvious that there is no compensation when they are injured, nor do they receive payment when sick.

In 1999, as a consequence of campaigning from members of the national Human Rights Commission, a circular to senior government employees informed them that henceforth it would be a disciplinary offence for them to employ servants in their households under the age of 14. Given that these are the very people who are supposed to uphold the law, there is very little hope that it will be applied generally. The Ministry of External Affairs (*sic*) embarked on a campaign to explain India's record of child labour to the world, given the increasing levels of protest against products manufactured by children. It even set up a website (http://www.meadev.gov.in/social/child/childlabour.htm), where one can read that 'joining the family trade at a very young age is tradition in India' (Swami 1998).

Not infrequently, the children working in the workshops of the informal sector are bonded labour, working for nothing more than their meagre keep against family debts (Human Rights Watch 1996). Although bonded labour was made illegal in 1976, the World Bank cites an estimated 15 million Indian children in bondage.

Burra, and many others, maintains that the problem of child labour will only be resolved when India makes education compulsory and enforces this. In response to the plea that families depend on the work of their children to survive, the counter argument is that the low wages paid to children deprive adults of higher rates of pay. The argument that Indian goods would not be competitive on the world market without children's cheap labour does not bear close scrutiny.

FIGURE 6.9 Child labour in a dye works, Madhya Pradesh

Street children

UNICEF calculates that there are around 11 million street children working and begging in India (*The Hindu* 30 November 1998). Mander and Rao (1996), working with street children's NGOs, argue that one should separate out children *on* the streets from children *of* the streets. The former do casual work and beg but return to their families at night; the latter live on the streets and have no effective families – often they have run away from abusive families. Mira Nair's film *Salaam Bombay* provides a picture of the life of children of the street. Nair made the film with the advice and co-operation of street children and employed them as actors. She portrays their resourcefulness but hopelessness and shows how they confront danger and exploitation at every turn. Many of her themes are spelled out by Mander and Rao who draw upon case studies to emphasize that the children of the street are multiple victims who try to scratch a living, are prone to disease, lack formal education, are prey to petty criminals and pimps, receive beatings from the police and lack any form of stability in their lives. They show that girls have a harder time on the streets than boys and that small girls will sometimes dress as boys to avoid being noticed; however, at around the age of 10 their 'freedom' is over and they are likely to be pulled into prostitution.

Mander is an Indian Administrative Service officer who, amongst his many other schemes for the most marginalized sections of society, has set up shelters for street children in the towns of Madhya Pradesh and enlisted volunteer workers to provide elementary education and to teach them to be aware of their legal rights. He is adamant that these are especially independent-minded children, keen to make something of their lives but unwilling to be taken over by authority, and he believes that any projects to help them must respect their desire for freedom and resist any temptation to try to institutionalize or confine them (personal communication).

These views are borne out in the work of the major northern Indian charity for street children, *Prayas*, where children are offered transitional education outside the formal schools and as they get older are taught trades. They run a childline telephone help service and will go out to pick up children in danger. *Prayas* does not attempt to stop children from rag picking, casual work or begging, but seeks to make it possible for the children to do more. Some live in shelters, but many continue to sleep on the pavements and railway stations or live with their parents in the slums. Those who believe that street children are a lost cause might be surprised to meet young adults who have 'graduated' from *Prayas*, running small printing businesses, beauty parlours or scooter repair shops, turning their hard-won resourcefulness into entrepreneurship – for *Prayas* does

FIGURE 6.10 A slum school in Delhi

have a strong pro-market orientation. The organization was originally set up by a senior police officer who realized that children were unnecessarily criminalized; many of its volunteers are still members of the police. Organizations like this, financed by grants from the Government of India and local charitable activity are nothing more than a mild palliative; they can only provide help to a tiny fraction of those 11 million children whose real need is to belong to families that are not trapped in destitution.

Children for sale

Periodically stories come to light of children sold abroad as workers or for adoption. Most recently a Christian organization called the Good Samaritan and Evangelical Welfare Association and an NGO, Action for Social Development, have been exposed for trading in children for export in Andhra Pradesh. It seems that between them they have sent about 400 babies to Europe and the USA over an eight-year period, and that the charitable work of placing children who would otherwise be institutionalized slipped into a lucrative business. The organizations realized that it was possible to buy the girl children born to poor families in the Lambada tribe for about Rs 5 000 and then charge adoptive parents $2 500–3 000 for them. The Lambada have been targeted because they have relatively pale complexions which are

more attractive to western parents (Kumar 1999).

OLD AGE

India is famous for the respect it accords to elderly members of society, but that does not mean that most old people are treated especially well. In a country where tiny children have to work to contribute to the household income, old people, too, have to struggle to do their share. The great virtue of extended families is that there is a pooling of resources and an internal welfare system whereby elderly householders can expect their sons and daughters-in-law to take care of them. Amongst the very poor this ideal has always been difficult to achieve.

The Hindu notion of stages of life assumes that people will accept the conditions appropriate to a particular age; the condition appropriate to old age is withdrawal from the affairs of the world and contemplation of death. Although the practice of renunciation is less common today than it was said to have been in the past, it is not unusual for older people to spend a good deal of their time in pilgrimage or staying in ashrams. Amongst conservative people, acting young for one's age is a source of criticism rather than admiration as old people are supposed to slow down and lead a more modest (and economical) life. The respect and care accorded to old

FIGURE 6.11 Working in old age

Figure 6.12 The time of life for pilgrimage, Haridwa

age is bought at the cost of having to accept the restrictions that go with it.

As has already been shown, the extended family is under considerable pressure in India. A consequence of the movement towards nuclear families in contemporary conditions is that many older people of all classes now live alone. Features are beginning to appear in the press about the plight of elderly people in the new India and older people frequently express their resentment about being the squeezed generation which looked after its parents but cannot expect the same now that it is their turn (Mitra 1998b). In this family-orientated society there is a very real concern about the loneliness of old age, now that the young wish to lead their own lives. Speculative builders have seen the opportunity in catering to the problems of affluent older people, promoting retirement communities and even placing advertisements for these which are directed at the guilt of non-resident children.

There are very few residential homes for elderly people and most of those that do exist provide for the destitute. When people become frail they are almost invariably taken into the homes of their children or other younger relatives, but today they often worry about being a burden and the household that is established in this way is not structurally the same as the old paternal joint family. Increasingly one reads in the newspapers about cases of domestic violence against old people, though, as in the case of wife beating, it usually takes a murder to reach the newspapers; it is suspected that there are many more concealed deaths. As I write, today's *Indian Express* reported that a young man, assumed to be in collaboration with his parents, was convicted in Delhi of the murder of his paternal grandfather who was living with them. The motive was inheritance of his property. Were it to occur, the revelation of abuse of elderly people on a large scale would strike at the very basis of the patriarchal system in a way that attacks on women do not.

One of the consequences of the New Economic Policy for relationships between the young and old of the affluent middle classes is that, whereas the older generation is liable to have retired with modest pensions derived from a career in government service, much of the younger generation is earning in the private sector. The younger people have rapidly adopted the consumerist values and global cultural forms promoted as intrinsic to the lifestyle of the new service class and I have frequently heard older people criticizing the way in which their own frugal ways have been rejected by their offspring. I increasingly gain the impression that elderly people of all classes in India feel threatened by the changes around them, not just the technological and fashion changes which perplex ageing people everywhere, but deep structural and value changes about people and relationships.

In 1998 the Union Ministry of Social Justice and Empowerment announced a new policy for elderly people, recognizing that the country is facing a major expansion in the numbers above the age of 60. However, this policy consists mostly of encouraging phrases about consideration towards old people and words of encouragement to lead an active life. Otherwise it is concerned with the speedier administration of already existing employment pensions and private medical insurance, preferential treatment in waiting lists for telephones and gas connections, reservation of seats on trains and in cinemas, and the sympathetic treatment of old people in public health provision. That is to say, it is an entirely cosmetic exercise. In a country where good medical care is exorbitantly expensive, where there are few support agencies and where there is no right to a state pension, elderly people can hardly be expected to greet an increasing individualization and market orientation with enthusiasm. They need to be able to claim their rights as citizens; however, old people, particularly frail old people, are less able than younger women to organize themselves in resistance.

7

VIOLENCE, CRIME AND CORRUPTION

Just before the 50th Anniversary of Independence, Pamela Phillipose used her column in the *Indian Express* to publish a 'possible script for a speech' for the Prime Minister to mark the occasion. It started, 'Long years ago we made a tryst with corruption, and now the time comes when we shall redeem our pledge, not wholly or in full measure, but very substantially.' It was, of course, Nehru's 'tryst with destiny' speech, with the inspiring words like 'freedom' and 'humanity' deleted throughout and replaced by the dull repetition of 'corruption'. 'At the stroke of the midnight hour, when the world sleeps, India will awake to life and corruption.' 'At this solemn moment we take the pledge to Indian corruption and the still larger cause of more corruption.' 'We have to build the noble mansion of corrupt India, where all her children may dwell.' She did not need to elaborate or interpret, but slyly cautioned that 'This is not intended to cast aspersions on the integrity of our politicians and bureaucrats, but only to celebrate their 50 years of freedom' (*Indian Express* 14 August 1997). What happened that the country which in 1947 bore the hopes of so many oppressed people throughout the world became so firmly associated with corruption and self-seeking?

C. Mitra (1998) cites the oft-quoted 'fact' that India is one of the 10 most corrupt countries in the world, but, as he acknowledges, this is a meaningless statement, since one obviously cannot objectively observe, measure and rank corruption. Singh (1997) cites a World Economic Forum survey which ranked 49 countries for honesty in various aspects of life – India came 45th for trustworthiness of public servants, 46th for business reliability and 40th for willingness to pay taxes. Corruption is, by its very nature, insidious and secretive, even though 'everyone' may know about it. The exact position in the league table does not matter; it is enough to acknowledge that corruption is rife in contemporary India and that it seems to be getting more blatant as market forces determine a new morality whereby 'rent-seeking' becomes normal.

Corruption is more than just crime – it implies the decay of the fabric of society, it can be seen eroding all institutions at all levels. The petty corruptions make small operators understand the motives of the big dealers; the major 'scams' justify the routine bribery, pilfering and nepotism. An insidious aspect of corruption is that it so easily becomes 'normal' – Rs 100 to the conductor to get a berth on a train which was supposed to be full; Rs 50 to the *chuprassi* to get into the queue to meet a public servant you are entitled to see; Rs 50 to the library assistant not to notice when you steal the book which all the other students in your year also need for their examinations; payments to get the telephone line installed or a gas connection; payments to get into a 'free' school or hospital; payments to the police when you are caught for trivial or major offences; payments for places in élite colleges; payments for good grades; payments to customs officials and officers in the revenue department; payments to municipal officers to 'grab' someone else's land for an urban development; payments to the ticket tout when you want to see a popular movie or get into a cricket match. And for every time someone bribes his way into a place, someone else forfeits it. There is a quick way round nearly every queue and a way out of almost every legal difficulty, and practically anything can be bought for a price. New regulations in terms of pollution controls, health and safety, and working conditions mean new ways for the 'enforcers' to earn money. As Amrit Lal says in his highly critical tract on the condition of India:

> Corruption in India has become synonymous with co-operation. Over the years this co-operative movement has acquired an unwritten constitution. The rules of the game are under constant revision; at least they can never become archaic. While everyone resents its omnipresence, nobody is able to check the monster because we are all in one way or another active abettors. (Lal 1995, p.43)

We can regard corruption as the tendency for people in the public realm who are supposed to be impartial to relinquish that impartiality for personal gain. However, there is a reverse side – the tendency of those with wealth or power to compel such relinquishment. Not all corrupt officials are greedy; some are very frightened. In India it is a crime to accept a bribe, it is not a crime to give one.

There is another form of corruption which takes the form of theft of public assets, diverting funds intended for the public good into private pockets. Common instances of this are over-invoicing on public works contracts, payments to fictitious workers on government projects, using substandard materials, underpayment on poverty alleviation schemes, fiddling expenses, selling government assets like timber from the forests and coal from the mines, allocating common land to wealthy farmers, purloining subsidized essential commodities from the public distribution system, feeding the children only rice whilst selling the vegetables issued

to a slum school; the list is almost endless. There are the government teachers who draw their pay but work elsewhere, the government doctors who spend all their time in private clinics and sell government medical supplies, the senior military personnel who get a little too close to arms dealers. Although there are those who like to believe that NGOs are somehow less corrupt than government agencies, as Amrit Dhillon (1997) shows, there is a parallel structure of NGO embezzlement of funds intended for the welfare of the poor.

Then there is nepotism. Here no money changes hands – the contract is longer term, as mutual favours in terms of unfair advantage are done within social networks of family and friends. Scarce places in college, jobs, promotion, government contracts, berths on trains, rooms in government rest houses, allocations of out-of-turn housing, telephone and gas connections, valuable information, blocks of political support, are not always paid for overtly. Nepotism shades off into sociability and yet so many are permanently excluded when jobs are found or contracts awarded this way. However, there is a sense in which, as an outsider, one feels oneself beginning to be integrated into Indian society when these sorts of facilities and obligations start to come one's way.

Vinod Pavarala (1996) believes that, depending upon their personal ideologies, people in India explain corruption in one of two diametrically opposed ways; some maintaining that it is a remnant of feudal patronage systems, others claiming that it is a product of a western-dominated, profit-motivated, market economy. It does not seem particularly worthwhile to try to choose between the two, since both strands are intimately intertwined in contemporary Indian life – corruption occurs when there is a pervasive lack of mutual respect between members of society and this can occur under virtually any political and economic system. Like decay in the supports of a building, it can also bring any structure down. India is a highly divided society; much of that division was systematically reinforced during British rule and there have been many twists and turns in the ways in which those divisions have operated since Independence, with the result that there is very little sense of social solidarity. To act corruptly one must have contempt for the welfare of other people and if that contempt has been built into one's consciousness, as it is when communalism is pervasive, no amount of moralizing will have any effect.

However, despite the pervasiveness of corruption, it is clear that there is a deep desire for things to be otherwise. In the end, only a few really benefit from corrupt dealing; many who accept bribes are likely to have to pay out similar amounts themselves and the great majority have no access to any scarce resource apart, perhaps, from their vote or their physical presence. The press not only regularly exposes major scandals, it also keeps up a constant background commentary on the corrupt nature of society; corruption may be widespread but if it still has the power to fascinate, shock and repel, the society cannot be said to have become completely blasé.

MAJOR 'SCAMS'

The past decade has been marked by three major instances of corrupt practice which have gained national and international attention. These are the Jain *hawala* (money laundering) scam, the securities scam, and the Bihar fodder scam. As C. Mitra (1998) says, these are not necessarily the largest in terms of money, but they are quintessential in that they involve major public figures and represent three major bulwarks of corruption, politicians, bureaucrats and businessmen.

The *hawala* scam dates back to the late 1980s when the Jain brothers made payments to a large range of prominent public figures – high-level politicians (predominantly members of the Congress Party) and senior civil servants. The Jains were socially and politically ambitious agents who acted as middlemen for overseas power companies anxious to enter the deregulating Indian market; but they also, and more famously, 'laundered' black money by passing it through overseas banks and businesses. They kept records of their payments, classified as 'political

expenses' and 'administrative expenses', and when they were rumbled by the Central Bureau of Investigation (CBI) in 1991 their diaries were confiscated, but kept closely under wraps. When these eventually came into the public domain in 1996, even the most cynical were shocked by the people listed: not only Rajiv Gandhi (whose name had already been tainted by the earlier Bofors scandal) but also the aristocratic Scindia and the seemingly incorruptible Advani. Eventually, when the CBI interviewed the Jains, the serving Prime Minister, Narasimha Rao, was named and the 'god-man' Chandraswami was implicated as a go-between (Jain 1995; Agha 1996; Joshi 1996; Muralidharan 1996). Though the scandal rumbles on to this day, convictions have proven difficult, thanks to considerable obfuscation. Although often dismissed as a 'white-collar crime' (as if this were somehow a more polite form of criminality), money laundering has been described as the mother of all crime for it frighteningly implicates petty criminality with major international crime.

The securities scam, too, came hard on the heels of liberalization and the partial deregulation of the stock market. The middle classes were encouraged by continuously rising share prices to enter the market, but when the inevitable crash occurred in 1992, it transpired that the boom had been engineered by unscrupulous dealing in unsecured bankers' receipts. This had required the connivance of bank officials, civil servants and stockbrokers, all of whom, plus their friends and family, had taken substantial profits as the market rose but withdrew before it dropped. It was of course the small investors who lost their savings but, just as important for the Indian economy, there was a grave loss of confidence in the financial markets. No one has been convicted, though in January 1998 the CBI was given permission by the Supreme Court to proceed against those named (Panchu 1998).

The Bihar fodder scam occurred in the State everyone likes to acknowledge as the most corrupt in the country. It took the form of invoicing for fictitious livestock, animal feed, transport, and veterinary medicine which were supposed to be supplied for poverty alleviation under the Integrated Rural Development Programme. 'The fodder scam is particularly illustrative of the sheer brazenness of the politician–bureaucrat nexus of corruption. In no other scam has officialdom been so dismissive of rules or indulged in such wanton disregard for probity' (C. Mitra 1998, p. 150). Because apparently 'everyone' was in on it, it seemed that the scam could go on for ever.

The fodder scam, however, is an example of how the powerful do not always get things their own way. India has a procedure known as Public Interest Litigation, whereby someone who is not directly affected by a misdemeanour can lodge a complaint with the CBI if it is deemed to be in the public interest. This can be done anonymously. Many such initiatives fall by the wayside, but this one was taken up and pursued through its many ramifications to implicate scores of politicians and civil servants right up to the level of the Chief Minister, Laloo Prashad Yadav. Yadav was charged, imprisoned and had to resign (although he never really relinquished power as the role of Chief Minister passed to his wife, who had shown no previous interest in politics).

Other 'scams'

Although these three have been regarded as the 'key' scandals of the 1990s, there have been plenty more, large and small. I have simply picked these, almost randomly, from a heap of press cuttings to give a flavour. Over and over again the businessman–politician–bureaucrat nexus emerges in some form.

In the winter of 1993–94 there was a shortfall in sugar production and the peak time of the year for sugar consumption is Diwali. The 'sugar barons' of Uttar Pradesh, the owners of the newly-privatized sugar mills, made a fortune on the spiralling sugar prices because the Minister of Food did not intervene to import sugar in time. He was charged with having deliberately delayed in order to allow the price to soar. Tharoor (1997) tells the other side of the story, citing a 1989 experience, that insiders give the tip-off to associates living in Britain just before India enters the world market for sugar; this enables them to buy at the crucial time and make a quick profit when the price suddenly and briefly lurches up.

In September 1996 several houses belonging to Sukh Ram, who had been Minister of State for Telecommunications in the Rao Government, were raided by the CBI. They found 22 suitcases full of money stacked in his prayer room and huge quantities of jewellery. He was found to have 19 bank accounts and to own two houses, a farm and an hotel, even though he came from a poor background and had been in politics most of his adult life. At the time of the raids Sukh Ram was in London and it was assumed that there were further assets abroad. He had presided over the Ministry of Telecommunications at the very time when tenders were sought for the private control of the telephone system; telephone networks in northern India were being modernized and fibre optic cable being laid. In Sukh Ram's absence the media turned much of its attention to an officer in the post and telegraph accounts and finance sector who was known to work closely with him – it was difficult for her to explain why a civil servant earning Rs 13 600 a month should have hoards of rupees and foreign exchange, a kilogram of gold jewellery and no less than 20 Rolex watches.

In December 1996 the leader of the Tamil nationalist party, AIADMK, and former Chief Minister of Tamil Nadu was arrested on an impressive array of charges of corruption. A former film star, she had flaunted her wealth as Chief Minister, never more spectacularly than when she turned the wedding of her adopted son into a State carnival with decorated streets, thousands of guests, ranks of mounted guards, lavish catering, and costly gifts to invitees (Subramanian 1995). The term 'assets disproportionate to known sources of income' was hardly adequate to describe the ostentatious wealth she had amassed, but this was only one of the many charges laid against her. She was also charged with abusing her official position to buy land; receiving kickbacks of Rs 8.5 crore from the supplier of colour televisions bought by the State for the villages of Tamil Nadu (coincidentally, her best friend);

receiving a share (with the Electricity Minister) of Rs 117 crore profit on imports of coal for the Tamil Nadu Electricity Board; and failing to complete her income tax form (Menon and Shekhar 1996). She was briefly jailed, but released on bail. Today, she is once again an active force in Indian national politics and has never been convicted.

On a smaller scale, in January 1997 two IAS officers were named by the Andhra Pradesh Anti-Corruption Bureau for allocating a prime piece of land in the élite Banjara Hills district of Hyderabad to a speculative builder. They had confiscated the land from its owner under cover of the regulations relating to urban land ceilings (this is a ruling which is intended to limit the size of urban land-holdings to prevent landlordism); land acquired in this way is supposed to pass into state ownership. This is a fairly routine swindle.

Also in January 1997 it was revealed that another IAS officer, the Chair of the New Okhla Industrial Development Authority (known as Noida – a new town in Uttar Pradesh which is on the outskirts of Delhi) had been allocating residential land to businessmen and politicians at special rates for official purposes, knowing that these would then be sold profitably at the going market rate. Given that Noida is a highly desirable residential area (despite its name) there was a substantial quick profit to be made whilst Delhi land prices were spiralling.

In February 1997 the Income Tax Department discovered that an IAS officer in the Uttar Pradesh cadre owned no less than six privatized, formerly state-owned, rice mills in the Terai region, all registered in the names of his relatives, and that he had committed offences under the Foreign Exchange Regulation Act (Awasthi 1997).

In June 1998 a scam came to light in Bihar whereby some Members of the Legislative Assembly (MLAs), who are entitled to free air conditioned first class travel on the railways, were seen to be spending virtually their whole lives on trains. They were conniving with an agent who cashed in their unused tickets (as the report in the *Hindu* of 12 June 1998 says, 'there were instances where the same legislator was travelling in different parts of the country on the same day').

In January 1999 the Superintendent of the Regional Passport Office in Guwahati was arrested for issuing forged passports to supposed 'army officers'. The Ministry of External Affairs was concerned that this might have been part of a racket relating to the entry of militant groups into India. It is just as possible that it was part of the extensive trade in illegal emigration.

In March 1999 police in Chennai uncovered a trade in fake certificates and marksheets which were being used to gain admission into the best colleges and to obtain high-salaried jobs. The gang responsible consisted of professional criminals, printers and members of the departments and colleges awarding genuine certificates. It was a lucrative game – basic qualifications were being sold for Rs 1000, engineering degrees for Rs 10000. But, as the police pointed out, since the fines on those caught have been only a few thousand rupees, there has been no real deterrence either to those who supply the documents or to the students who fraudulently use them.

In April 1999 the Minister for Social Welfare in Maharashtra was charged with receiving Rs 40 lakhs as a kickback from the Awami Bank for making deposits of Rs 4.5 crore belonging to State welfare agencies.

Then there is the rumour of bribes paid by Enron to Maharashtran politicians to secure a contract; the adulteration of mustard oil (winked at by food inspectors) which resulted in deaths from dropsy and so on and on and on.

THE BUSINESSMAN–POLITICIAN–BUREAUCRAT NEXUS

Though none of them was averse to making a small fortune on the side, the sole motivation of those 'corrupt' politicians was not invariably self-enrichment. In India it is virtually impossible to gain or retain political power without the financial backing of the business community and, as the present Prime Minister, Vajpayee, said when the *hawala* scam broke in 1996, 'No one looks at the colour of money when accepting donations' (Rekhi and Shekhar 1996, p. 13). In virtually every country, businesses make donations to political parties and this is a matter which is in the public domain, but in India donations are made not to parties but to individual politicians to fight individual seats and the donations are not subject to public scrutiny. It has frequently been suggested that the way to stop the business community entering into private contracts with politicians would be to make the transactions overt, but the suggestion always fades away without trace. The businesses want to be able to use the 'black' money which they cannot declare; they need to have a hold over the politicians and the politicians prefer that there is a margin which enters their private reserves.

Even as deregulation is gaining pace, the 'scams' cited demonstrate that there are still plenty of avenues for illicit profit through dealings with government. The politicians can only act through the bureaucracy so they put pressure on civil servants to grant favours and bend rules; some of the time they pay for this in money, much of the time with promises of lucrative postings or threats of punishment posting, and sometimes they resort to threats of violence against officers or their families. Corrupt bureaucrats and corrupt politicians gravitate towards one another in mutual benefit; straight bureaucrats try to avoid direct confrontation with politicians but they also are happy to negotiate themselves into those jobs which have few pickings attached to them where they will not be put under pressure. Bureaucrats and the business world can, and do, make direct connections without the intermediary of the politicians, but without the politician neither knows how long a public servant will stay in a particular post so it is an altogether more secure deal if the classic triumvirate works together.

In March 1996 *India Today* ran a series of articles about the way in which an election is financed for an urban and a rural constituency, estimating the former at Rs 1.25 crore and the latter at Rs 35 lakh (Rekhi and Shekhar 1996). However, politicians do not just need funds for fighting elections; they need to be able to maintain a permanent relationship of patronage with their constituents. Laloo Prashad Yadav, for example, rarely makes a tour without distributing sarees, dhotis, blankets and such like to his poor followers. Politicians keep open house, feeding great retinues of helpers and visiting constituents; their salaries come nowhere near to meeting their obligations.

POLITICS AND ORGANIZED CRIME

It is now taken for granted that crime and politics enjoy an almost symbiotic relationship in India. Not all of those businessmen who support politicians are in legitimate trades. Drug traffickers, smugglers, kidnappers, extortionists and brigands all need 'protection' and pay for it. Sometimes they go through elaborate intermediaries in their dealings with politicians, at other times they are startlingly direct. Mumbai has long been dominated by two major gangs – one predominantly Muslim, run by Dawood Ibrahim, the other, run by Amar Naik, predominantly Hindu. In 1998 Romesh Sharma, a senior member of Dawood's gang, was arrested – a large swathe of élite Delhi had been closely associated with him and his lavish hospitality. Many politicians in Uttar Pradesh took fright when the Special Task Force gunned down Shri Prakash Shukla and started to investigate his contacts. It was alleged that he had been used by them as a hit man. *India Today* quotes a senior police officer as reporting that at least 40 senior government officials, including IAS and IPS officers, were in league with him and another as saying, 'Those wanted by the law have begun to lay down the law. We won't be surprised if one day we see some of these men surrounded by Black Cats' (Mishra 1998, p. 32) (Black Cats are an élite squad used as the bodyguards of senior politicians). In neighbouring Madhya Pradesh, an opium dealer, who is safe from conviction, forms an alternative structure of law and order covering large tracts of the State.

The political use of criminals is not limited to expenses. Criminal gangs are used for intimidation of voters and also to maintain routine power, particularly in the urban slums. Organized crime is also frequently the source of supposedly spontaneous rioting on political/communalist issues, as Kalpana Sharma demonstrates of the 1993 riots in Mumbai where the *Shiv Sena* mafia connection was clear (Sharma 1995). In 1999 the President of India declared that he would deprive Bal Thackeray, the leader of the *Shiv*

Sena, of his vote for six years in punishment for inciting communal hatred. It is unlikely that Bal Thackeray would be chastened by the removal of just one vote. On the other side of the communal divide, the link between organized crime and politics is assumed to extend to the international level with the Pakistan Inter-Services Intelligence reputedly maintaining links with the Muslim Mumbai gangs (Baweja 1998).

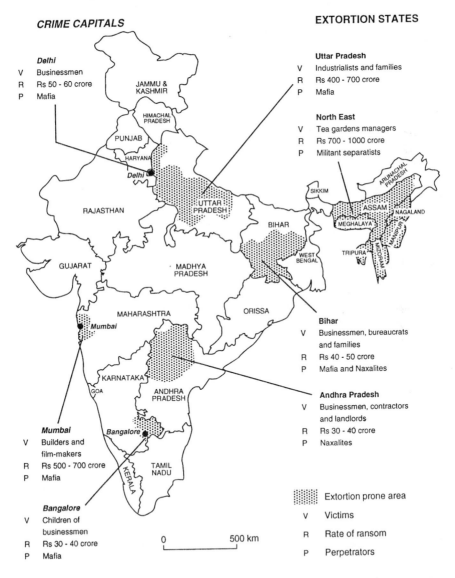

FIGURE 7.1 The ransom business
Source: based on information published in *India Today*, 6 October 1997

A relatively new development is that criminals are now entering politics directly. The Election Commission maintains that 10 per cent of the 13 952 candidates in the 1997 General Election were facing criminal charges at the time (*Infoseek News* 14 January 1998). This does not just mean minor crimes. Singh and Ahmed quote Veena Das as saying in an interview, 'Earlier criminals helped politicians get elected. Today criminals occupy the seats themselves,' and an unnamed *Shiv Sena* leader in Mumbai admitting 'Criminals routinely demand (party) tickets. If you ignore them you've had it. Other parties will accept them – and win' (Singh and Ahmed 1995, pp. 29–30). The Representation of the People Act forbids convicted criminals from contesting elections; this deters few, since gaining a conviction under Indian criminal law is a difficult and tedious process and there have been cases of people fighting (and winning) elections from the cells whilst under charge. The Vohra Committee was appointed by the government to look into the question of the criminalization of politics; its report was presented in 1995. Although it came up with little in the way of hard detail, it reaffirmed the intimate involvement of organized crime in both State and national politics. (The committee made its report just as the Congress Government was suffering a certain unease because it had been revealed that the leader of Youth Congress had murdered his wife and tried to dispose of her body in the *tandoor* of a government-owned hotel in Delhi.)

N.K. Singh (1999) argues that little will happen to control the increasing criminalization of politics until a *Lok Pal* (ombudsman) is appointed with the specific mandate of addressing people's complaints regarding electoral corruption. This post should be backed up by a statement of assets from each member of parliament. The BJP (which has campaigned on an anti-corruption platform) introduced such a bill early in its administration.

VIOLENCE

Perhaps the best known criminal to enter national politics is Phoolan Devi, the 'Bandit Queen' who is the Samajwadi Party Member of the *Lok Sabha* for Mirzapur in Uttar Pradesh, but she does have a special status as a champion of *dalit* people against upper-caste landlords and, for all her violence, is certainly not part of the Indian mafia. She had made her special cause the protection of women and the plight of child labourers as well as caste issues in general. Morally, hers is a difficult case, since her actions were motivated by a desire for revenge on the caste which had oppressed hers for generations and whose men had raped her – but they were still brutal and illegal (Shankardass 1996). The Phoolan Devi phenomenon of alternative systems of 'law' is echoed many times over in the States of Bihar and Uttar Pradesh where landlords' private armies (*senas*) control the rural areas and spill over into the towns. These are then opposed by armed *dalits* and Naxalites. As Arvind Das eloquently demonstrates, the practice of landowners maintaining armies goes back to feudal times, but it is only relatively recently that there has been lower-caste organized armed resistance:

> And how different is the violence of the political *goonda* who captures polling booths from that of the *lathi*-bearing arrogant rich peasant who holds up a long distance bus on the highway so that his family can walk leisurely to catch it? The assertion of wealth and power in its most elemental form is the basis of this kind of violence in Bihar. In a putrefying society where order is maintained by the *lathi* and the gun, there is also the regenerative, creative violence of resistance. (Das 1992, p. 73)

Gun ownership is normal in rural Bihar and there is no pretence that these are hunting weapons. They are sometimes illegally imported from Pakistan where there are numerous workshop-based gun factories, but they are also locally manufactured. The *senas* are linked to landlord castes and periodically descend on villages of *dalits* to demonstrate their power and intimidate the people in orgies of murder, torture, burning and rape. The poor look to the various Naxalite groups for their sole protection, as the neutrality of the police cannot often be relied upon (Chaudhury 1999). The graffiti of the *senas* adorns the mud walls of village dwellings, marking their domain. After a spate of atrocities in early 1999, the journal *Frontline* published a series of articles on the subject, including a count of the incidents. One group, the *Ranvir Sena*, was involved in no less than 80 attacks on *dalit* and poor communities between April 1995 and February 1999. 19 of these were massacres in which a total of 277 people were killed, 44 of whom were children (Ramakrishnan 1999). The last of these massacres was the excuse for the BJP Government to establish President's Rule in Bihar, dismissing the elected government – a supreme irony since the atrocities were committed by right-wing forces and the State government, for all its manifest faults, was broadly pro-poor and anti-landlord. It was widely recognized that this was an expedient action against political enemies rather than a genuine attempt to impose law. Central government soon had to back down and reinstate the Chief Minister.

Gun culture

The major cities of India are becoming routinely violent. Chapter Six has considered domestic violence and gender-based harassment but there is also an increase in violent robbery. For decades Mumbai has been associated with organized crime and gang warfare focussing particularly around protection rackets, real estate deals, and drug trafficking. Dawood Ibrahim, who remains out of reach in Dubai, is the major mafia don controlling the Mumbai gangs and, though his henchmen such as Romesh Sharma may occasionally be arrested (Gupta and Singh 1998; Bavadam 1998), there is no sign of this denting the power of the underworld which has remarkably close relationships with politics (Swami 1998b).

The business community is increasingly finding that it is becoming the target of organized crime, blackmailing, extortion, and kidnapping with death threats (V.S. Aiyar 1998a). Many of the very wealthy in the major cities are withdrawing into bulletproof vehicles and guarded residences; their children are heavily chaperoned. A kidnap victim was quoted as saying 'We deal directly with the kidnappers. The police charge their own fee' (Halarnkar *et al.* 1997).

The organized gangs, however, are increasingly moving into new operations. The new Vice Chancellor of the University of Lucknow resigned in February 1998 because she was demoralized to find that she could not control the systematic criminalization of the students' union. Though this could be traced back to the late 1980s when Neeraj Jain approached criminal contacts to help him win a students' union election, in the late 1990s the campus became dominated by mafia activities. In the 1998 students' union election, both contestants for President had criminal charges against them – the victor for attempted murder, using explosives and intimidation, the loser for murder, attempted murder and gangsterism. The dormitories of the university were being used as an arms store, rival students' union officers were toting Mausers – one was shot dead. Students were being used to run protection rackets in Lucknow and the university was a recruiting ground for organized crime. As Neera Jain pointed out, 'every student leader nurses political ambitions and when he sees people getting into the Assembly or the *Lok Sabha* due to money or muscle power, he does the same to graduate into politics' (Ahmed 1998, p. 23).

The ranks of the disillusioned middle-class educated young are becoming increasingly prone to crime in the new consumerist India; their tastes and aspirations have been moulded according to globalized fashions and yet they are locked into a life of few prospects and limited spending power. When this is blended with cults of individualism and competition in a climate of pervasive corruption, it is no surprise that they are easy recruits into organized crime (Thapa *et al.* 1999). Babloo Srivastava, a kidnapper and extortionist member of the Dawood empire, exclusively recruited educated young people into his gang so that they would not seem suspicious to their victims. His second in command was a sophisticated young woman graduate from Lucknow University. With the aid of portable telephones and co-operative guards, three years after his extradition from

Singapore on 45 counts of murder, he was still running his operations from jail in Allahabad (Mishra and Chakravarty 1999).

In April 1999 a crime which had long been anticipated took place in Delhi. At the Tamarind Court, a restaurant owned by one of Delhi's 'beautiful people' and frequented by the cosmopolitan super élite, a party was taking place. When Jessica Lal, a model employed to serve drinks, refused to serve the drunken son of a former Congress Party minister, he drew his gun and shot once into the ceiling, the second time into her head. The violence which underpinned so much of the wealth and power in India had come home (Baweja and Chakravarty 1999). Manu Sharma had led a charmed life and his indulgent father had made him Director of a Harayana sugar mill when he was only 20. After the murder, it began to be revealed the extent to which the usual nepotism, extortion and violence had underpinned the wealth of the family. The acquisition of the sugar mill was accomplished with the assistance of the Chief Minister; Manu managed it corruptly, not paying his suppliers in full, terrifying them into silence with his gang of youths (Baweja 1999). It was also revealed that the elegant and popular Tamarind Court did not have a liquor licence and that its owner had the bloody evidence of the shooting cleared up by her servants. As Tarun Tahiliani, a fashion designer who was at the party, said, 'The killing reflects the total anarchy in north India.'

VDIS

The previous pages are intended to show that the accumulation of large amounts of wealth in India is frequently associated with violent crime, directly or indirectly. There is a lot of 'black' money washing around the system and, indeed, some payments can only be made in 'black' (speculative builders will commonly quote a price for a house or apartment as partially made up of 'black' money, so that they need not declare their excessive income; this can cause problems for people who do not have routine access to it).

In 1997 the government decided to take liberalization to its logical conclusion and to grant a moratorium, from July until December, on previously undeclared income in the hope of bringing it into the mainstream economy. Under the Voluntary Disclosure of Income Scheme, no questions would be asked about the source of income and, as a further inducement, the highest rate of tax would for this special purpose be 30 per cent instead of the 40 per cent (still) paid by those who were in the habit of declaring their incomes and paying their taxes. The Chairman of the Central Board of Taxes explained that the scheme was 'aimed at tapping the money lying outside the mainstream of the economy and an effort was being made to bring it into official circulation for better utilisation'. He declined to be pressed on the morality of the issue. He announced that 'the scheme has received a very positive and warm response from the various sections of society', and claimed that the new enthusiasm marked a 'cultural and attitudinal change from tax defiance to tax compliance' (*The Hindu* 23 December 1997). The earlier pages of this chapter give some hints as to where 'outside the mainstream of the economy' lies; suddenly the government was cutting in directly on illicit profit – not confiscating it, just asking for a voluntary 30 per cent with no questions asked, not even when future tax assessments were made. The Finance Minister dared to say, 'Earlier the income tax rate was as high as 97.5 per cent and because of this even a most honest person used to hide his income' (*The Hindu* 15 December 1997). This seems a very peculiar attitude for a minister to take to the rule of law – what if one happens to think even 30 per cent too high?

In December, when the six-month VDIS period ended, it was announced that 350 000 people had come forward to declare formerly undisclosed income to the value of Rs 25 000 crore (Mitra and Rekhi 1998). That would not really be a very large number of people by Indian standards, but for the fact that one is looking at the people who were willing to come clean over illicit income. It certainly averages out to a large amount of money per person by any standards.

India's income tax system has been

notoriously easy to cheat; less than 2 per cent of the population pays any income tax at all and records have been almost impossible to maintain. A new computerized system which started up in late 1997 to collate tax declarations with such things as car licensing, house purchase and applying for foreign travel is intended to widen the net of tax payers. It will be interesting to see how it works. In mid 1998 the Finance Minister declared that, in order to ensure that the money being used was legal, it would become compulsory for people to quote their computerized income tax account number when buying high value items. The announcement was greeted with derision, since the tax offices had not got around to issuing such numbers in most places. There is never any shortage of regulations to deal with the problems, just an apparent shortage of will to apply them.

CONTROLS

The system has many procedures for monitoring corruption in all aspects of public life. The Central Vigilance Committee (CVC) has an overarching responsibility to guard against civil service corruption, though, until recently, its powers were severely limited in relation to senior officers. It is, however, notoriously difficult to punish a corrupt official and a recent report shows that 'in 136 government organisations monitored by the CVC there are 5 310 cases pending departmental inquiry for periods up to 35 years' (S. Mitra 1998, p. 16). Mitra reports the CVC Commissioner as saying that it is difficult to demotivate a corrupt public servant given that the risks are so low and the profits so high. In theory, the Prevention of Corruption Act allows for the forfeit of property owned by civil servants beyond their 'known sources of income'. Civil servants are supposed to fill out a declaration of all of their property at the time of joining the service and update their property returns file annually with explanation and receipts for purchases over Rs 10 000 (Agnihotri and Mittal 1995) (I remember the jeers of disbelief from some of the officer trainees when this was mentioned in a session on personal affairs at the National Academy of Administration).

On the matter of corruption in politics, the Election Commission is charged with running fair elections; under the leadership of Seshan it made considerable headway in reducing the amount of illegal expenditure and use of violence on election campaigns (C. Mitra 1998). The Election Commission has adopted an overt policy of curbing the criminalization of politics through the stringent application of the Representation of the People Act, which debars convicted criminals from standing as candidates, but again, the difficulty is in tracing the records of each and every candidate.

In an attempt to control 'black' money, there is a new stringent Prevention of Money Laundering Bill (still awaiting approval as I write); this seeks approval at the same time as a bill to relax the foreign exchange laws, reflecting the conviction amongst the advocates of liberalization that deregulation is the best way of curbing corruption. This will only be the case if the rules which are in place are rigorously applied – deregulation is one thing, flouting regulations is quite another.

OPPOSING CORRUPTION

It is too easy to fall into the trap of seeing India as inherently corrupt; this is absolutely not the case, but everyone feels the impact of corruption on their daily lives and many attempt to resist it. This resistance ranges from the individuals who routinely refuse to give bribes, the upright public servants who refuse to receive them or to perform favours for politicians, to the activists in the people's movements, the outspoken elements of the media, right up to the judiciary. Here, I would like to pay tribute to a young hero, an IAS officer, Dasharath Prashad, who was shot in his office at point blank range by a contractor's gunman in January 1999. As Manipur Tourism Director, he had refused to subvert the tendering process for tourism promotion, even though considerable pressure had already been put on him from local politicians. He had been in government service for only three years; his widow and his young family paid the price of his honesty in a corrupt system and one can begin to understand the officers who are less honest.

The Uttar Pradesh IAS Officers' Association surprised the country when in 1996 some of the younger officers proposed a resolution whereby the Association would conduct a ballot to identify the most corrupt officers in the State with a view to naming and shaming the three 'winners'. Amidst a flurry of disapproval, the resolution was passed and the ballot conducted (Aswathi 1997). Though not published, 'everyone' knows the names and the potential for the Service to regulate itself has been established.

There is considerable respect in India for both the print media and the judiciary. The press has a reputation for outspokenness and keen investigative journalism and the judiciary for its impartiality and willingness to step in with innovative judgement where the law-makers seem to be deficient, exposing their sins of omission and commission. This can be easy to forget. Long ago it was pointed out that disclosure of malpractice made the polical wheels turn: 'Corruption – the fact itself, but, even more important, the talk of it – occupies a great place in Indian politics' (Morris-Jones 1971, p. 62).

We can see the popular respect for the press going back to the important role it played during the Independence Movement, but we can also see the defence of a free press being enhanced by the experiences of Indira Gandhi's Emergency (1975–77) when censorship was imposed. Undoubtedly, the press played an important role in bringing the Jain *hawala* scam to the public attention, when it seemed it was being quietly hushed up. But the press does not just convey news, it also helps to form opinion by maintaining an awareness of corruption and inequality. The Indian press is refreshingly critical of society and politics in a way which should be the envy of a great many wealthier countries. Its Press Institute maintains standards rigorously, for example censuring the mighty *Times of India* for bribing 'persons close to the Prime Minister' to effect the transfer of a difficult bureaucrat (Bhattacharjea 1998b).

Likewise, the judiciary has, on the whole, managed to remain free from the taint of pressure from politicians and the business community. The Supreme Court retains considerable independence, even though it does have its own built-in selectivities on the basis of class. But justice grinds exceeding slow in India; cases take years to come to court and trials seem to go on almost indefinitely. The principle of Public Interest Litigation is a valuable tool in the hands of people and groups attempting to resist entrenched privilege and power. The courts can take up social and environmental causes at the instigation of an individual or group and organizations such as the Commission for Human Rights can bring cases from which laws of precedent can be derived.

People's resistance movements

In 1997 the members of the *Chhatisgarh Mukti Morcha* (CMM) (Chhatisgarh People's Struggle) won their battle for the conviction of the killers of their leader, the trade union activist Shankar Guha Niyogi. The gunman was sentenced to death and the two executives of the Simplex Group who had hired the killer received life imprisonment, but these sentences were to be overturned on appeal in 1998. The CMM attribute the murder in 1991 to a consortium of five large business corporations operating in Bhilai-Durg and are continuing their struggle for the others to be brought to justice (*Indian Express* 30 June 1997). Niyogi had not only organized the workers of the Bhilai Steel Plant and the associated Chhatisgarh Mines, he had also been the driving force behind an anti-liquor movement and forest protection work. He had many powerful enemies and had been imprisoned and beaten up many times. Although his activities were legal, the local industrialists had the backing of the Madhya Pradesh BJP Government and it was not difficult to mobilize the forces of law and order against the workers. In July 1991, workers protested against the sub-contracting of work from the public sector-owned Bhilai Steel Plant and the consequent deregulation of production, with casualization of labour, low pay and dangerous conditions. They sat on a railway track in typical Gandhian passive resistance. The police opened fire and killed 16 of them. Two months later their leader was murdered (Dogra 1998; Seabrook 1993).

There are numerous examples throughout India of groups and individuals working against the corruption of the system, most using legal means, others, like the various Naxalite groups, resorting to armed struggle (Banerjee 1980; Routledge 1996; Singh 1995).

Right to information

Many activists in India today claim that the greatest weapon in the fight against routine corruption is information. Virtually everything done by public servants is protected by antiquated British laws of secrecy. Until it is made public how contracts are awarded, for what payment and to complete exactly what work, it is impossible to know whether cheating is taking place. Once lists of workers on schemes are available to the public, it will be possible to check whether all of them really exist and whether they are paid the rates that are claimed. When the accounts of the Public Distribution System (ration stores) can be inspected it will become difficult to divert supplies into the open market (Mander 1998). As a former Supreme Court judge, Justice P.B. Sawant, is quoted as saying in *India Today*, 'The barrier to information is the single leading cause for corruption in society. It facilitates clandestine deals, arbitrary decisions, manipulation, and encourages embezzlements' (Bhaumik 1996, p. 76).

Transparency will blow open the cosy relationships between businessmen, politicians and bureaucrats. An ex-bureaucrat turned social activist, Aruna Roy, realized that if she mobilized people in demand for open government a transformation in the routine operation of public works could be effected. She initiated a people's organization in rural Rajasthan, the *Mazdoor Kisan Shakti Sangathna*, which has blossomed into a national Right to Information Campaign (Dogra undated). This campaign has enlisted the backing of the National Human Rights Commission and the Press Institute of India and is growing into a powerful force (Bhattacharjea 1998a).

In the States of Rajasthan and Madhya Pradesh, Right to Information legislation has been passed (and a watered-down bill is before the *Lok Sabha*). In Rajasthan this gives people the right to inspect, but not photocopy, records relating to the public distribution system, public works, poverty alleviation schemes, and land deals amongst other things. In Madhya Pradesh photocopying is permitted; in a largely illiterate society the right to photocopy is particularly important. When I accompanied members of the Right to Information Campaign to a ration shop in Madhya Pradesh, the people in the queue were amazed and gleeful (and the shopkeeper palpably terrified) when they asked to inspect the records. It is such a very simple device, to pass the monitoring of corruption into the hands of the people who really can understand the projects being funded. They are now required to inspect the records. Combined with the strengthening of local democracy through *panchayati raj*, this could be the means whereby the carefully constructed network of graft and corruption finally falls.

A method used by the *Mazdoor Kisan Shakti Sangathna* has been the public hearing, at which activists obtain and read out the details of local development and poverty alleviation schemes so that the assembled people can compare these with their experiences. Dey *et al.* (1995) testify to the way in which a mixture of disbelief, amusement and anger commonly greet revelations that 'muster rolls' of paid workers include themselves, when they have been neither employed nor paid, or list people they have never heard of or who have died. They protest when buildings they know not to have been completed are declared officially to be finished to high standards. These public hearings are videoed as evidence and used as the basis of prosecutions of public servants who have been found to be operating corruptly. These movements tell of the way in which contractors and civil servants are becoming aware that they cannot get away with corrupt practices, and officers are even beginning to come forward to confess to previous misdemeanours. Activists contrast the success of the public hearing approach with the lonely struggle recounted by Mander (undated) (fast becoming a classic in the field) where a district collector revealed theft of Rs 10 crore in development schemes to the value of Rs 18 crores, but the organized might of politicians, from the level of *sarpanch* to MP, combined to get the zealous DC rapidly transferred, then to have the official report on the subject shelved.

Obviously there is considerable opposition, not only to the proposed legislation for the right to information, but also to its application. The Commissioner for Bilaspur, a driving force behind the Right to Information legislation in Madhya Pradesh, declared that he would open a new government depart-

ment to public audit every two months. He found himself transferred out of his post at a day's notice at the insistence of a coterie of contractors and MLAs. No worthwhile struggle is easily won.

In 1946, as part of his election campaign, Nehru took a stand against corruption which he saw as an outcome of British rule, claiming that, when Congress came to power, he would 'hang the next black-marketeer from the next lamppost'. One assumes that he was speaking metaphorically, but there has been a noticeable lack of corrupt practitioners adorning the street lights.

8

DIVISIONS IN SOCIETY

As should have become apparent in the earlier chapters, society in India is riven with divisions so deep that sometimes it stretches one's credulity to think of it as one country. But one country it very definitely is and its internal contradictions are responsible for the dynamic which is India at any point in its history. It is far too easy to think of the major divisions of society as if they generated completely separate units or were based upon separate issues, rather than thinking of the units or issues in isolation as topics in their own right. If one goes along that path, one finishes up with nothing more than trite and touristic commentaries about India being a land of contrasts. India has to be taken as a whole and it needs to be appreciated that the lines of cleavage define the way that society is at any juncture; this means that opposing groups and interests define themselves in relation to each other and each other in relation to themselves. They do not have essential characteristics beyond this. Inden (1990) is at pains to demonstrate that many commentators have been happy to see India as a land of essences (postulating essentialist views of religion, the caste system, regions, etc.). This is a largely western and *brahmanical* construction, which suits a particular use of knowledge as power; it is not something which captures any absolute reality. Of course, the construction is itself an interesting phenomenon which demonstrates the world view of a small, but very influential, section of contemporary Indian society.

Acknowledging connectedness makes for a more nuanced understanding of India, but it also means that one has to forego the simple explanatory structures which are generally offered.

COMMUNALISM

The idea of membership by birth of separate ascribed groups, based on caste or religion, each with supposedly inherent characteristics, is very much a part of Indian life. Unfortunately, this idea in its 'communalist' form becomes the basis of a political reality in which communities present themselves as having not only clear identities, but also separate and conflicting interests. It has become as ingrained as racism is in many societies. In its Indian usage, the term 'community' invariably cuts across neighbourhood and locality; one would not normally think of a village as a community comprising people with different caste and religious characteristics, rather one would think of those characteristics constituting communities which extend beyond and divide villages. Like racism, communalism is built upon illogical beliefs in innate characteristics, reinforced by selective observation, evidence-building and pseudo-science. Also like racism, the illogic is based upon a desire to maintain or achieve unfair advantage, or, as Tambia (1996) indicates, *jati* and ethnic groups with 'self-proclaimed collective identity' seek preference in the name of equality. This chapter will consider the nature of communalist politics and also the 'secularist' opposition to it.

Everything that is socially constructed can also be deconstructed and we find that increasing numbers of Indian intellectuals (Ahmad 1994, 1996a; Sarkar 1993, 1994; Taneja 1994) are turning their attention to the historical and philosophical underpinnings of European fascism in their quest to theorize the new forms of communalism emerging in the conditions predicated upon liberalization and globalization. There are certainly similarities, but theory cannot be imported wholesale (Vanaik 1997). Communalism is such an important issue in contemporary India that some of the very highest quality academic work is being done in this field, none better than Achim Vanaik's (1997) excellent study of religion and secularism, *The furies of Indian communalism*. Much of the analysis of communalism in India deserves a far wider readership than just people interested in the sub-continent since it is at the forefront of the theorization of the sub-national divisions which bedevil so much contemporary politics worldwide. Vanaik writes of Hindu nationalism that one should see:

> the principal danger not as residing in something that lies *behind* Hindu communalism or as residing in some fascist core *contained within* or *hidden* in Hindu communalism, but as Hindu communalism *itself* as the specific manifestation of the politics of cultural exclusivity and right-wing reaction.
>
> The long term and ... more basic focus would not be on its potential or likelihood for a 'fascist' suborning of the state but on politicized *Hindutva's* deep roots and growth in civil society well beyond its capacity to appropriate the state. In a sense the phenomenon is *more deep rooted* than fascism, *more enduring* and more difficult to completely or comprehensively destroy. (Vanaik 1997, pp. 279–81)

Here he is referring to an ideology which requires the total suffusion of society with a single idea and a single value system.

This is power well beyond government, ingrained into the constructed Hindu 'tradition', with no need to consider the structures as anything other than self-evidently right and pre-ordained. This is the ultimate communalist dream.

CASTE AS A COMPLEX

There have been numerous western/*brahmanical* accounts of the caste 'system' as the key to understanding the Indian society. The most influential of these in modern times has been the work of Dumont (1970) whose structuralist imperative caused him to believe that there was a pan-Indian hierarchy of *jati* (see Introduction) arranged like a squash ladder (if one goes up another has to come down). His influence caused caste to be represented as a closed system, based around the concept of ritual purity as laid down in the Vedic scriptures. Whilst structuralists see internal positional flexibility as possible, they represent the system itself as having a constant shape. Partha Chatterjee (1993a and b), however, emphasizes that caste should be seen as fragmentary and dialectical, agreeing with Gupta's (1984) claim that, though notions of inequality are certainly important, a simple linear hierarchy is not the determining principle. A dialectic generates a very different sort of whole from a closed system.

I want to say, loud and clear, that there is no such thing as the caste *system*. There is nothing *systematic* about it, although it suited earlier western intellectual fashions to think otherwise (Cohn 1987; Kaviraj 1992). Caste is, rather, a *complex* – a loose assemblage of practices, rules, ideas, relationships, beliefs and prejudices, which forms around hereditary membership of corporate 'communities', together with a recognition of inequality of rights. Often it is convenient for those who wish to maintain the *status quo* to represent this with all the power of a logical system, but this complex assumes very different forms and characteristics when experienced from different subject positions in society. There is not even any agreement about the shape and nature of inequality. *Jati* are groups which act for the mutual advantage of their members.

Since they are also endogamous, virtually all kinship and interpersonal ties of friendship are concentrated within them. They are obviously a powerful form of social organization and it is not difficult to see why they persist, changing form and function with different modes of production and political systems. There is no reason why modernization or globalization should be assumed to be intrinsically liable to erode caste.

Obviously there have always been more representations of caste from the point of view of the *brahmins* (the occupational specialists in literacy and the management and control of formal knowledge) than from any other social group's perspective. I should add that here I do not mean individual people born *brahmin*, many of whom are some of the most critical analysts of Indian society – I am referring to *brahmins* acting with consciousness of their group identity and interest. The loudness of their claims to ancient knowledge is no guarantee of their superior understanding of the totality. The dominant position of the *brahmins* in the construction of knowledge in and of India is, however, a perfect example of the Foucauldian concept of the equation of power and knowledge (i.e. that it is the powerful who define the parameters of the knowledge system and thereby enhance their own power).

Taking the view that caste is a complex, we can distance ourselves from any sense that the way in which caste is configured in present times is a perversion of a former ideal system. It becomes axiomatic that caste will always be the manifestation of the current modes of inequality of power, prestige and wealth. It was not, somehow, more logically 'perfect' in the past when there were feudal systems of land tenure and division of labour, or trapped by the rigidities of British imperialist classification or liable to degenerate under globalized systems of capital accumulation – all of these forms echo and amplify their times.

Caste has always been political; most of the classic accounts of it demonstrate the forms taken under feudal economic and political systems, where the complementary forces of landownership and ritual laid down the dominant principles of profane and sacred (*kshatriya* and *brahmin*). Today's political systems take account of new configurations of caste, some of these based on economic change, others on new mobilizations in relation to the state. Kothari (1970) warns that to decry the involvement of caste in politics is naïve, since caste, as an important social principle in India, is bound to be politicized. By 1997 Kothari argued that caste-based politics is not just a matter of the protection of privilege but that it can also become the basis of resistance through both political parties and new social movements, since it can offer a basis for minority mobilization against 'majoritarian' forces.

'UNTOUCHABILITY'

The term 'untouchable' was unsayable by all but the most insensitive until a few years ago, but the people at the bottom of the heap have started confronting the rest of society with the full implication of their status by challenging them with the word. Gandhi employed the term *harijan* (children of God) but was naïvely unmindful of the fact that in the villages this word was used pejoratively for the children of *devadasis*. Of late, the favoured term is *dalit*, which translates as ground-down or oppressed. It is only with a sense of anger and self-recognition that 'untouchable' can be appropriated.

There has been a long, but largely unrehearsed, history of *dalit* resistance, including the *bhakti* tradition, going back as far as the seventh century. Mendelsohn and Vicziani (1998, p. 22) quote Kabir, the fifteenth-century *bhakti* poet, who rejected caste hierarchy:

> *Pandits* sat and read the law
> Babbled of what they never saw

> and

> *Pandit*, look in your heart for knowledge
> Tell me where untouchability
> came from, since you believe in it.

An early modern example is the conversion of Keralan 'untouchables' to Christianity in the nineteenth century which resulted in high rates of literacy, through attendance at mission schools, consequent rural development

Figure 8.1 Born to sweep

and left-wing State government. Prior to this, Malabar (as it was then known) had some of the most vicious and degrading devices for separating 'untouchables' from others. In the late nineteenth century there was a *bhakti* revival in northern India; gaining ground among urban 'untouchables' in the early twentieth century, it offered an organizational structure for the development of explicitly anti-*brahmin* ideology. In the South it was parallelled by Phule's inversion of the caste hierarchy and rejection of *brahmin* interpretations of religion. The important Non-*Brahmin* Movement in the Madras Presidency (Tamil Nadu) in the 1920s led to the very first instances of government reservation and Periyar's Self-Respect League. Best known are Ambedkar's Independent Labour Party and Scheduled Caste Federation of the 1930s and 1940s with their opposition to Congress as 'a *brahmin*-bourgeois party' (Omvedt 1995).

At Independence, positive discrimination in favour of the Scheduled Castes was continued and extended. It was initially assumed that this would be a transitional phase and that, by conferring access to government employment and preferential treatment in rural development, there would eventually be a collapse of the division between the caste Hindus and others. This has not been the case. The majority of members of Scheduled Castes have seen none of the benefits of reservation but remain not just trapped in dire poverty but still on the receiv-

ing end of the contempt of the those who believe themselves to be their superiors. However, individuals and sometimes whole communities have been able to take advantage of reservation to acquire education and high-status jobs; there are significant numbers of *dalit* school teachers, doctors and bureaucrats. Even more important, *dalits* have been able to organize themselves into political units and have become a force to be reckoned with. With the exception of the Republican Party of India, formed in the 1950s, *dalits* have mostly operated in organized politics through the established political parties; the regional parties in Tamil Nadu and Andhra Pradesh have strong *dalit* elements and Congress continues to pay lipservice to the *dalit* cause. The phenomenon of seat reservation gave *dalits* a good basis for recognition within the parties. However, with the development of the *Bahujan Samaj* Party and the growing power of Paswan in the *Janata Dal* in the 1980s, *dalit* politicians became significant players in the Hindi belt of northern India. Mendelsohn and Vicziani (1998) write of 'A new untouchable politics that is radical and assertive but also ruthlessly pragmatic. For the first time across large parts of India the *dalits* have to be taken seriously rather than viewed as a vote bank to be exploited by their social superiors' (p. 204). There is certainly plenty for these politicians to fight for.

Practices of 'untouchability' are most obvious in the rural communities where people have personal knowledge of each other and where any individual's caste status is known to all. A routine practice is to debar 'untouchables' from using the same water source as caste Hindus and to force them to live in separate settlements. It may seem trivial, but in 1999 in Tamil Nadu there has been a fair amount of publicity given to the 'two glass' phenomenon at village tea shops. It is a common (and illegal) discriminatory practice for the people who run tea stalls to keep two sets of vessels, one for serving 'clean' castes, the other for 'untouchables', who are served separately and must wash their own receptacles. Pro-*dalit* politicians have been descending unannounced on tea shops to catch the owners out (of course it is a publicity stunt in the run up to an election). Trivial? In the same villages *dalits'* homes are being burned down and pitched battles are being fought between other castes and untouchables. There has been a ban on naming bus concessions after 'caste heroes' – this because the concessions were granted by MLAs to their supporters who often showed their gratitude by naming them after leaders of their own community, publicly flaunting their relationship with powerful forces. There has also been a ban on casteist graffiti because it inflames violent reaction. These are feeble measures in the light of the fact that in Tamil Nadu, as in the northern States like Bihar and Uttar Pradesh, caste-based armies with both home-made and purchased weaponry are taking control of the rural areas.

In Bihar no one is striking poses outside tea shops – there is war between the *dalits* (here still called *harijans*) and the landowning castes, as the latter try desperately to cling to their feudal privileges. In the late 1970s, caste-based atrocities started to come to light whereby *dalit* men who were deemed to be getting above themselves were reminded of their lowly status by premeditated blinding with acid. With the passing of formal political power into the hands of the Other Backward Classes in the 1990s, new levels of caste violence have emerged. Marginalized landowners, distrustful of the State government, are setting up alternative local structures of 'law and order', raising their own

'armies' (*sena*), often with the deliberate indifference or unofficial support of the police. To provide a counterweight, Naxalite guerrilla groups offer protection to the Scheduled Castes, whereupon the excuse given for attacks on villages becomes the need to flush out Naxalites.

In the past, caste-based violence and caste insults generally went unreported; today there is more publicity and this is a measure of progress, however limited. Though it is a relatively small shift, the media is increasingly representing *dalit* people as individuals with whom readers can identify, rather than as a category to pity or despise, though, as Kothari (1997) cynically remarks, this has become something of an empty show of concern. On 16 July 1999 *Frontline* published a story about routine insults to *dalit* women in Tamil Nadu (Sivaraman 1999) in which a woman is quoted as saying 'I am a midwife who helps their women. I get some tea for my labour, never in a tumbler but in old soda bottles, sometimes in coconut shells. I can touch their babies, but not their vessels.' (Women giving birth and their babies are regarded as impure and polluting.) In the same issue was a report about the Mallahs of Bihar claiming back their fishing rights (Sharma 1999). Deepak Bharti, their leader, draws attention to the fact that *dalits* are not only becoming organized but are also gaining a sense of self-worth, saying that they now call government officials *bhaijee* (honoured brother) rather than *huzur* (lord) and sit in chairs in waiting rooms rather than cowering on the floor. That these are considered to be significant advances shows just how far there still is to go, but it is not long since it would have been hard to interest English readers in the insults borne by the people at the bottom of the social ladder. Of course, the greatest symbol of *dalit* pride was the appointment of Narayanan as President of India.

Broken people, a Human Rights Watch report (1999), is essential reading for anyone who doubts the depths of the continuing neglect, exploitation, indignity and brutality to which *dalit* people are routinely exposed. It reports upon a series of cases from around India, including the atrocities of house burning, systematic rape and butchery in Tamil Nadu in 1998 when caste Hindus turned upon *dalits* in a series of incidents. The details read like something one might think of in the context of war crimes, not actions which even the most depraved members of the same society could contemplate against the neighbours in conditions of peace. 'Why are they driven to this extent? Because for them *dalits* are nothing. They give more respect to their animals', said one woman. It considers the rioting in Bombay in 1997 which escalated, fuelled by the enthusiasm of the *Shiv Sena*, when 10 *dalit* young men, protesting against the desecration of Ambedkar's statue by caste Hindus during Independence anniversary celebrations, were shot dead by the police. It gives details of the many massacres perpetrated by *Ranavir Sena*, one of the landlords' armies in northern Bihar. It also looks at the routine callousness against *dalits*, revealing the plight of the manual scavengers, the people from the *bhangi* (sweeper) caste whose hereditary role it is to remove human excrement. Exposed to disease, whether they are working for municipalities, businesses or private households, they are paid a pittance but are so despised by virtually everyone that it is near to impossible for a *bhangi* to get other employment.

The absolute degradation of *dalits* is an essential part of caste differentiation as it secures the status of caste Hindus in terms of the distance they can put between themselves and these stigmatized people. It is arguable that if *dalits* could achieve effective, not just legal, citizenship, the hierarchical aspect of the complex of caste would unravel.

It is certainly not only the members of the highest ranking *jati* who have an interest in maintaining the depressed position of the *dalits*. In the case of the Tamil Nadu atrocities referred to, the perpetrators were members of OBC groups who resented the fact that *dalits* were moving out of their oppressed position. This had happened as a consequence of a combination of increasing educational achievement under reservation and remittance income from relatives working abroad (Human Rights Watch 1999, p. 82). In a single incident in 1998, 400 *dalit*

homes were destroyed, young women raped and murdered, and the old people beaten as a consequence of OBC resentment of *dalits* with money trying to bid in a government auction for village assets. Human Rights Watch reports that in 1996–97 there was a 34 per cent increase over the previous year in reported incidents and that in by far the majority of 282 cases, the violence was between OBCs and *dalits*. Not only were some *dalit* groups becoming economically more advanced, they were also organizing themselves into new and challenging political units. Established politicians, the police and the bureaucracy had much to gain from attempting to maintain the *status quo*. In the 1999 general election campaign, *dalit* politicians announced a new regrouping to take on what they perceive to be the degeneration of the Tamil politics which has discarded the core principles of the *non-brahmin* movement for a populist form of *Hindutva*.

It should not be assumed that caste animosity stops at the 'line of pollution'; there can be considerable conflict between Scheduled Castes on the basis of entitlements granted to them. The Scheduled Caste quota at national and State level does not differentiate between different *jati* – technically it would be possible to fill the quota exclusively with members of one group. In Andhra Pradesh in 1998, a controversial new ordinance allowed for the generation of sub-quotas to represent the divisions between *malas, madigas, rellis* and *adi andhras*. Other states have similar problems.

NEO-KSHATRIYA

Although all anthropologists are brought up on the importance of Sanskritization (emulating the behaviour of the *brahmins* as a strategy for a *jati* to improve its status), it is noticeable that in India today a new social mobility is forming around the principle of usurping the roles of the ruler/landowner groups. The Other Backward Classes (OBCs) are the castes which are deemed to be above the (totally unsanctioned) 'line of pollution' in which the majority traditionally had a low standard of living. They are generally classified as *shudra* but increasingly apply the term *bahujan* (mass/majority) to themselves. In several regions, particularly in northern India, significant numbers of members of cultivator *jati* moved into positions of relative power and wealth when old feudal systems of land tenure gave way to independent farming (Varshney 1995). The 'Green Revolution' further transformed the lives of farmers, often in receipt of considerable government subsidies and assured a controlled market (Jeffrey 1997). In what is popularly referred to as 'the forward march of the backwards', new political configurations emerged in the 1980s, campaigning for reservations in government and education which would allow them to catch up with the old élites in terms of political influence. In 1992, under pressure from the new political parties of the OBCs such as the *Janata Dal* and the *Samajwadi* Party, the Union Government accepted the recommendations of the Mandal Commission on extending reservation categories.

The new 'bullock capitalists' (Rudolph and Rudolph 1987) of Uttar Pradesh are busily establishing neo-feudal modes of interaction with their employees and bonds of kinship and patronage with local administration as they reap the benefits of newly deregulated markets for agricultural produce, particularly sugar cane. There is no doubt at all that the rise of emerging capitalists from these communities goes hand-in-hand with corruption, violent crime and sabotage of democratic processes as new informal power structures emerge (see Chapter Seven for the 'sugar scam', the 'fodder scam' and the Jessica Lal murder). The success of the affluent sections of the OBCs subverts what Vanaik (1997) sees as the 'natural centre of gravity' of Indian political life, the numerical strength of the mass. This subversion takes place because people are enticed to vote according to caste loyalties, even though these cut across their class loyalties. There is a trite, but true, saying about no longer casting a vote but voting a caste in the newly restructuring India.

However, OBC politics has to retain some vestiges of populism. This is frequently manifested in direct patronage (in Bihar it is joked that one can map the home areas of Members of the Legislative Assembly by observing the distribution of tube wells). As always, there is built-in caste-based favouritism, but it is undeniable that in its new form the largesse is being distributed further down the social scale than in the past. The élitist English-medium press often delights in snobbish criticism of the 'vulgar' style of politicians such as Laloo Prashad Yadav of Bihar and Mulayam Singh Yadav of Uttar Pradesh, both members of the upwardly mobile *yadav* (milk producers) caste. Even Deve Gowda was mocked as Prime Minister for his country ways (particularly his language problems and his attachment to his large extended family). The sneering is a mark of the anxiety of old élites in the face of emerging new forces they cannot easily control.

RESERVATION

When it was announced in 1992 that the recommendations of the Mandal Commission would be implemented, there was considerable consternation amongst *brahmin* and *kayastha* university students, particularly those from lower middle class backgrounds who feared that their anticipated employment in the clerical ranks of the bureaucracy would be threatened. Many took to the streets; wearing black armbands, they burned copies of the Mandal Commission Report. There were even suicides. Mandal's recommendation of extending the principle of reservation to include the OBCs meant that, taken together, the three reserved categories would control about 50 per cent of all places, more in those States where the government, for reasons of popular support, chose to interpret the legislation generously. Since these three categories constitute more than 50 per cent of the population, one can understand the logic. The Mandal Commission Report showed that, though they formed only 15 per cent of the population, the 'most forward castes' held almost 70 per cent of all government jobs and 90 per cent of the Class I positions. Reservation was the obvious way of breaking this exclusion of the caste majority.

As Ilaiah (1996) is at pains to demonstrate, a typical *brahmin* socialization emphasizes the avoidance of manual work, but encourages the specialization in knowledge-based employment, including administration, teaching and research as well as priestly functions and the liberal professions. Government posts had long been an important preserve, but access to college places was even more crucial. Higher education was the gateway to the modern professions and had been virtually monopolized by young *brahmins*, brought up in literate households and taught from their infancy the importance of learning how to pass examinations. Mandal threatened this domination. Many members of the upper castes criticized Mandalization on the grounds that places should be awarded on the basis of 'merit' alone (Shah 1991), but this championing of excellence was far from impartial, since their upbringing, contacts and everything about their culture ensured that they could command the highest levels of 'merit' (which, of course, they defined).

Reservation has a range of outcomes and even those who support it in principle have misgivings. Most obviously it gives the chance of self-improvement to individual members of 'backward' communities, who would otherwise be held back by their birth and rearing. It also extends dignity to whole groups when it is perceived that their members can achieve prestigious positions and, additionally, it gives the dispossessed sections of society networks of contacts into power and influence. Less beneficially, reservation has resulted in the creation of the 'creamy layer' (the language of caste is full of ugly terminology) – those affluent people who, having used their deprived caste status to rise to the top, then distance themselves from others. It is impossible not to notice that, for some individuals, reservation has been a matter of jumping onto a 'gravy train' rather than a means of diffusing advantage through the community. Reservation for OBCs is supposed to exclude its 'creamy layer' from job quotas on grounds of parental income; however, scaling down one's declared income is routine. The first 'Mandal' intake into the prestigious Indian Adminstra-

tive Service in 1996 showed a marked intensification of a trend towards increasing numbers of recruits coming from the small towns. This reflects what was already realized, that it is the élites of the OBCs – the people who have moved into the marketing and processing of agricultural produce – who are cornering the gains ostensibly intended for mass 'uplift'. The descriptive lists of the new trainees showed remarkably small parental incomes for such sophisticated young people.

Reservation has had the effect of changing the status of government employment and all but the most competitive of state-funded higher education, both of which are perceived by the élites as having declined in prestige. The extra concessions to the formerly excluded sections of society were made close on the heels of the New Economic Policy. There was no direct causal link, but the backward sections came to a significant position in administration just as the power of the state was being questioned and society was becoming more orientated towards the market and privatization. There is a very real sense in some sections of society that the bureaucracy is now no longer significant in its own right but has become the plaything of politicians and their related business interests.

THE 'TWICE BORN'

Shashi Tharoor (1997, p.43) said of the super élite, of which he is a member, they are 'able, but not electable'. With the decline of feudal landlordism and *brahmanical* bureaucratic hegemony, combined with the organization of mass political parties, the upper castes can no longer expect to dominate Indian politics, even though they have a good deal of influence. Though still important players in Indian affairs, we find that the upper castes are aware that their best chances are in terms of finding a niche in the international realm. For the most accomplished and best connected members of the upper castes this implies foreign higher education and employment overseas; for others it means private higher education, through fee-paying colleges and foreign-franchised courses in India, followed by the scramble for managerial positions in private companies; for the middle-class majority there is relentless studying to get the unreserved places at university and networking to gain acceptable employment which would recently have been seen almost as a matter of right.

Box 11   Able but not electable

Shashi Tharoor (1997) expressed the mood of the élite in the late 1980s:

> Rajiv Gandhi had brought to power the kind of Indian almost completely unrepresented in Indian politics. *My kind of Indian.* There are many of us, but among India's multitudes we are few. We have grown up in the cities of India, secure in a national identity rather than a local one, which we express in English better than any Indian language .... And in Indian politics we are pretty much irrelevant. We don't get a look in. We don't enter the fray because we can't win. We tell ourselves ruefully that we are able, but not electable. We don't have the votes: there are too few of us, and we don't speak the idiom of the masses .... Until Rajiv Gandhi, the accidental prime minister came to power. (pp. 42–3; my emphasis)

(Tharoor is a cosmopolitan Indian with an American Ph.D.; since his early twenties he has worked for the United Nations, currently as Executive Assistant to Kofi Annan.)

Coinciding with 'the forward march of the backwards' in the public sector, we can witness the parallel development of an upper-caste domination of the corporate private sector, a new twist to caste-based division of labour (Dhesi 1998). Thus, in a situation of radical restructuring, the élite sections of the upper castes are still to be found where the real influence lies, but they now have a vested interest in weakening the power of the state, devaluing the status of the bureaucracy and thinking globally. This does not always mean working for an international firm; there is also a noticeable gravitation of members of the upper castes into the international organizations and the newly fashionable NGOs, given the mushrooming of possibilities for well-paid research and consultancy. An interesting new class of urbane upper-caste report writers and international conference attenders is emerging in the new globalized India.

But not all members of the *dvija* – the supposedly 'twice born' upper castes – are affluent, highly educated and cosmopolitan. The people who once dominated the clerical posts in the public sector – the functionaries who moved files painfully slowly in government offices, banks and railway booking halls and resented serving those they considered to be their inherent inferiors, the mediocre school teachers and State college lecturers – now find themselves excluded by both the policies of Mandalization and the competitiveness of globalization. Lower middle class members of the upper castes, like the mass of the lower castes, are finding themselves squeezed into new configurations. Out of these new caste alignments a new politics is being forged which shakes the former certainties of many people.

RELIGIOUS COMMUNALISM

In the same way as caste formations constantly change, the larger identities based around religion are not essential, despite the insistence from more entrenched Hindus that one is born to a religion and conversion should not be possible. A friend offered to compile a map for this book showing the distribution of membership of religions; I refused it, explaining that the very act of mapping not only perpetuated outsider perceptions of India as riven by clear-cut religious oppositions but also constituted a small reinforcement of the divide. The data available on religion never addresses the question as to who is a Hindu, and divisions, once unambiguously assigned, become very difficult to transcend. This is not to say that identity based upon membership of religions is not important to a great many people, or that religion is not the basis of powerful groupings – it is simply that one can refuse to help strengthen the construction. The social politics of religion is intimately involved with the social politics of caste and, just as caste is in a state of radical transformation, so is religion.

HINDUTVA

Out of all of the churning, an old idea has emerged with a new significance – the vision of a Hindu *rashtra*, a nation built around the principles of Hindu culture, not just a nation where the majority of people are Hindus. The view of Hinduism taken by the proponents of *Hindutva* has to be seen as firmly grounded in hierarchical ideology, that is, one cannot understand *Hindutva* if one tries to divorce it from caste, even though it purports to be inclusive of all Indians.

The underlying philosophy is nationalist and the aim is to construct a monolithic culture regulating the values of all Indians. This may seem a strange claim in the face of the multiplicity of strands within Hinduism, but Praful Bidwai catches the contradiction perfectly when he writes that 'Polytheism may have helped Hindus accommodate to other faiths, but it did not make them tolerant' (Bidwai 1998, p. 105). Other religions are acceptable so long as they become a part of Hinduism, not if they remain 'other'. Bidwai quotes Joshi as saying, 'Hindu Rashtra is the basic culture of this country. All Indian Muslims are Mohammadiya Hindus; all Indian Christians are Christi Hindus. They are Hindus who have adopted Christianity and Islam as their religion,' and Sudarshan as saying, 'If Muslims have to stay in India, they will have to submit to the Indianisation of their religion' (ibid. 1998). Bidwai also demonstrates the way in which contemporary militant Hinduism tries to claim that Buddhism is no more than a sect of Hinduism, whereas in truth it was one of the many breakaways from the tyranny of caste-based Hinduism (Bidwai 1998, p. 104).

THE RSS

The *Rashtriya Swayamsevak Sangh* (RSS) (National Association of Volunteers) had been the custodian of a dream of nationalist Hinduism since it was founded in 1925. Godse, Gandhi's murderer, was a part of a *Sangh*-based conspiracy and the RSS never made any secret of the fact that it believed that Gandhi had betrayed Hinduism. After a period in which it was banned (and went underground) the RSS rehabilitated itself and gradually built up a strengthened web of influence. In 1996 it even felt confident enough to hold a public 'felicitation' of Godse's brother to which it invited the widows of his co-conspirators, just to show it had no regrets (Padmanabhan 1996).

The RSS is a powerful and efficient organization which works on a cell structure. It recruits its members at a young age and has a policy of sponsoring them to gain places in all professions and major organizations, including trade unions and the media. This allows the *Sangh* to conduct effective propaganda work and gather information, but, most of all, it creates powerful interpersonal networks. In some ways it is rather like a freemasonry. Its aim is nothing less than the unification of the whole of India under a common culture. Romila Thapar explains that this has required the invention of a new form of Hinduism to fit contemporary conditions – a new, codified, inflexible, 'syndicated Hinduism' in imitation of the Semitic religions (Thapar 1989). In a study focusing on the significance of Ram in this process she maintains that:

> Characteristic of the Semitic religions are features such as a historically attested teacher or prophet, a sacred book, a geographically identifiable location for its beginnings, an ecclesiastical infrastructure and the conversion of large numbers of people to the religion – all characteristics which are largely irrelevant to the various manifestations of Hinduism until recent times. (Thapar 1990, p. 159)

This has largely been achieved through the work of the RSS in spreading a northern

Indian, *brahmanical* version of the religion which elevates Ram, as the king *avatar* of Vishnu, into an equivalent position to Christ. As Thapar mentions, the popular television serialization of the *Ramayana* was influential in reinforcing the adoration of Ram and propagating a single version of the story which imposed a knowledge of heroic, masculinized Hinduism, the authority of the Vedic scriptures, and Ayodhya – Ram's birthplace and capital – as a place of origin. All of this fed back into the RSS project.

The RSS also undertakes a considerable amount of welfare work, disaster relief and fundraising and runs its own chain of schools. It is famous for its practice of bonding its members from youth into *shakhas* – local assemblies which combine consciousness-raising with physical fitness. There is early morning drill with prayer, lectures and nationalist sloganizing to establish a sense of discipline and group; this emphasizes praise for the motherland and the quasi-military nature of these defenders of the faith. In addition to the local daily assemblies it also holds uniformed mass rallies. The gatherings particularly appeal to lower-middle-class males who have few opportunities for group solidarity and there are obvious parallels with the scouting movement. Outsiders sometimes ridicule them as paunchy old men in gym shoes and khaki shorts, but it should be remembered that the RSS adopted its ideology of discipline of mind and body at the same time as other 'Aryan' groups in Europe. Their embracing of a virile image of Hinduism under the warrior god Ram, along with emphasis on purity and control, is a chilling combination when one remembers that some of the chubby knees belong to men in very influential positions and boys who will rise fast.

THE SANGH PARIVAR

The RSS is the core organization; clustering around it are the associations which form the *Sangh Parivar* (the *Sangh's* Family). The most significant of these is the political wing, the *Bharatiya Janata* Party (BJP) which came to power in 1998 as the majority member of a coalition government. In Atal Behari Vajpayee, the RSS has its first Prime Minister. The exact relationship between the RSS and the BJP in government is never made clear, but it is acknowledged that Vajpayee is not a free agent as Prime Minister (Mitra and Baweja 1998).

Other members of the *Sangh Parivar* are various youth and student movements, women's groups, development associations, policy committees, groups committed to establishing policies of *swadeshi*, groups with a briefing for education, the thuggish *Bajrang Dal* and the sinister *Vishwa Hindu Parishad* (VHP) (World Hindu Council). As Ahmad (1996c) clearly shows, the RSS works through the formation of 'distinct but overlapping mass fronts' which he lists as being: '(1) the front of students and intellectuals, (2) the fronts that help it cement ties with the traditional sector for religious legitimation, (3) the fronts which connect it with the urban lumpen elements and (4) the crucial parliamentary front' (p. 297).

Through these fronts it has influence in virtually all of the socially and politically significant arenas in India. The *Sangh* uses direct propaganda, distributing its own publications, tapes and videos, but it has also gained a considerable footing in the print media and television which helps to establish its ideology as mainstream (Ahmad 1996c; Basu *et al.* 1993; Basu 1995). It has a website too. Basu *et al.* emphasize 'the attempt of the VHP and BJP to dominate the oral culture by means of the audio-visual media' (p. 89), using propaganda videos which offered depictions of heroic confrontations with marauding Muslims or popular television stars appearing in 'amusing' anti-Muslim sketches. There was free distribution of inflammatory speeches on audio-tape, calling for sacrifice and martyrdom. In a country with low levels of functional literacy the tape cassette is an ingenious means of establishing hegemony.

The *Sangh* combine manages to be popular and élite; to back both the *khadi* industry and the construction of big dams; to offer a spiritual home to statesmen and peasants. Some of its component groups are fervently *swadeshi*, others (like the BJP) attract members of the globalizing business élite. It masterminded the campaigns against Kentucky Fried Chicken and for testing the nuclear bomb. It has enlisted the support of the *sadhus* and appropriated the fervour of major religious gatherings like the *Kumbh Mela* (though Pinch [1996] maintains that many of the *sadhus* came to feel that they had been used in the Ayodhya movement). It claims to *be* India and it can seem very persuasive. The *Sangh* is able to offer a sense of security to people who felt that their world was being turned inside out. By stressing the wholeness and virility of Hinduism it was able to give an illusion of potency to weak people. In its VHP incarnation it stresses that, though there are many forms of Hinduism ('one garland, many flowers'), to be Indian is to be unambiguously Hindu, since Hinduism is the Indian way of life in its entirety. This sounds like the epitome of tolerance, but it means that to be Indian is not to be Muslim, Christian or Buddhist (it is ambivalent about the status of Sikhism, which it claims as militant Hinduism). It is crucial to *Sangh* ideology that all who accept Indian nationality must accept *Hindutva*, which can only be defined circularly as not not-Hindu. The VHP has sought to establish a degree of uniformity within Hinduism, focusing on Ram, the ruler of an earlier Hindu *rashtra*, and establishing common core symbols, including the use of the colour saffron, in an attempt to invent the fundamentals of a non-fundamentalist religion.

Pragmatism

Although the ethos and the higher level leadership of the *Sangh* is upper caste, it has had to attract support from the masses, particularly in terms of its political wing, the BJP. It cannot ignore the voting power of the lower castes and uses a mixture of alliance and inclusion to gain power (Basu 1995). Perhaps the most blatant piece of cynical pragmatism on both sides was the coalition with the *dalit* party, the BSP, in Uttar Pradesh in 1995 and power sharing in 1998, negotiated on both occasions in order to frustrate their mutual enemy, the OBC *Samajwadi* Party (Mohan 1998; Zerinini-Brotel 1998). In the Madhya Pradesh Assembly elected in 1996, the BJP

representation not only contained more SC/ST/OBC members than the Congress Party, but these outnumbered its own upper caste members (Jaffrelot 1998). None of this implies any compromising of *Sangh* principles – it depends upon recruiting members of the lower castes who are personally ambitious and have a popular following.

Securing this following requires the delivery of concessions. In the run up to the 1998 General Election, the incumbent Punjab administration – consisting of an alliance between the Sikh Party, the *Shiromoni Akali Dal*, and the BJP – extended free electricity to the households of poor members of Scheduled Castes and OBCs and handed out senior citizens' pensions. In the same campaign the Election Commission banned State governments from extending the lists of communities classified as OBC – such classification, with all its built-in entitlement to quotas, being an obvious way of establishing group loyalty to the ruling party.

WOMEN AND THE HINDU RIGHT

Whenever there is a patriarchal system, the control of the honour of women becomes a primary symbol for the strength of social units, whether we are looking at the family or at the state (Menon and Bhasin 1996; V. Das 1995). The most reliable form of control is always self-discipline, the internalization of the rules by the subjects themselves, and, in the case of female honour, this means that women develop a reverence for such concepts as chastity, fidelity, maternity, humility, self-sacrifice and domesticity. Women's values then form around ideals constructed in the light of the relationships within the patriarchal family and they become the custodians of such value systems, ensuring the piety of the household. In the conventional wedding ritual, the example of the long-suffering Sita, the consort of the hero-god Ram, is presented to the bride as one she should emulate and she is told that she should bow to the 'wisdom' of her husband and see virtue in duty. Bacchetta (1996) demonstrates the way in which the Sita story is incorporated into the ideology of the *Rashtra Sevika Samiti* (Women's National

Service Association – the women's association within the *Sangh Parivar*)

Women who have internalized these values and shaped their lives around them find their very self-esteem threatened by the economic, political and social changes of the present. They resent the new images of women being presented in the media, the devaluation of their homely skills, the western fashions, the 'brazen' behaviour of young middle-class women, the threat to arranged marriages and extended families. It is not surprising to find that they are attracted to the conservative ideology of *Hindutva*, especially since the *Samiti* offers these womanly values up in an aggressive and militant form. It glorifies the warrior Rani of Jhansi and, using the symbol of the conquering form of the goddess, Durga, it gives women the opportunity to be strong and angry at the same time as being very virtuous. Basu (1995) recounts the way in which

> Hindu nationalism has created new spaces for women's activism. It has done so

FIGURE 8.2 The goddess Durga

partly by creating an aura of passionate commitment to a cause that demands tremendous sacrifices of its followers. Urban middle and lower-middle-class families – who tend more than others to practice female seclusion – have allowed women considerable freedom. (ibid. 1995, p. 76)

She explains that people permitted their daughters-in-law to take part in riots, when they would not normally have allowed them out at night, because they were 'safe in the midst of the *Sangh Parivar*' (ibid., p. 77).

As is observed in situations where there are deep social divisions, the protection of 'our' women from the rapacious intent of the 'other' is placed at the centre of the maintenance of normality. In India one finds numerous examples of the assumed predatory intent of Muslim men in relation to Hindu women. Similarly, higher-caste women are assumed to be vulnerable to lower-caste men. Kannabiran, in a paper on rape and the construction of communal identity, argues that

> The upper caste Hindu sees himself as threatened and under attack on two fronts, from the outside by 'immoral minorities' [Muslims] and from the inside by 'unclean' castes; and women form the core target in both the perception of this threat and the use of violence to suppress it. (1996, p. 33)

Bacchetta (1996, p. 145) refers to the way in which the RSS uses the Partition as a 'recurring theme'; 'Muslim rape of Hindu women' constantly repeated alongside 'Muslim pillaging of Hindu property'. Mani Ratnam's film *Bombay*, which was made in the aftermath of post-Ayodhya rioting, found it symbolically necessary that the husband should be Hindu and the wife Muslim in the inter-communal marriage which stood for communal reconciliation. Had it been otherwise it could have been used to perpetuate the fantasy of the Muslim desire to possess the women of the majority.

The prominent women on the Hindu Right are few in number and very varied in style and appeal, but common to all of them is an emphasis on personal strength. Sadvi

Rithambara is probably the best known, a passionate and violent orator whose audiotapes urged the storming of the *Babri Masjid*; in contrast there is Vijaya Raya Scindia, a gracious aristocrat; the tough and glamorous Uma Bharati (Minister of State for Human Resource Development in the BJP government); and the vulgarian Jayalalitha who has managed to introduce principles of *Hindutva* into the party which is the descendant of the Tamil Non-*Brahmin* Movement. All, like their supporters, are convinced of the need constantly to be vigilant against the Muslim and Christian foreign menace (Sarkar 1996).

MUSLIM SCAPEGOAT

Islam is the obvious target, but Muslims, as the most numerous minority, are primarily a scapegoat which permits the forging of a corporate Hindu identity. In his study of Hindu/Muslim rioting in Hyderabad, the psychoanalyst, Sudir Kakar, refers to the Hindu 'cultural memory' of Muslim tyranny under rulers such as Tipu and Aurangzeb, saying that 'cultural memory is the imaginative basis for a sense of cultural identity ... for isn't imagination a memory of vital moments of life freed from their actual, historical context?' (Kakar 1995, p. 22). As Basu *et al.* (1993) show, this means unifying Hinduism, when formerly it was unorganized; it also means giving preference to the religious forms of the upper castes in the Hindi-speaking 'heartland'. Whatever anyone might say about Muslims receiving special treatment, reproducing too fast or plotting with enemies of the state, India's Muslim communities are on the whole deprived, politically cautious and very aware of their minority status. This does not make them any less suitable for demonization by the forces of Hindu chauvinism, for the goal is not so much the defeat of a threatening minority as the establishment of the power of a Hindu force for its own sake. Hasan (1996) warns against thinking of India's Muslims as a homogeneous group and shows that Muslim intellectuals have often, to their own cost, built upon a British notion of Muslims constituting a separate nation.

Ideas about *Hindutva* were becoming more popular through the 1980s as the VHP doggedly worked at encouraging Hindu households to fly a saffron flag, to display *om* stickers on their crash helmets and posters of Ram in heroic mode in cafés and other public places. It staged pilgrimages and organized group projects to increase solidarity. In 1990 the senior RSS/BJP figure, Advani, embarked upon a rallying *rath yatra* through northern India to Ayodhya in Uttar Pradesh, the supposed birthplace and capital of Ram, the godking. The translation 'chariot pilgrimage' does not quite do justice to the dignity of the symbolism of the vehicle of the conquering hero, Ram, but neither did the truck, decorated with a chariot cut-out and bearing an ageing politician, unless one were a devotee (Davis 1996). There was a call for the demolition of the small sixteenth-century mosque, the *Babri Masjid*, which enthusiasts claimed had been built on the exact site of the birthplace of Ram at Ayodhya. When a new wave of international influence combined with the rumblings of Mandalization in the early 1990s, the hour of *Hindutva* had come.

On 6 December 1992, in an act of collective vandalism, RSS storm troopers tore down the mosque whilst the police looked in other directions. This date is taken as a milestone in the development of communalism in contemporary India. It provoked waves of communal violence across much of India, notably in Bombay where the attacks on Muslim citizens were co-ordinated by the ruling *Shiv Sena*. (I am using the old name Bombay in preference to Mumbai, since that was still its name. The change of name in 1995 was yet another sign of the *Shiv Sena's* authority.) Bal Thackeray, the leader of the *Shiv Sena*, said that the Muslims in Bombay had acted like the Jews in Nazi Germany and should not, therefore, be surprised to receive the same treatment. Mani Ratnam's film *Bombay*, banned and then released in 1995, is a sentimentalized but powerful treatment of the events.

As Ludden (1996) explains, *Hindutva* forces construct Muslims as foreigners – outsiders, invaders, infiltrators – and there is a constant discourse of 'othering'. They complain that politicians outside the BJP 'pander'

One must accept that Hinduism has by far the largest following in this country. This must be remembered. Always. Those who refuse to accept this will have no right to live in this country. Those who have all their lives spoken ill of *Hindutva* are not going to be spared. Embrace this country in its entirety as Hindustan. Else leave.

We have to create a Hindustan for Hindus. We have to create a country where Hindus are respected. The country where *Hindutva* will shine in all its glory. A country where the anti-Hindu shall bow before the will of the Hindu. That is the country we have to build.

Secularism in our context is nothing but an opportunistic impartiality … but the intent is deadly. Look under the covers of this impartiality and you will find unholy incest between purpose and intent. Opportunism is the prophylactic [*sic*] but the demon will surely be born. Someday, someday very soon, when the purpose and intent stand at cross purposes, the membrane will be torn. And the bastard will be conceived. The monster will be born. And our land will be cursed.

(This is an extract from a manifesto for 'Saffron Week', a celebration of *Hindutva*. It was written by Bal Thackeray, the leader of the *Shiv Sena*, which with the BJP forms the government in Maharashtra. *Source: The Hindu* 16 October 1998.)

FIGURE 8.3 A muslim patriarch in Jammu

to Muslims, who receive too many concessions, particularly their right to retain Islamic personal law instead of accepting a common civil code. (This came to public attention in the infamous Shah Bano case, in which the Supreme Court upheld a decision under Islamic law that a man was not required to pay alimony to his elderly divorced wife.) They use sleight-of-hand to present Indian Muslims as Pakistanis, never more so than during the Kargil confrontation. Marqusee (1996) demonstrates the way in which Hindus checked Muslims for their reactions to India's win over Pakistan at Banglore in the quarter-finals of the cricket World Cup. They become disturbed by illegal immigrants coming across the porous Bangladesh border, deporting Indian Muslims who cannot prove that they are not Bangladeshi. Muslim-majority Kashmir is, of course, a constant source of anxiety. The military might of India, including the nuclear bomb, is constantly poised to repel attack from Pakistan, the Muslim state whose birth demonstrated the separability of India.

The same forces encourage routine harassment such as defiling mosques with pig carcasses or ransacking the studio of M.F. Husain, one of India's most eminent artists, on the spurious grounds that he had painted the goddess Saraswati irreverently.

There is no justification for the pretence that Islam is anti-Indian or does not have a place in contemporary India. As Hasan

(1990) demonstrates, there are plenty of historical precedents for peaceful co-existence of Hindu and Muslim people in India. If one thinks that pedigree is important in conferring rights of citizenship, the majority of Muslims are the descendants not of invaders but of *dalit* converts, attracted by the egalitarian ethos of Islam. India has the second largest Muslim population in the world (after Indonesia); even though this constitutes only 12.1 per cent of the total, it is still a significant share. In any case proportions are irrelevant; there is no justification for demonizing a minority, whatever its size.

The events of 1992 have served to make Muslims – always conscious of their minority status – feel ever more beleaguered. There is no doubt that fundamentalist forces within Islam gained increasing support (Hasan 1996). The election of a BJP majority in 1998 did nothing to calm their fears, especially when extracts from a 1995 article written by Vajpayee for the RSS journal, *The Organiser*, were published. Vajpayee (who became Prime Minister) maintained that the solution to 'the Muslim problem' was that Muslims should be 'changed and then restored to the mainstream after providing them with the right *samskaras*'; his alternative to this was that they should be rejected as compatriots (*The Hindu* 1998a). During the election campaign a bomb had devastating effects in Coimbatoire; it was planted by Islamic militants. In June there was rioting, with loss of life in the old city – the Muslim quarter of Hyderabad.

Their organizations protested that Muslims were full members of the nation and that their loyalty should not be questioned. They complained that Muslims were underrepresented in all governmental institutions and that the small number of Muslim MPs and MLAs in the secular political parties did not actively represent their interests, leading to a campaign for the regionalist Muslim parties to merge into a national party. They did this in November 1998, forming the *Milli Jamhoohri Mahaz*. Its first assembly passed resolutions demanding the reconstruction of the *Babri Masjid* on the same site, proportional representation in the State legislatures and Parliament, and quotas in the govern-

ment services (*The Hindu* 17 November 1998) – one further step in the deepening of communalization in Indian politics.

AYODHYA

The demolition of the *Babri Masjid* was not a single finite act. The dispute had rumbled on for centuries, sometimes lying dormant, erupting in times of communal strife, acting as a symbol and a catalyst. Ramachandra Gandhi (1992), writing before the demolition, used Hindu philosophy and local mythology to argue that a narrow interpretation of the literal birthsite of Ram diminishes belief, confines the spiritual to the physical. 'The zone as a whole is Rama's birthplace; and every part and portion of it and every point on its surface. Any number of birthplace shrines can be established there' (p. 16). He explains that a far wider area is known in local mythology as 'Sita's Kitchen' and assumes that this must have been the site of a pre-Hindu sacred grove, leading him to argue that 'a deeper understanding of the site's significance can not only resolve the Ayodhya dispute but also help dissolve the pervasive dualism of "self" and "other" which is hurling civilization headlong towards annihilation' (p. ix). The point is not to know who came first on the site but to understand why some people choose to rally around its ownership as a symbol of their own conflicts.

Archaeologists starting from different ideological positions have long found evidence to back the claims of their 'side' and the sequencing of the accumulation of supposedly objective scientific facts makes a fascinating story (Prakasam 1992). The latest round in the struggle for the ownership of this history occurred in 1998 when the BJP Government, as one of its first actions, purged the Indian Council of Historical Research – the main historical research institute – of secularist historians who had questioned the archeological evidence for a Hindu temple below the mosque (Muralidharan 1998a).

After the demolition, people all over India were urged to send money and bricks, inscribed with the name of Ram, for the construction of a new temple, giving widespread symbolic ownership of it. When it was revealed that pillars were being carved in Rajasthan for assembly in Ayodhya, *The Hindu* (1998b) commented that 'The construction-related activities establish beyond doubt the continuing agenda of the Sangh Parivar to systematically erode the secular spirit of the national polity.' The control of sacred geography and history continues to be of the utmost importance in the maintenance of communal conflict.

In 1997 the VHP launched another initiative in Utter Pradesh which never gained the same emotive following as Ayodhya. This was the *Krishnajanbabhoomi* agitation, aimed at liberating Krishna's birthplace at Mathura from under yet another mosque; its initial rally was timed to coincide with the Muslim festival of Bakrid. Lest anyone think that this 'religious' movement was not a political gesture, one of its organizers told a *Frontline* reporter, 'We would like to see how SP leader Mulayam Singh Yadav opposes an agitation dedicated to liberating the birthplace of the principal deity of his community' (Ramakrishnan 1997, p. 29). (The *yadavs*' traditional occupation is cattle rearing and milk production. The god Krishna was a cowherd. More importantly in today's politics, Mulayam Singh Yadav is a leading secular politician and former Chief Minister of Uttar Pradesh.)

CHRISTIANS

The Christian minority is tiny – just 2.34 per cent of the population – and though it is highly concentrated in the north-eastern States and Kerala, elsewhere it consists of small pockets of converts of *dalits* or tribal people who have used Christianity as a strategy for escaping caste status. The Syrian Christians of Kerala claim a lineage stretching back to St Thomas the Apostle, asserting that their ancestors were *brahmins* who wished to escape from the matrilineal descent system. They are an élite and exclusive category of people with very high levels of education, professional skills and business acumen; they have little in common with the

Keralan *dalit* Christians who are more recent converts and are more typical of Indian Christians. Clark (1998) and Massey (1995) both emphasize the *dalit* identity of the majority of Christians and the ways in which this is not obliterated by membership of the church.

As part of the paranoia of *Hindutva*, Christians have come to be seen by right-wing elements as an enemy and conversions are regarded as a subversion of the power of the Hindu *rashtra*. Calls were made for a law to be passed banning conversions, on the grounds that, since Hinduism was a broad enough religion to contain any faith, conversions by force and trickery must be taking place. Administrators working in areas with Christian minorities say that they had seen the violence brewing for the five years beforehand, but it erupted in late 1998. Churches were burned in the Dangs district of Gujarat; nuns were raped in Bihar and RSS officers suggested that they had only themselves to blame. In January 1999 in Orissa, Graham Staines, an Australian missionary, and his two young sons were burned to death in their vehicle. With remarkable lack of sympathy, the VHP Vice-President said that Staines' work with leprosy patients was a mere 'facade' for conversion work (Muralidharan 1999). Many explained the current upsurge of opposition to this politically inconspicuous community as a device to emphasize that to be Indian is to be Hindu, stressing that the Congress Party had disloyally selected a leader, Sonia Gandhi, who was foreign by faith as well as by birth. (So much for the idea of the loyal wife and the sanctity of mothers of the nation.) An *India Today* article quotes an RSS member as saying of missionaries, 'They are not only changing the religion but converting nationality' (Mahurkar and Raval 1999, p. 20). Because of the presence of foreign missionaries it is easy (and often justifiable) to make the link between proselytizing Christianity and western imperialism.

Against all of this there were forcible 'reconversions' of Christians to Hinduism, even though tribal people generally were not Hindu before conversion to Christianity and the issue of *dalit* Hindu status is unclear. It is reported that, in the first two weeks of 1999, 1 200 members of the *Bhil* tribe in the Dangs district were reconverted (Mahurkar and Raval 1999, p. 19). There was also violent 'liberation' of Christian institutions like schools which were seized in order to be run by Hindu organizations.

The leading figures in carrying out the atrocities were members of an organization of young men known as the *Bajrang Dal* (Bajrang is another name for Hanuman, the monkey god who was famous for his devotion to Ram). It is generally seen as the unruly but passionately-devoted wing of the *Sangh Parivar*. Halarnkar and Mahurkar (1999) show that there is paranoia amongst poorly qualified men of the upper castes about the way in which *dalits* and tribal people are able to gain education through adherence to Christianity. They cite an interview with a youth from the *Bajrang Dal* who had taken a leading part in a raid on a kindergarten in an Ahmedabad slum and who felt that seizing it for the VHP was a noble act. It is obvious that the *Dal* offers the chance of the glow of heroism to people with few prospects. Although the battle is presented in religious terms, it is fairly obvious that we are also looking at a caste and class struggle in which religion is being used, on both sides, as a rallying point.

EDUCATION

Much of the most prestigious schooling in India is in the hands of the Roman Catholic church. 'Convent educated' is a term often used to describe the English-speaking élites. This domination is not surprisingly resented by many people, as an educational system lays down the value system of a country. Virtually all of the teachers are Indian nationals and by no means all of the staff at these schools are nuns and priests or even Christians. Direct proselytizing is absolutely forbidden, but religious symbols and texts are everywhere. The RSS complains (and who can blame them?) that the church is influencing the élite.

Government schools are supposed to be religiously neutral, in keeping with the principles of the secular state. Schools usually interpret this by employing ecumenical devices, addressing an unspecified god, pruning out sectarian symbols, but it is very obvious that Hindu motifs creep in as uncontroversially 'Indian'. The current BJP Government, however, with the RSS constantly prompting it, has attempted a stealthy Hinduization of civil life in general and education in particular. The RSS has long complained that Hindu values are underplayed in formal education. In 1998 at a conference of State education ministers, convened by the Human Resource Development Ministry (Minister Uma Bharati), the *Vidya Bharati*, the educational wing of the RSS, made a series of proposals for school education to be 'Indianized, nationalized and spiritualized', with the teaching of 'the essentials of Indian culture'. Everyone knows that this meant Hindu education. Things were deemed to have gone too far when the Uttar Pradesh Government made it compulsory to start the school day with renderings of the Hindu songs *Vande Mataram* (*Praise to the Motherland*, a freedom song which, to the resentment of many, has been appropriated by the Hindu Right) and the *Sarawati Vandana* (the hymn of praise to the goddess of wisdom, the arts and learning) (Muralidharan and Pande 1998). The Muslim League forbade Muslim schoolchildren to join in the worship.

Besides maintaining its own schools, which often offer the only functioning education in rural areas, the *Vidya Bharati* demands the teaching of Sanskrit (the language of the scriptures) in all schools. It sponsors the revision and adoption of school textbooks which give a *Hindutva* construction of history and use *Hindutva* examples in grammar and comprehension exercises (Menon and Rajalaksmi 1998). With a BJP government in power, its project has greater power than ever. It has already been mentioned that uncongenial historical research is being stifled. There is a similar trend in all academic disciplines which gains respectability by dressing in the clothes of anti-imperialism, which western scholars, mindful of their own imperial guilt, frequently take at face value. A recent example is Singh's paper entitled

'Rethinking development in India' in the collection edited by Simon and Narman (1999); it asks seemingly innocent questions like, 'Is it possible to discern any sense of sacred in the "alternative development" strategy?' (p. 55) and builds up an argument full of the sort of 'tradition' which rests upon old divisions of caste, religion and gender.

SECULARISM

Many commentators believe that since Hindu nationalism has invaded Indian politics, there can be no assumption that the state is neutral any longer, with a resulting growth of cynicism about government (Brass 1997; Jaffrelot 1996). More than mere factionalism, this is arguably the greatest price of communalism, whereby the assumption that violence is normal creeps into one's political consciousness (van der Veer 1994).

The counter to the communalist forces is secularism, which was seen by Nehru as an essential component of the independent India. The term 'secularism' is used in India in a range of rather different ways. The obvious meaning is the separation of religion from state; this requires that the law is independent of religion and that religious motifs are not incorporated in the symbolic construction of the state. However, this use of the term has been extended into a peculiarly Indian usage – that the state should be evenhanded towards all religions. There is also the strange communalist appropriation of the idea of secularism, which claims that all (acceptable) belief can be incorporated within Hinduism which is uniquely tolerant of all. This last usage results in accusations of 'pseudo-secularism' being levelled at people who support either of the other more conventional uses.

To criticize *Hindutva* is very definitely not to criticize Hinduism. There are forms of Hindu belief which consider that the nation-state is a modernist irrelevance; stress equality not only among people but also between people and nature; emphasize giving and selflessness; value non-violence and tolerance. There are many people who are not supporters of the Hindu Right or of communalism who regret the way in which Hinduism has been perverted into *Hindutva*. One sometimes sees the slogan 'Keep your politics out of my religion!' in protest against this. Such people often express an anti-secularist view, claiming that the way forward for India is to reject western ways and to espouse traditional Indian values, including a suffusion of spirituality in all aspects of life. Leading figures with this view are Ashis Nandy (1983, 1994, 1995b, 1998b) and T.N. Madan (1997a and b) who have been influential in establishing an anti-modernist trend in Indian intellectual life. Their arguments are very appealing, particularly to people with orientalist leanings, as they offer the hope that there could be a way to shut out the unpleasantnesses of global competition and reorientate oneself into a whole different way of life. However, they present a romantic notion of traditional India which is difficult to apply to real conditions. Achin Vanaik (1997) and Partha Chatterjee (1994) are disinclined to believe that one can achieve true equality and heal the divisions within society within the bounds of tradition; both argue for a non-consumerist and totally secular modernity as India's contribution to contemporary global politics.

A HINDU BOMB

When India exploded nuclear devices at Pokhran in the Rajasthan desert in May 1998 there was jubilation in the streets of the major cities. The new BJP Government had been promising the tests in the light of the country's refusal to sign the Comprehensive Test Ban Treaty, seen as a western plot to enfeeble India. Crowds danced in celebration of this manifestation of national strength, even though the delight was soon to be tempered by Pakistan demonstrating that it too had the Bomb. Containers of sand from the site were distributed around the country as relics of the achievement. The tests were interpreted by all but a minority as being a matter for pride and patriotism, a demonstration of India's scientific and technical achievement. They were also a message not just to

Pakistan, but also to the western nuclear powers that India would not be pushed around.

The secular Left (Roy 1998) is conducting an uphill campaign to educate people about the nuclear threat. Whilst the Left draws attention to the ironies of a desire for nuclear force in a country which fails to deliver clean drinking water to all its citizens, the Hindu Right appropriates the glory and the powerful imagery of weaponry named after gods.

In the 1999 Kargil War, the most enthusiastic supporters of *Hindutva*, such as Bal Thackeray, periodically threatened to 'go nuclear'. The war was about national sovereignty – it was not a matter of Hindu versus Muslim; however, in contemporary situations in which state and religion are being brought into greater intimacy, the risks of conflation of national interest with faith become frightening.

9

THE CENTRE AND REGIONAL MOVEMENTS

Although Independent India was constituted as a federal republic, it has always been highly centralized – the Union Government having power over defence, foreign affairs, planning, currency, major aspects of taxation and legislation. The majority of funding for the States comes from the Centre and the senior administrators are members of the All-India Services, though they are attached to State cadres (see Chapter Eleven). Each State has a Governor, who acts as the representative of the Government of India; this person is appointed by the President and does not necessarily have a prior connection with the State. The President of India can, under Article 356 of the Constitution, suspend the individual State governments if these are deemed to have lost control of law and order, if there is a breakdown of the State economy, or during war (Pattabhiram 1997). The Centre can also declare a general State of Emergency where all State legislatures are dissolved, as did Indira Gandhi between 1975 and 1977.

The strong Centre is largely the product of the Independence Movement, whereby India was imagined as a single nation in opposition to the colonial power. This sense of nationhood was intended to cut across community and region to create a strong and unified modern state and to prevent the emergence of sub-state nationalisms. One can see this vision of the unified state as being in the idealized image of the Congress Party – modern, pan-Indian but upper-caste

dominated. However, we can also see the new India reflecting the centralized structure of the colonial power, the States replicating the British administrative provinces, with the addition of the princely States. Nehru's modernizing project was opposed to the autonomous development of the States as ethnic and linguistic regions but it was in Indira Gandhi that the Centre strengthened to become all-dominating. Virtually all decisions at State level needed to be ratified by the Centre and State politics was conducted with an eye to Delhi.

Brass (1984) introduces the idea of a 'dynamic interpenetration' as being essential between Centre and State in a federal structure but considers the greatest weakness in Indian politics to be its ever-increasing centralizing tendencies (1994). This is a view shared by many Indian political theorists of the Left, perhaps most cogently expressed by Partha Chatterjee in his celebration of the potential demise of centralized power following the 1996 elections (1997).

Brass contends that the overcentralization of Indian politics, associated with Hindu majoritarianism, is the direct cause of minority regional and ethnic discontent, leading to secessionist and autonomist movements. He does not believe that inherent regional identity provides the motive force for autonomy or secession. As he shows, the response of the Centre to demands for autonomy has always been the use of repressive measures, sometimes the use of considerable military or para-military force, since there is a fear that the Centre will not hold and that India will fragment into its component parts. For Brass, and many others, the only solution is to devolve power to the States and then right down to the level of local government, rather than to attempt further concentration.

Forms of decentralization at the lowest level, such as *panchayati raj* and the favouring of NGOs, have been incorporated into the structural adjustment programme as a major aspect of the project of rolling back the bureaucratized state. The States vary considerably in terms of their economic fortunes and their influence nationally. This is not just a matter of location and physical geography but of histories of previous trade relations and investments, development strategies, and internal political relations. Today we see State governments increasingly promoting themselves directly on the global stage, seeking foreign investment, advertising their tourist attractions, offering concessions and bidding for international aid. There are regular State supplements in overseas newspapers and journals and State-based foreign deputations are becoming routine.

ARTICLE 356

However, there is little devolution of real power to the States, as was brought home very clearly in January 1999, when President's Rule was (briefly) imposed upon Bihar. Certainly the status of law and order in Bihar was at crisis point, but, as its Chief Minister was quick to point out, there were other States, such as Gujarat, Maharashtra and Uttar Pradesh, which also witnessed communal violence but were protected from President's Rule by having BJP/*Shiv Sena* governments. In the case of Bihar, the Samata Party – a member of the Union Coalition Government but the minority party in the State – was determined to bring down the RJD administration.

Other States had already been investigated over their law and order status. Tamil Nadu's former Chief Minister, Jayalalitha, had been campaigning for President's Rule as a way of ousting the State's DMK Government and in

June 1999 the leader of the AIADMK Parliamentary Party (part of the coalition government) walked out of the *Lok Sabha* on her instructions. In West Bengal, Mamata Bannerjee of the Trinamul Congress, yet another coalition member, stirred up a demand for President's Rule in opposition to the ruling CPI(M) government.

Since Independence, Article 356 has been invoked more than a hundred times, but in 1998 it became the subject of considerable controversy because it seemed to be being used very opportunistically. The scope for abuse of Article 356 is obvious. A precarious government at the Centre can intervene in State matters, so long as it can gain the agreement of the President. Refusing to meet the Central Home Ministry team of enquiry into alleged *panchayati raj* election violence, the West Bengal Home Minister declared:

> It appears that the Trinamul Congress is pressurising the Centre to serve its own narrow political interests. The Centre, too, cannot do a thing as it is dependent on the support of parties like the Trinamul. If it is really worried about the law and order situation, it should send a team to Uttar Pradesh. (*The Hindu* 19 June 1998, p. 1)

On the same page of *The Hindu*, the All-India Congress Committee accused the BJP Government of 'trying to erode federalism. This is nothing but an attempt of the *Sangh Parivar* to spread its wings all over the country.' The BJP was accused of having 'elastic standards' relating to its concern for law and order in the States, given that it was not imposing President's Rule in Rajasthan (with its appalling rate of violence against women and *dalits*), Uttar Pradesh (with its *dacoity*, kidnapping and rape record), or even Jammu and Kashmir with its troubled political situation (Swami *et al.* 1998). The leading in-depth journal of current affairs, *Frontline*, brought out a special issue (Muralidharan 1998c) on the implications of the cynical attitude of the BJP-led coalition to the suspension of democratically-elected governments at the State level, arguing that the main problem was the Centre rather than the States.

As the previous chapter indicated, besides the simple expediency of retaining power, the BJP must adhere to the ideology of the RSS, with its ultimate project of a single Hindu *rashtra* with a strong central authority. Ironically, at present it can further this aim only by compromising with the minority parties in the regions. The intense debate in the late 1990s about the nature of federalism and the continuation of democracy in India formed around the realization that Article 356 is a loophole whereby a dictatorship can be imposed, regardless of the political will in the regions. As Kuppuswami maintains:

> The frequent misuse of Article 356 [is] possible ... because of the Governors aiding and abetting the Centre in imposing President's Rule when the state was ruled by a party in opposition to the ruling party at the Centre. The Union Cabinet appoints as Governors retired bureaucrats who were accustomed to serving the interests of the Union or politicians belonging to the ruling party who are not able to find a suitable place in the political arena ... The framers of the Constitution intended that a Governor be a person above party politics. (Kuppuswami 1997)

Although the RSS works through the umbrella organization of the *Sangh Parivar* which contains many traditionalist elements, as the previous chapter showed, its impetus is very definitely in terms of modernist imperatives. It gains its majority support from those lower-middle-class people who are squeezed by modernizing forces but who were also constructed by them. For this section of society, a strong centralized, even militarized, state seems an essential bastion against the potential power of the mass, located at regional level.

NEW STATES

It is impossible to draw the State boundaries in India in such a way that each is ethnically and linguistically homogeneous, even though there have been boundary reorganizations as a consequence of agitation on linguistic grounds. In 1956 Madras Province was divided between Tamil Nadu and Andhra Pradesh; in 1960 Bombay Province became Maharashtra and Gujarat; in 1966 Punjab split into Punjab, Harayana and Himachal Pradesh. However, it is impossible for each minority to have its own State since each new State formation, as well as making former minorities into majorities, also does the exact opposite. It becomes essential that the States, just as much as the Union, should generate policies in which their own minorities are accorded equal rights. States, however, do not just segment internally along linguistic lines – like the nation, they contain religious, caste and tribal divisions, which rarely have more than a loose fit to territory.

The language and ethnicity issue is important not just for reasons of identity but because of economic and political opportunities. It is inevitable that as economic and political formations change, there will be new demands phrased in terms of old divisions. Recently, the stated policy of the BJP to encourage the formation, wherever possible, of smaller States has been far more significant than any grass-roots agitation for autonomy. Like the abuse of Article 356, this policy is intended to strengthen the Centre by fragmenting the States and removing the power base of some important players.

Jarkhand/Vananchal and Chhattisgarh

One of the oldest demands for a new State is that of the Jharkhand Movement, whose history stretches back into pre-Independence days. It consists of an alliance of tribes in southern Bihar, western Orissa and eastern Madhya Pradesh which had long campaigned for a separate state called *Jharkhand*, where tribal people (*adivassis*) would be in the majority. It was intended that this new State should be carved out of all three existing States (Ghosh 1998).

The southern part of Bihar is very rich in minerals; India depends upon this region for coal and iron in particular, but it is also becoming very important for the mining of uranium. It contains the steel city of Jamshedpur which is virtually controlled by the major industrialist firm of Tata. It is this wealth which so long stood in the way of separate statehood for the tribal people with

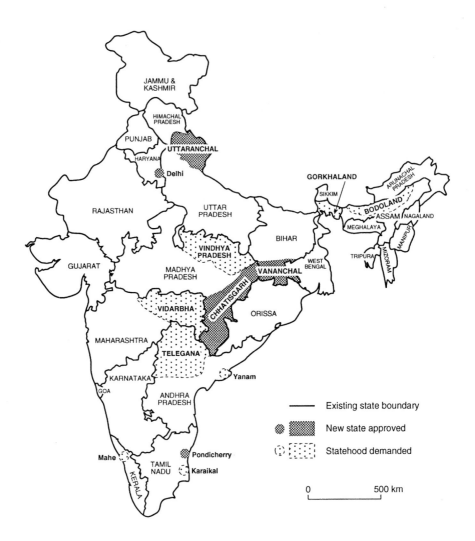

FIGURE 9.1 New States

Source: based on information published in *Frontline*, 31 July 1998

Note: In 1998, the BJP Government approved the formation of three new States – Uttaranchal (Uttarakhand), Vananchal (Jharkhand) and Chhatisgarh – to be carved out of Uttar Pradesh, Bihar and Madhya Pradesh respectively. The status of a State of the Union was also conferred on Delhi and Pondicherry.

their predominantly forest-based economic system. Like most sub-state nationalisms worldwide, the Jharkhand Movement was led by frustrated educated minorities who saw opportunities in a new political structure; it also drew upon the aspirations of the poorly unionized industrial workforce, drawn from the tribal rural areas.

In the political transformations of the 1980s and 1990s we can see the status of the tribal people of the Jharkhand region changing in the light of changes in the politics of the component States. At the national level, Bihar took on the role of the scapegoat State, the one which could always be called upon the show how bad things would get in terms of corruption, favouritism, disorder, caste violence and economic backwardness, and much of this was attributed to the way in which Bihar had become dominated by OBC politics. Its Chief Minister, Laloo Pradad Yadav, was perceived by both Congress and

BJP governments at the Centre as an overly powerful player in the national as well as State arena. The *yadav* power base is northern Bihar – the densely-populated, agriculturally-based, Hindu/Hindi heartland – but 70 per cent of the tax revenue of Bihar is generated through the mining and processing of the South. It is perhaps inevitable that this economic and political configuration, rather than the long struggle of tribal peoples for self-determination, should lead to successive Union governments becoming increasingly friendly to the idea of a separate Jharkhand State.

In 1994 the Jharkhand Autonomous Areas Council was established in the southern districts of Bihar as a consequence of economic pressure and popular unrest; it was predominantly composed of members of the *Jharkhand Mukti Morcha* (JMM). This organization had travelled a long way to the political Right since its days of violent agitation and association with Naxalite groups in the 1970s. The initial impetus for Jharkhand grew out of demands for the rights of tribal people, particularly regarding access to forests and compensation for land acquired for mining and industry, but gradually, with increased investment, the non-tribal population of the region grew to constitute a majority; this was largely as a consequence of migration from northern Bihar. The movement then came to represent far wider economic interests than those with a subsistence base and to have as its main focus a divorce from the impoverished and OBC-dominated North, which was seen as draining away the South's wealth. In 1993 there was a 'money-for-votes' scandal when it was alleged that seven JMM members of the *Lok Sabha* were bribed with more than eight crores of rupees to prop up the tottering Congress Government, and the JMM was revealed as being as opportunist an organization as any. There was growing BJP support in southern Bihar and the party at the Centre increasingly turned its attention to the region, promising that, if elected to government, it would grant a separate State. This new State, however, would consist only of the southern districts of Bihar and would be known as Vananchal (land of the forest) to distinguish it from the

Jharkhand which had aspirations towards districts in Orissa and Madhya Pradesh. In 1998 the necessary bill was tabled.

On the Madhya Pradesh side of the border is the proposed new State of Chhattisgarh, (already mentioned in Chapter Seven in connection with the struggles of the *Chhattisgarh Mukti Morcha*). The original demands for a greater Jharkhand as a tribal people's State included two of the 13 districts which would make up the new Chhattisgarh, but the BJP set its sights on creating a new State in its own right, in which tribal aspirations would be incidental. The similarities with Vananchal are considerable. It is a mineral-rich region in a poor State and provides 45 per cent of the State's revenue. It has a substantial but fragmented tribal population which provides cheap labour for mining and industry and it has a new immigrant population of caste Hindus with commercial interests, who have swollen the non-tribal population to such an extent that it now constitutes a majority.

Uttarakhand/Uttaranchal

The hill districts of Uttar Pradesh are different in many ways from the more populous plains which constitute the greater part of the State. Most obvious is the difference in terrain which means that there is little rural opportunity other than a precarious living from forests and from terraced small-holdings. The hills have long sent substantial numbers of young men into the armed forces and they rely on government employment, some tourist activity and remittances from wage-earners on the plains. There are other less obvious differences, such as the predominance of the Pahari language and an unusual caste configuration, whereby *brahmins* and *rajputs* make up about 80–85 per cent of the population, as against about 11 per cent for the whole State (Mawdsley 1997).

Uttar Pradesh is India's largest State in terms of population (152 million) but the hill districts account for only 4 per cent of this. The lifestyles and economic interests of the hills are radically different from those of the plains and there have long been suggestions that the hill region could form a separate State; however, as Mawdsley shows, until

---

Box 13 Khand v. anchal

The suffix 'khand' denotes a piece – that is, a tract of territory. It has its roots in *Urdu*, the language which is increasingly being narrowly associated with Muslims, even though it has been in general use in Northern India.

The suffix 'anchal' is more metaphoric. Literally it is the edge of a sari, the part which a woman pulls over her head or uses to cover a baby she is feeding; it stands for ideas about motherhood. As part of the name for a new State it implies a part of the motherland.

The BJP has sought to appropriate separate State movements by divorcing them from their origins and imposes the latter term, which poetically incorporates the separation back into the Centre. Uttaranchal – the Northern Motherland; Vananchal – the Forest Motherland.

---

recently there was little serious enthusiasm for this. These differences surfaced as an active demand for separate status in 1994 when the Chief Minister, Mulayam Singh Yadav (leader of the OBC-dominated *Samajwadi* Party), announced that he would apply reservations according to the Mandal recommendations in all districts in the State. More specifically he instructed the higher education institutions in the hills to reserve 50 per cent of places for SC/ST/OBC. There was a sudden realization that the government service and the colleges would be swamped with lower-caste outsiders and that valuable jobs and opportunities would be lost (Ramakrishnan 1994a). The Uttarakhand Movement was initially launched by students who saw their job opportunities receding, but it soon grew, particularly after violent confrontations with the police in September 1994 in which 20 protestors were killed. As the campaign escalated, State and central government institutions were picketed, a district collector was murdered, *bandhs* (closure of shops etc.) were organized, trains were stopped. When a bus carrying protestors to Delhi was fired at by the

police in Muzaffarnagar, 15 of its passengers were killed and women allegedly raped (I have to say 'allegedly', since it has not yet been proven), and the tide of public opinion in India swung in favour of the movement (Ramakrishnan 1994b and c).

In 1995, a coalition of the BSP and the BJP replaced the *Samajwadi* Party as the State government. Mayawati, the first *dalit* woman to hold the rank, was Chief Minister and was opposed to demands for Uttarakhand; she was also demonstratively anti-upper caste and made life a misery for sympathetic civil servants by transferring them at will. However, the BJP part of the alliance was in full support of the separate State and it demonstrated this clearly on the anniversary of the rioting by helping to organize a rally in commemoration of the martyrs (Pande 1995). The Uttarakhand Movement is predominantly upper caste, middle class and BJP-voting; its demands are those of the new India, with very few echoes of the forest activists of the past. It has experienced violent opposition from both the State government and the Centre but with the BJP's accession to power at both levels, Uttarakhand (to be known as Uttaranchal) was assured its separate statehood. Reservations will be in proportion to its own unique caste composition.

Despite support from the Centre, the problem still rumbles on. The minority Sikh population of the Terai region on the borders of the proposed new State are resisting inclusion, enlisting the support of the Punjabi party, the *Akali Dal* – a partner of the BJP. The Sikhs in question were refugees from Partition and had been given grants of forest land which were not subject to the State's land ceiling laws. They had become affluent large farmers and owners of sugar and rice mills and had much in common with the rest of Green Revolution western Uttar Pradesh. They feared that Uttaranchal would impose land ceilings on them, and also that their products would have to pay duties when they crossed what would become a State border into Uttar Pradesh. They had nothing to gain from revised reservation laws and felt that there was much to lose from joining a smaller, poorer unit.

Vidarbha and Telengana

Vidarbha, on the north-eastern side of Maharashtra, is similar in many ways to Chhattisgarh or Vananchal in that it has a significant tribal population and is mineral rich. It is also a major cotton and orange producing region, but has received limited amounts of development funding from Maharashtra and is regarded as a 'backward' region. Where it differs from the claims for statehood already mentioned is that, this time, the opposition to its formation comes from a State government which is an ally of the BJP. Whilst the BJP at the Centre was willing to stand up to Congress-ruled Madhya Pradesh and RJD-ruled Bihar, its policy in relation to the opposition to claims from Vidarbha has been to back down (Bavadam 1996; Rangarajan 1999). Similarly the bid for Telengana in northern Andhra Pradesh has been a virtual non-starter because of the ruling *Telugu Desam* Party's valuable opposition to the Congress Party in the State.

Union Territories

At the same time as it tabled bills for the creation of the new States of Uttaranchal, Vananchal and Chhattisgarh, the central government announced the creation of the new State of Delhi and shortly afterwards, Pondicherry – both hitherto Union Territories. The Tamil Nadu opposition party, the AIADMK, immediately organized a victory procession to celebrate the new status of Pondicherry. As *The Hindu* of 15 March 1998 commented of Pondicherry, 'There is hardly any scope for the proposed State sustaining itself. In fact the clamour for statehood has very much to do with the thirst of the political class for more executive authority.' It was widely believed that Pondicherry received statehood only as a condition for AIADMK support for the Delhi Statehood Bill, which had long been a major ambition of the BJP.

The State of Delhi will exclude the separate area of the administrative capital but will consist of the major residential areas. It will be the most affluent and politically influential State in the Union and, most importantly, will be able to administer the allocation of some of the most valuable urban land in the country. Part of that power will extend to being able to displace illegal residents from good development land. Even as a State, Delhi will however still have all its old problems regarding the release of water by Haryana.

THE NORTH EAST

The States of the North East (Assam, Manipur, Meghalia, Nagaland, Tripura, Arunachal Pradesh and Mizoram) have always sat uneasily in independent India. With majority tribal populations they differ in virtually all respects from the rest of the country and have more affinities with neighbouring countries such as Burma and Bhutan. Mountainous States, connected to the rest of India by the narrow 'panhandle', it is easy to forget that they are part of the Union. They are off-limits to casual visitors from India because of the long-running armed struggle of separatist movements of two kinds: first, the radical demand for the secession of Assam from India, and second, the local demands for internal fragmentation to create Bodoland, based on tribal ethnicity, out of the present Assam.

Brass (1994, pp. 201–15) gives an excellent account of the issues involved until the early 1990s. These revolve around problems of multiple minority status and immigration. Assam's indigenous population is Assamese-speaking and Hindu, but this was overlain by Bengali administrators, estate owners and traders, both Hindu and Muslim. The Bangladesh War caused a huge immigration of Bangladeshis (Muslims) and Assam claimed that it was becoming flooded with foreigners. Assam's indigenous Hindus wanted its borders more effectively policed and to be able to deport outsiders; they also successfully campaigned for Assamese as the only official State language, gaining an advantage over the Bengalis. The United Liberation Front of Assam emerged as a militant separatist organization, agitating for independence from India; its main base was educated, unemployed middle-class youth, frustrated by the lack of prospects in the

State. As time progressed, its anti-immigrant stance waned and it became increasingly left-wing. It maintains bases in neighbouring Bhutan, a country with an uneasy relationship with India (Ray 1995). Meanwhile, tribal minorities in Assam resented the influence of the Assamese Hindu community and claimed that they were excluded from many State benefits on the grounds of both language and networks; they began their own violent campaign, under the Bodo Liberation Tigers, for separate statehood for Bodoland. Currently there are central government accusations that the Muslim schools in the area are harbouring Pakistani ISI-funded trainee terrorists.

There is little question of splitting or granting independence to Assam (Choudhury 1999). The government's tactic has been to strengthen the Bodo Autonomous Council and to fund its development projects directly, rather than through the Assam Government (Chaudhuri 1998). It has also sought to cut off the funding of the Liberation Tigers by getting tough with the big tea companies, demanding that they cease paying the militants protection money. Given that planters have suffered shootings, kidnappings and intimidation of their labour force, it is hardly surprising that they are willing to pay up; there are also plenty of indications that they are more interested in a stable regime than in giving any enthusiastic support to the Government of Assam (Chaudhuri 1997).

The other northern States continue to be plagued by terrorism as militant elements fight for the same independence as Bhutan, and yet there are also women's peace movements, as in Manipur, where there are counter-campaigns simply against violence.

Gorkaland seeks the status of an autonomous State, independent from West Bengal, whose CPI(M) government is sympathetic to its demands but intractably opposed to dividing the State, following the expressed party policy of support for strong States. We can probably expect Gorkaland to be in the next round of proposed States, unless its sensitive border position makes the Centre fearful of complete secession.

THE PUNJAB

The Punjab lies on India's most sensitive border. The line dividing it from Pakistan is nothing more than the slash of a cartographer's pen – more than half of the Punjab lies on the other side and many people have their ancestral homes there. The Punjab bore the brunt of the violence of Partition and has never quite shaken off its legacy. Muslim Pakistan may be the enemy, but part of the country itself is 'home'. It continues to be a State with its heart severed in two, never forgetting that everything can be taken away, nothing can be relied upon. In the three wars with Pakistan the Punjab has found itself in the front line. Even in the Kargil 'War', continuing as I write, Punjabis are moving their families, livestock and valuables away from the border, just in case it escalates. It is no wonder that the State is never quite settled or that it sees itself as distinctive. For the present, the Punjab is relatively stable, its tensions channelled into internecine disputes between religious factions rather than political groups, but the stability cannot be taken for granted (Swami 1999a).

The Punjab has been betrayed many times over; it has a long history of invasions which trained its people to be aggressive and protective at the same time. Its population consists of both Sikhs and Hindus and there is a distinctive Punjabi culture irrespective of religion (Hershman 1981). The RSS would have us believe that Sikhism is nothing more than the militant wing of Hinduism; historically that is true – perhaps it is even beginning to become true again – but it is a long time since ordinary Sikhs and Hindus thought of themselves as one group and the dreadful events of the 1980s served only to increase the distance between them.

The State is probably the best example of Brass's claim that separatist tendencies are a consequence of over-centralization. In the 1980s, in an attempt to diminish the regionalist base of the Akali Dal and its demand for a confederation within India, Indira Gandhi's government actively encouraged rival Sikh fundamentalist groups, championing Bhindranwale, a Sikh *sant* (independent holy man). These groups quickly slipped out of governmental control and started to make demands for a separate State of Khalistan outside the Union. The movement drew, as usual, upon young men with some education but limited prospects; it was heavily backed by the Sikh diaspora with fantasies of Khalistan. In 1984, after a prolonged campaign of rural terrorism, Indian troops launched Operation Blue Star and stormed the Golden Temple at Amritsar, which Bhindranwale and his supporters had established as a defensive position. Bhindranwale was killed, as were many of his supporters, and the temple was badly damaged (Shurmer-Smith 1984). A year later, Indira Gandhi was assassinated by Sikh members of her bodyguard. Delhi erupted in vengeful attacks on innocent Sikhs, particularly those living in the poorest quarters. The memories of Operation Blue Star and the Delhi riots are still too raw for Sikh Punjabis to trust the rest of India (Das 1990; Singh 1999; Srinivasan, 1990).

The Punjab had been the showcase for the Green Revolution, but by the 1980s the miracle was fading. There was a general feeling that India had been prepared to see the advance of the Punjab as an agricultural producer but was not willing to allow it to progress beyond this. Affluent Punjabis felt frustrated by the lack of backing for local investment in industry and for the modernization of the economy. Others saw the gap widening between rich and poor. The educated children of wealthy farmers frequently developed aspirations beyond agriculture and felt discriminated against when they could not find the sorts of employment they had anticipated (Madan 1997; Jodhka 1999). There has been massive emigration from the Punjab to the USA, Canada, Britain and the Far East and the non-resident Sikhs have not only invested back in buildings and small businesses in the Punjab, they have also maintained strong personal and emotional ties.

Terrorism was more or less extinguished in 1992, but the Chief Minister of the Punjab was killed by a car bomb in 1995 and there are still sporadic outbreaks. There is no effective demand for a separate country called Khalistan, but the desire has not been extinguished in the minds of frustrated young people or the romantic patriotism of those who will probably never return to live in India but continue to support fundamentalist tendencies 'at home'. India alleges that Pakistan's Inter-Service Intelligence is actively promoting pro-Khalistan terrorist activities by funding such groups as the Bhabar Khalsa International, the Khalistan Zindabad Force and the Khalistan Commando Force. Whether it is Pakistan or the non-resident Sikhs, or both, who provide the finance, bombs on buses and at railway stations are still not a thing of the past – but the groups responsible are small and fragmented. At present the Punjab is ruled by an Akali Dal/BJP coalition and the Akali faction is promoting itself now as a Punjabi party, rather than exclusively a Sikh party (Pandher 1998a). It would however be rash to say that the Punjab is no longer a possible secessionist state.

KASHMIR

As I write, young men are dying on the frozen wastes of the frontier between India and Pakistan in the Kargil 'War', the war we are not supposed to call a war, because it has never been declared and because the 'intruders' into India from Pakistan are not (are not supposed to be?) Pakistani soldiers but independent *mujahideen*. Kashmir is perhaps the main reason why the Indian government has a built-in centralizing urge. It stands as a permanent, unsolved, and insoluble remnant of the Partition of India. However, although the roots of the Kashmir problem lie in the past, like all political disputes it has to be interpreted in terms of the present; young men and women are not fighting their grandfathers' battles.

At Independence, Kashmir, then a princely State, was allowed to opt whether to become part of India or Pakistan. The Maharaja was a Hindu, as were many of the élite minority – the *pandits* – of the Kashmir Valley, but the majority of the population was Muslim. The Maharaja chose India and signed the Instrument of Accession of Jammu and Kashmir State. It was given (temporary) special status under Article 370

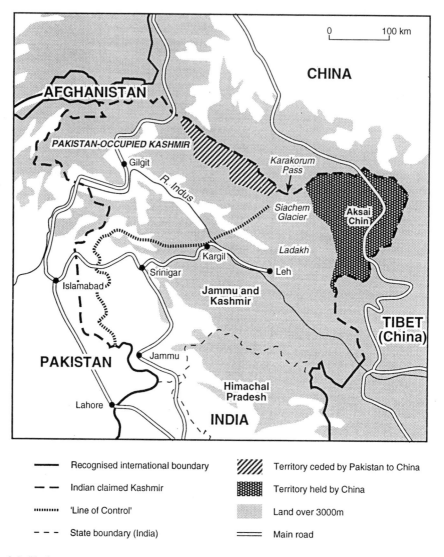

FIGURE 9.2 Kashmir

of the Constitution, which limited the powers of the Indian government over Kashmir. Its status has been contested ever since and it has been the cause of three declared wars with Pakistan and ongoing border skirmishes. Kashmir's northern boundary is not an accepted international border – it is a 'line of control' established in 1972 by the Shimla Agreement at the end of the 1971 Indo-Pakistan War. It is conventional in India to refer to the territory to the north of the line as 'Pakistan-occupied Kashmir', not

conceding it to Pakistan. Ahmad (1999) sums the situation up concisely:

> The Kashmir problem ... has proved to be so very difficult to resolve *politically*, in accordance with the actual wishes and interests of the population, precisely because the territorial dispute between the two nation-states is based in irreconcilable geopolitical objectives (p. 18).

But Kashmir is far more than just disputed territory; many Indians claim that,

Figure 9.3 Kashmir before the violence

with its Muslim majority, it is evidence of the validity of India's claim to be a secular State – one which is not composed along religious lines.

There is not sufficient space to outline the details of the background to the current insurgency, which dates back to 1986, but the political scientist Sumit Ganguly (1997) gives a masterly interpretation of this complex situation and Tavleen Singh's (1995) *Kashmir: a tragedy of errors* is a meticulous and engaging personal account by one of India's most provocative journalists.

Although the problems of Kashmir may seem unique, some of the underlying issues are general to those Indian regions which seek autonomy, at whatever level. Most obvious is the matter of ethnic identity, but we know this to be something which emerges and recedes in the light of circumstance. Then there is the question of peripherality – Kashmir is remote from the rest of India and difficult to access. Most important in the late twentieth century, however, has been the consciousness of lack of economic opportunity, inability to share in the fruits of the new economy, and this consciousness is always felt most acutely by middle-class young men with some qualifications but few chances. It is easy for their ambitions to be channelled into ideological struggles. Apart from tourism (now shattered), Kashmir had little modern economic activity and felt neglected in terms of development initiatives. Many

saw themselves as colonized by India rather than a part of the nation. There is ample evidence that development funding has been syphoned off by 'the political middlemen who helped New Delhi keep a grip over its population, whose democratic aspirations were exceptionally high, thanks precisely to the promise that was once made but never kept' (Ahmad 1999, p. 18).

One can sum up the political positions in Kashmir as consisting of those who believe that Kashmir should be a part of Pakistan; those who believe that it should be a part of India (as at present); and those who believe that it should be a separate country in its own right. These are not reconcilable views. The situation is, of course, perfect for the activity of the Pakistan Inter-Service Intelligence which provides training, weaponry and bases for Kashmiri freedom fighters/rebels (according to one's perspective). It even recruits committed young men in foreign universities and infiltrates them, in the guise of NRI students on holiday, to carry the Kashmir campaign of terror into the cities of India. Virtually all of the Kashmiri *pandits* have left the valley and many will probably never return, whatever the outcome, given that they have set up successfully in business in the booming Indian cities.

Although I have been referring to Kashmir throughout as if it were one place, the name of the State is Jammu and Kashmir and it contains Laddakh and Leh. In April 1999 the

Regional Autonomy council recommended setting up three provinces in Kashmir and three more in Jammu, all generated along ethnic/religious lines. It is obvious that the policy is to fragment a difficult region so that defensive action can be concentrated where it is most needed (Kargil), and other areas can begin to rebuild. Jammu has a more mixed population than Kashmir, with substantial numbers of Buddhists as well as Hindus and Muslims. Pakistan exercises no claim over Jammu and local business interests are pressing for a severance of Jammu from Kashmir altogether (Swami 1999b).

Should Kashmir become an independent nation in its own right it is fairly clear that, given the circumstances of its history and location, it can never become economically independent or be left to its own devices politically. Its very geography means that it will not only be reliant upon international aid but that it will always be fraught with tensions generated outside its borders.

But Kashmir is an issue for the rest of India as much as it is an issue for itself. It is because of disputed Kashmir that *Hindutva* forces can construct Muslims as the enemy within, undermining a united India. Those forces could never contemplate letting go of Kashmir for, if they did so, they would forfeit their most emotive cause. Not only was the Kargil War waged in 1999 but so also was an election campaign. The BJP-led coalition was brought down in mid 1999 by the withdrawal of support from a minority regional party, but the caretaker government remained to conduct the war. It is clear that the war was used as political capital by all factions: the Left condemned the BJP for allowing the situation to escalate so far and for inefficiency in running the war; the BJP indulged in a rhetoric of heroism and patriotism which was hard to resist. *India Today* devoted entire issues to paying tribute to the fallen and to sacrifices made by ordinary people for the war effort, quoting children who donated their pocket money as saying that they wished they could go to fight on the frontier. The battle of the Centre to control the States is encapsulated in the Kargil War but that battle is for more than just administrative control – it is for the deeper project of the Hindu *rashtra*. Praful Bidwai maintains that the costs of Kargil are greater than the loss of life and the military expenditure: 'They involve militarism and chauvinism, and "loyalty" tests for the minorities; growing intolerance in sections of the media towards those who question the conduct of Operation Vijay; and abridgement of democratic freedom through censorship and manipulation' (Bidwai 1999, p. 104).

10

WHAT PRICE THE ENVIRONMENT?

The religions and traditions of India emphasize a society in which there is a seamless continuity from nature to culture, and a respect, which merges into reverence, for the natural world (Mishra 1991; Prime 1992). The theme recurs in Gandhian philosophy, which teaches a lifestyle with a low impact upon the environment and an acceptance of the place of human beings within nature rather than ascendant over it. However, even the most cursory encounter with India reveals a landscape of exploitation, denudation and pollution.

Everywhere in the world, the issue of the environment is fraught with conflict at all possible scales, ranging from questions of global pollution and international responsibility, such as those left unresolved by the Rio Earth Summit, to the micro-level interpersonal disputes about use of local resources. At all scales, however, there is a commonality in the conflict which invariably turns on rival claimants' views of their own perceived entitlements to material wealth and conditions of life. This often appears to be a conflict between the ideological claims of development versus environment, but the crucial questions which need asking are: whose development? Whose environment? As the Introduction to this book suggested, India often makes one confront, head-on, questions which sometimes present themselves in the West as abstract arguments. Nowhere is this more apparent than when considering the environmental consequences of economic change.

To start at a local level example, Figure 10.1 is the view from the balcony of a training

FIGURE 10.1 Sewage plant in Delhi

centre and refuge for street children in Delhi. The building itself is attractive and modern and was designed to make maximum use of natural light with plenty of space to provide an inspiring environment; it is situated in a high-density, low-cost housing area close to the Yamuna River. The building and surrounding area reeks with the smell of the sewage plant in the picture; the black effluent is on its way, without further processing, into the already dead waters of the Yamuna. In present conditions, there simply is not enough water capacity in Delhi to provide every resident with access to a flush lavatory; plants like this one deal with the effluent of the relatively wealthy, whilst others suffer the product of modern sanitation. Slum dwellers have to use the open gutters and waste land and the ladies in the bathrooms of South Delhi think that it is the poor who are the polluters. It does not have to be like this – there are many low-cost ways of treating sewage. For example, the Titagarh township of Calcutta has adopted *panchayat*-managed sewage utilization, whereby a totally biological system converts the waste into cultivable soil (Chakraborty 1995).

WATER

McCully quotes Ravi Chopra and Debash Sen of the People's Science Institute in Dehra Dun as saying that 'Each time the flush handle is yanked in an average urban Indian home, the entire daily consumption of an arid-zone dweller in India goes down the drain' (McCully 1997, p. 208). Shortage of water is one of India's greatest problems, in both urban and rural areas, and control of water goes hand in hand with dominance over other people at all scales. The upper castes in villages routinely deny *dalits* access to 'their' well; the urban middle classes install private storage tanks to smooth out the problem of water rationing, whilst slum dwellers wait with buckets for a water tanker; the cash croppers of Gujarat appropriate the waters of the Narmada River. Tamil Nadu is in long-running dispute with Andhra Pradesh over the waters of the Cauvery, and Delhi is annually held to ransom by Haryana.

The Union Urban Affairs Ministry has set itself a five-year target of 100 per cent provision of adequate urban water supply and sewerage facilities and estimates that this will cost Rs 81 000 crores. This plan projects a use of 135 litres per person per day where there is a tap inside the dwelling and 40 litres where there is a shared standpipe. It aims at one standpipe per 20 families and a maximum walking distance of 100 metres to fetch water. This is a fairly parsimonious provision but it is generally acknowledged that it is unlikely to come about (Sunderarajan 1998).

In the rural areas, water for crops obviously radically improves the standard of living. At one end of the scale there are the water-hungry monocultures like sugar cane production with overhead irrigation and

FIGURE 10.2 Water-harvesting, Bihar

Figure 10.3 It runs straight into the drain. Dye works, Madhya Pradesh

commercial grain production, where multiple harvests are taken thanks to diesel-pumped water from deep wells. These lower the water table, with the consequence that still more pumping is required, and deplete the shallower wells used by the poorer people. At the other end of the scale are small local schemes for watershed development and water-harvesting in small lakes and ponds which raise the water table and recharge the wells in addition to providing irrigation and water for animals. In 1997 Chandrababu Naidu, the charismatic Chief Minister of Andhra Pradesh, launched a scheme for watershed development in the State, aiming for '10000 checkdams before the next monsoon' (*The Hindu* 1997a). The trouble is that water-harvesting is routine, unglamorous village work with few opportunities for quick profits for contractors and it is often left to NGOs to promote it. Recently, far-sighted local authorities have encouraged the incorporation of urban rain-water collection in the design of new housing, drawing upon almost forgotten techniques common in traditional house design in Kerala.

Quantity is not the only water problem in India; the quality of drinking water is cause for considerable concern. The urban élites fit expensive filtration and purification units to their kitchen water supply and many drink bottled water (a bottle of which costs about half the minimum daily wage). Many other people, urban and rural, are exposed to water which is rich in herbicides, pesticides, industrial chemicals and sewage. The environmentalist journal *Down to Earth* frequently alerts its readers to the water problem and the way in which 'solutions' such as the sinking of tube-wells are not a sustainable answer (*Down to Earth* 1999a).

INDUSTRIAL POLLUTION

Tons of raw industrial waste are routinely emptied into the rivers of India. The waste chemicals from the extensive leather tanneries and cloth dyeing plants are major culprits, but there are many others. Polluters are supposed to pay the cost of cleansing despoiled land and water and there are regulations about the treatment of industrial chemicals, but dealing with the waste in an environmentally friendly way wipes out a significant part of India's competitive advantage in the world markets for these products. The question is often asked: which counts for most, profits and employment or environmental quality? It is a hard question to answer when we are thinking about people on the verge of destitution. In Tamil Nadu, a State with an important yarn-dyeing industry, plants which simply release untreated chemicals are currently threatened with closure by the Supreme Court because they have delayed installing their own effluent treatment plants. Common treatment plants (opted for by small producers) have not been completed 'due to a host of problems, including the initial lethargy of the dyeing unit owners, red tapism and later delays caused by contractors' (*The Hindu* 18 November 1998). 'Workers in these and allied industries, such as weaving, clothing manufacture, packing and transport, all fear for their jobs and resent the hard line being taken on this important environmental issue. We have reached an impasse. The profits and jobs were being created at the cost of the health of the workers and other people living locally as well as the natural environment. So why were the plant owners lethargic? Building a treatment plant clearly erodes profits and the export market for textiles is already in recession. Why was there 'red tapism'? Government officials who are not well paid demand their kickbacks. We need to think deeper than the immediate conditions to consider global pricing if we are to begin to understand India's environmental problems.

In March 1999 the Vellore Citizens' Welfare Forum in Tamil Nadu petitioned the President of India for compensation for loss of livelihood of farmers and agricultural labourers due to air and water pollution caused by the leather tanning industry. Workers are set against other workers in environmental struggles because paying and benefiting rarely coincide.

For mainly historical reasons, the State of Gujarat is one of the wealthiest in India. It was early to industrialize, has generated considerable capital for local investment, but also draws upon the capital of its migrants to the West. Its environmental controls have been notoriously lax and industrialization has not only meant wealth, it has also brought very high levels of pollution of air, water and soil. The so-called 'golden corridor', from Vapi to Mehsana via Surat, Baroda and Ahmedabad, is a virtually continuous strip of industrial development containing not only large modern plants but also small units where costs are cut by permitting untreated chemicals (predominantly acids) into the public sewers (from which they leak). Bruno (1995) asserts that 'Gujarat is well on its way to becoming a toxic wasteland and international "sacrifice" zone, its environment forfeited for the sake of industrialization, chemical consumption and com-

petitiveness in global chemical product markets' (p. 163). But, as the cover story of *Capital Market* was at pains to point out, when controls are implemented, much of the suffering is passed directly to the workforce: 'Work at 756 chemical units in Vatwa, Naroda and Odhav [near Ahmedabad] came to a standstill, resulting in a loss of over Rs 30 crores per day and 50 000 workers rendered jobless' (Kakodhkar *et al.* 1995, p. 14). The Government of Gujarat is acutely aware of the issues relating to environmental health but has to negotiate a difficult line between environmental and industrial interests. Given that the State has long been solidly BJP, it is clear that the industrial base cannot be easily alienated.

Surat, famous for its gem-cutting industries, became notorious world-wide in 1994 when cases of plague were discovered; these were inevitably confined to the congested and rat-infested slums of this affluent city. Plague is guaranteed media attention that the routine misery of tuberculosis or dysentery cannot command. Officials in Surat became very conscious about the need to clean up the city, but this took the form of overly enthusiastic and unsympathetic slum clearances and hygiene campaigns which did nothing to relieve the poverty which had forced people into these unsanitary and overcrowded conditions (Shah 1997).

It is lower on the scale of seriousness, but the road north from Delhi through Uttar Pradesh forms another industrial corridor, this time predominantly of sugar processing and brickworks, but also rubber, chemical and fertilizer plants, engineering works, steel making, textiles and flour mills. The air smells of molasses and is full of insidious black flecks of soot from sugar cane waste because owners economize on the height of factory chimneys; these then deliver particle-laden smoke down to breathing level. Sugar and chemical effluent runs off untreated in open drains, the sugar attracting swarms of flies. Ultimately it finds its way to the Yamuna River. When geographers from the Alligar Muslim University undertook an intensive study along the Meerut Road, passing through Muzaffarnagar, they found that the worst pollution came from the smaller sugar refineries. This was making locally-grown fodder inedible and also causing a considerable drop in the size of the mango harvests (Rawat 1993). There are many more similar local examples to be found all over India.

Sometimes there is effective resistance against large-scale industrial 'development'. Nilesh Naik, a landless farm worker, was killed by a police bullet during a protest against the building of a factory near to his village of Keri in Goa. Villagers were afraid that the proposed Thapar Dupont plant, which was to produce Nylon 6,6 (a material used in the manufacture of heavy duty tyres) would poison their wells with chemical wastes. Additionally, they argued that truck-loads of chemicals would have to negotiate rural roads and proved that the blasting of tube wells for the plant had caused shortages of water for agricultural purposes. Eventually Thapar Dupont abandoned the site, even though it was insistent that the chemicals involved are less hazardous than those used in the production of the more established Nylon 6. As a subsidiary of a large multinational, it was highly sensitive to the potential global cost of adverse publicity caused by local resistance (Noronha 1995). Rajendra Kakodhkar and others, writing for the business journal *Capital Market*, are not convinced that the protestors won the battle, for they maintain that in India 'The environment becomes a local testing ground for politicians who fear an erosion of their authority if industry brings in its wake greater literacy and well-being. And it suits them to feed the local population on misinformation, inciting agitations' (Kakodhkar *et al.* 1995, p. 9).

Quite possibly they are correct in this assessment of the motivations of politicians with rural constituencies, but it needs to be considered why it would be that work-hungry people would be willing to be won over by such strategies if they had not, all too often, seen the results of mismanaged industrial development. The Bhopal disaster surfaces quickly in the opposition argument whenever a large-scale plant using toxic materials is planned; perhaps this is sometimes alarmist, but one can hardly be surprised at the reaction.

The world's most horrific industrial disaster was the leakage of methyl icocyanate from the Union Carbide Corporation (UCC) pesticides plant in Bhopal in December 1984. Estimates of the numbers of dead vary at around 6000 and the controversy about the number of people whose health was affected still rumbles on. More than 400000 people have lodged claims for compensation, but the Government of India has still not released so much as half of the $470 million interim settlement paid by UCC. The legal case surrounding UCC's liability is confusing, since Union Carbide Eastern was deregistered in 1992 and the attempts to bring the case in the United States (where compensation would be higher) have so far failed. The Indian Government has delayed starting the process of extradition of the former UCC chairman to India. Meanwhile, relatively little has been done in Bhopal for the victims. A large new international standard hospital is slowly being built, surrounded by financial wrangles. It will probably be of more benefit to the affluent middle classes than to the slum dwellers who suffered.

Meanwhile, social activists of the Sambhavna Trust run the Bhopal People's Health and Documentation Clinic to provide free medical care and to monitor sickness and exposure-related deaths for the purpose of bringing legal action (Venkatesan 1998). Its 1999 report highlights the lack of official research on the continuing and transgenerational consequences of the leak (*The Hindu* 15 January 1999). The memory of the disaster is never far away. When wealthy young men started to race motor launches on Bhopal's Upper Lake, people began to worry that they would stir up poisonous sediments. No one trusts the city's drinking water, though many have to use it (the well-off have installed separate cisterns for their drinking water which they have delivered by tanker). One might have thought that, with all its awareness of the risk of environmental disaster, Bhopal would today be very conscious of the problems of pollution, but this is far from the case. Not only is the lake in the centre of the city putrid with untreated sewage from eight major drains and dumped garbage, but the Bhopal disaster victims, with their damaged lungs, have to live in an atmosphere where the level of suspended particulate matter is far above the WHO norm – largely as a consequence of traffic congestion (Shastri 1997, p. 93). Whilst addressing Bhopal's environmental problems should be a high priority for the State government, this is not currently the case. Perhaps it helps one to understand if one has seen that the poor and the relatively powerless live in the congested old city and in shacks along the railway line, whilst the affluent areas and the brand new parliament building are on the pleasantly wooded slopes above the pollution. Bhopal's environmental condition is far from unique, but with the memory of so many dead and incapacitated, it seems especially poignant there.

INTERNATIONAL DUMPING

As if there were not enough locally generated hazardous materials to deal with, India has begun to import waste on a large scale. This occurred in the wake of the 1989 Basle Convention on Transboundary Movements of Hazardous Wastes and their Disposal, when many other poor countries withdrew from the international traffic in toxic wastes (the Basle Convention outlawed dumping, but permitted recycling). There is every indication that much of the 'recycling' in India is simply dumping. Praful Bidwai suggests that the hazardous wastes lobby is growing stronger in India and is putting pressure on the government to continue to accept wastes for 'recycling' on the grounds of the profitability of the exercise. As Bidwai says,

> It is either disingenuous or unethical to argue that waste imports are good because they generate employment, without considering the quality of that employment and its consequences for the employee as well as the larger environment – water, air, flora and fauna and, above all, people. Beyond a point, jobs at any cost is a totally perverse argument (Bidwai 1996, p. 191)

He points out that multinational firms operating in India find it easy to import their own waste products, giving the example of soft drinks companies manufacturing bottles in India to export for use abroad, but importing used bottles, 'transferring both hazardous technologies and used products from the North to the South' (p. 191).

The Indian case exemplifies the view of Lawrence Summers, the former chief economist of the World Bank, when he famously commented that, 'The economic logic behind dumping a load of toxic waste in the lowest wage countries is impeccable and we should face up to that' (Summers 1991. Quoted in Bidwai 1996).

FORESTS AND COMMONS

There is no shortage of environmental awareness amongst people living in rural areas. Many of the most effective rurally-based social movements are environmentalist, but this environmentalism is not just an abstract reverence for nature – it is a symbiotic relationship where livelihoods are immediately at stake. The *Chipko Andolan* of the Himalayan regions of Uttar Pradesh is world famous as an example of popular action in protection of a natural environment which was crucial to livelihood, and many other less well-known local movements throughout India have emulated it (Gadgil 1998). *Chipko* is best known for the way in which villagers hugged trees to prevent logging contractors from cutting them down. Women from the Gandhian movement who had moved into the Garwal Himalaya to work for principles of village self-sufficiency were instrumental in co-ordinating the resistance of rural women (Shiva 1989). Certainly the women believed that the trees were beautiful and had a right to life, but beyond this, they knew that their own lives would be impoverished by their removal. Trees are the source of animal fodder and firewood, their leaves are used as utensils, and tools and furniture are made from their wood; all these are obtained by harvesting them without cutting them down. Anil Agarwal (1986) points out that an important impetus to the *Chipko Andolan* was the Forest Department's refusal to let villagers take the very tough wood of the ash tree, which they needed as the traditional material for making and

Figure 10.4 Harvesting the forest, Bihar

mending ploughs, whereas it was selling the right to take the same wood to sports-goods manufacturers.

When nature is an important part of people's spirituality, it is almost always because it is an important part of their every-day lives. When new processes of exploita-tion of natural resources intervene, the livelihoods and the value systems of ordi-nary people are all too often threatened. They are unlikely to take this lying down. The resistance is not always organized or overtly political, but it can be seen in the everyday acts of people, such as deliberate encroach-ment on reserved forest lands and theft of forest products. Inevitably, India's new export orientated economy has impacts which reach as far as the forest dwellers. Market orientated forestry has increasingly driven out indigenous multi-use trees like the sal in Uttarakhand, and even the famous Himalayan deodar is under threat. In their place are commercial trees like the pine and the eucalyptus, both grown for pulping. Nei-ther is useful for fodder, neither yields fire-wood without being felled, neither has indigenous medicinal properties.

The two major biomass demands in India are for fuel and fodder. By far the greater part of fuel for domestic use in both the towns and the countryside in India comes from veg-etable sources. This does not necessarily mean the use of logs, for access to these is controlled by the Forestry Department and when rural people can obtain firewood they

frequently sell it for cash in urban markets, depending on twigs, leaves, agricultural by-products and dried weeds for their own fuel needs. This, combined with the use of dried cattle dung, deprives the soil of essential humus and nutrients. In the towns, gas con-nections are scarce and gas far too expensive for most households; electricity is not univer-sally available, is relatively expensive and power cuts are frequent. Logs from India's forests flow ceaselessly from the countryside, as does charcoal. Some of this is legal, but much comes to the towns as head loads col-lected by rural women. As Guha (1989) and many others have pointed out, the rights over forest products have long been con-tentious, going back well beyond the scope of this book. During the British raj, when forests came to be managed for the most efficient production of timber and conserved on the basis of existing botanical knowledge, many of the traditional uses were seen as conflict-ing with scientific notions of conservation. The long-standing opposition between local people and conservators was under way and it is only relatively recently that outsiders to the system have come to appreciate as sus-tainable the ways in which forests were man-aged long before professional scientific forest management was introduced. But this recog-nition has come almost too late, since the people living on the margins of the forests have been forced into short-termism in their attitude to forest products, using and selling whatever they can lay their hands on.

FIGURE 10.5 Logging in Kerala

The ravenous paper industry is a major consumer of pulpable wood, whole tracts of forest being sold to contractors. The bamboo forests of the North East have long been a major mainstay of the subsistence economy – leaves being used for fodder, the bamboo itself serving as a building and roofing material and as the raw material for a huge range of village crafts. Officers of the Forest Department, however, prefer to sell the bamboo in bulk, rather than bother with the small-scale needs of traditional producers. They either refuse to sell to them altogether or demand prices far higher than those they charge the contractors. In 1998 the Forest Department charged paper mills Rs 15 a tonne for bulk purchases of bamboo but traditional basket weavers at rates which worked out at Rs 1 500 a tonne (*sic*). This disparity is due to a combination of bribes, perceived inconvenience and straightforward contempt for the lifestyles of tribal people. Plantation production of pulpable products on marginal land might seem to be the the answer to stem the denudation of forests, but the long-term investment deters many (CSE 1995).

When the forests recede, the consequences extend beyond the loss of fuel and fodder; there is also the loss of minor forest products, to say nothing of wildlife habitats. In hill regions, trees slow the rate of run-off of rain water and when they go the soils are washed away and major landslips can occur; some of the Himalayan regions will never be cultivated again. Trees raise the water-table and also stabilize the evaporation of moisture, with valuable outcomes for rain-fed agriculture; yet the forests are disappearing fast and it is estimated that only 19.5 per cent of the total area of India is now forested (Agarwal 1995). The Survey of India's *State of the forest report for 1997* revealed 5 482 sq. km. of forest cover totally lost in the previous two years and 17 777 sq. km. of dense forest reduced to scrub (Mahalingam 1998b). Despite the claims for schemes such as the People's Participation Programme, introduced in 1990 in Bihar (Jewitt 1995), the policies of joint forest management (where rural people are directly involved in the conservation of the forests) and social forestry (where villagers are encouraged to plant trees for their own use in and around their villages) have not been particularly successful. Failure is due to a combination of factors, often relating to relationships with forestry officers. These often prefer to see their role as that of policing the forests against those whom they classify as ignorant tribals (Kothari 1994) and rank social forestry low on the scale of both prestige and illegal remuneration. Successes are achieved where *van samitis* (forest watching groups) are set up independently of the local foresters and monitor their corrupt use of forest products as well as local abuses (Sainath 1994).

ECOLOGICAL REFUGEES

Gadgil and Guhar (1995) have devised a three-fold classification system which helps us to think about the different relationships between people and the environment. They apply the term 'omnivores' to those wealthy enough to take as much as they like of what they desire and then look for new supplies elsewhere. These are the global asset-strippers with a profit orientated economy. (Most of us who live in the West have to face up to our omnivorous characteristics, for we are the people who deny others their ploughs in order to get exactly the cricket bats we want.) 'Eco-system people' are those who interact in an immediate sense with their environment, ensuring its sustainability in order to ensure their own. 'Ecological refugees' are those forced out of their harmonious relationship with the environment by the actions of 'omnivores'. They become reluctant urban dwellers and landless poor, often compelled by desperation to act in ways which have devastating effects upon the already depleted natural resources around them. Of course the model is a simplification and it is easy to romanticize the 'eco-system people' whilst demonizing the 'omnivores', but it does help to reveal not just India's naked environmental conflicts but also the ways in which these are enmeshed into global economics. Virtually every person working in polluted and dangerous conditions in factories, brickworks and agricultural processing plants or struggling to live in the slums and on the pavements of India's cities would qualify as an 'ecological refugee'.

THE BIG DAMS

Nowhere is this schema more apt than when thinking about the issue of big dams – those huge symbols of 'progress' which promised so much, and delivered so little. From his early position, when he hailed these vast engineering projects as temples of modernity, Nehru came to regret what he called the move to gigantism and to question its human outcome. When one looks at a dam site and contemplates the intended refashioning of the environment, it is hard to understand the thinking in favour of stopping the flow of ancient rivers, flooding forests, fields, homes; destroying natural habitats; shifting whole populations and changing patterns of production. Where people's lives are intimately entwined with their environment, changes on this scale can be devastating – economically, socially and emotionally. In the heady days when modernism seemed to hold all the answers to the world's problems, dams stood for the power of rational men over capricious nature. In theory, at least, one could weigh the costs of what would be lost in terms of nature and traditional systems of production against the gains in increased productivity in terms of electricity and irrigated farming. But, as Smitu Kothari (1995a and b) says of sacrifices made by the poor in the name of the 'national interest', it is essential to think about who defines the 'national interest'. It then becomes important to ask why it is that the interest does not stretch so far as the adequate compensation, in similar land, of the people who are displaced by large dams. Kothari is adamant that there is no absolute shortage of land, just misallocation of resources.

There is no better account of the argument against big dams than Patrick McCully's (1997) *Silenced rivers*, which demonstrates that, worldwide, almost invariably, big dams do not repay even the monetary costs involved in their building, let alone the environmental and social costs. The large dams were predominantly financed by the World Bank, which favoured huge, expensive schemes (George and Sabelli 1994). In turn, these white elephants became an element in the debt crisis which precipitated India into acceptance of structural adjustment.

In the 1950s and 1960s there had been a conventional wisdom that investment in large-scale, heroic projects could facilitate the catching up which India needed to do in terms of development. There were fantasies about the greening of India through extensive irrigation and about the unleashing of industrial potential once there was access to abundant cheap hydro-electricity. The sacrifice of subsistence cultivation seemed a small price to pay in this great march of progress. However, the simple truth was that the people whose lives were disrupted were not those who benefited from the fruits of the modernization, and gradually the 'oustees' (as they are termed in India) turned to organized resistance in the face of the despoliation of their homes, fields and forests.

McCully begins his book with the recognition that 'the unshakeable commitment and integrity of the *Narmada Bachao Andolan* (NBA) (Save the Narmada Movement) and the deceitfulness of the backers and builders of the Sardar Sarovar Dam' (1997, p. ix) had inspired his research and writing. The NBA ranks alongside *Chipko* as an inspirational people's movement, particularly since it managed to humble the mighty World Bank and contribute to a global change of policy on investment in dams.

The Narmada runs east–west through Central India, a life-giving and sacred river. Plans for a massive Narmada Valley Project were first raised seriously in the 1960s; the total project consists of 30 major dams supplemented by more than 3000 small irrigation schemes. If completed it will displace about a million and a half people. The Bargi Dam was the first to be begun and completed. The people from the 162 villages to be flooded found that there was no plan for their resettlement. With the help of young activists, led by Medha Patkar, the tribal peoples formed an action committee in 1986 which became the NBA in 1989. They trans-

ferred their local struggle to the national and international arena.

The next two dams in the project, the massive Sardar Sarovar and the Maheshwar, became the focus of their attention. This is not the appropriate space to summarize the NBA's struggle, achievements and setbacks. This can be accessed on their website (http://www.angelfire.com), in McCully's text, and most recently in the eloquent and moving *Frontline* article by Arundhati Roy (1999). Using the Gandhian techniques of hunger strikes, passive resistance (including refusal to move as the waters rose), petitioning and mobilizing international environmentalist support against the dam's funders, the NBA was able to demonstrate not only the human suffering caused by the scheme but also that the environmental balance sheet did not add up. The large dams could be shown to be unsustainable (Singh 1997). The real value of newly-irrigated lands in Gujarat would not be substantially greater than the lands forfeited to flooding in Madhya Pradesh; silting and salinity would be inevitable consequences; the dam would not be able to produce the promised levels of hydro-electric power in the dry season; and, finally, the plans had 'forgotten' to include the cost of piping and distribution of the promised drinking water. The World Bank pulled out in 1993. Then, in 1995, the Government of India required the State of Gujarat to limit the lowest point of the dam wall to 63 metres (half of what was

FIGURE 10.6 The life-enhancing Narmada River, Madhya Pradesh

intended). The Indian Power Minister declared 'We are not going in for large dams any more; we want run of the river projects and to have smaller dams, if they are necessary at all, which will not cause any impediment whatsoever to the environmental needs' (quoted in McCully 1997, p. 306).

The aim of the NBA is an end to dam-building on the Narmada and the lowering of the existing dams, but in February 1999 the Supreme Court gave the State of Gujarat the right to raise the highest part of wall of the Sardar Sarovar to 85 metres, causing 33 000 more families to be moved for no reason other than political symbolism and vested interests. Even the constructors admit that 'the dam will only be able to serve any purpose in terms of irrigation water or electricity once it crosses 110 metres' (*The Hindu* 24 February 1999). Currently the campaign continues against the Maheshwar Dam and for a complete review of the whole Narmada Valley Project, hunger strikers are being forcibly hospitalized by the police and the veteran environmental activist Baba Amte is demanding an apology from the Chief Minister of Madhya Pradesh (*The Hindu* 23 April 1999). In July 1999 people who would lose their livelihoods lined the Narmada in a *satyagraha*. Medha Patkar and her supporters declared that they would drown rather than submit (Venkatesan 1999). In August the 'Rally for the Valley' took place with thousands of tribal people taking part in addition to the much-publicized artists and intellectuals from Delhi giving their support. Arundhati Roy donated the whole of her Booker Prize to the cause and drew the attention of the world's press.

Meanwhile the Tehri Dam in the Garwal Himalaya is nearing completion. The town of Tehri will disappear under the waters and the luckier inhabitants have a brand new overly-planned concrete settlement to move into. Sunderlal Bhaguna (of *Chipko*) has mounted a long protest and a series of hunger strikes against this project which turns the confluence of two tributaries of the Bagirath into a mere lake, the purpose of which is to supply electricity to Delhi – regardless of the terrifying level of seismic activity in this region. Popular wisdom says that villages will be flooded all the way to Dehra Dun if the wall were ever to break.

GENETICALLY MODIFIED CROPS

Just as the benefits in increased yields of the Green Revolution have plateaued and the real costs are being counted, a new 'miracle' in the form of genetically modified crops is being offered to India. The opening of the country to multinational firms has seen the establishment of the South Asia division of Monsanto in Mumbai and a series of experimental crop testings across southern India. Opinions are, of course, sharply divided about GM crops; they may well offer remarkable new yields. I am unwilling to offer an uninformed view about the biological implications (which are no different for India from those rehearsed elsewhere in the world) but there is very justifiable concern about the economic outcomes of patented seed, particularly if it contains 'terminator' genes. There have been farmers' protests and fields of cotton have been burned. Without rigorous governmental supervision the logical outcome would be the emergence of a small class of highly successful farmers and the progressive squeezing of marginal producers.

AIR POLLUTION

The WHO ranks Delhi in the 10 most polluted cities in the world. Many of the other cities of India are not much better, as the *Hindu survey of the environment*'s review of environmental conditions in major centres demonstrates annually. The pollution is multiple, but it is air pollution which gives the greatest cause for concern.

The Centre for Science and Environment (CSE), a Delhi-based NGO, launched an Air Pollution Campaign in 1998 to raise people's awareness of the health risk involved in breathing in Delhi and to petition the Prime Minister with a People's Charter on Clear Air. It used a cartoon captioned 'Roll down the window of your bullet proof car, Mr Prime Minister. The security threat is not the gun, it's the air of Delhi', which captured exactly the way Delhites without air-conditioned vehicles feel about venturing onto the streets. To visit Delhi is to develop a cough and hope it is not more. As the CSE's petition reminds us:

> While India's Gross Domestic Product has increased two and a half times in two decades (1975–1995) the pollution load from industries has gone up four times and from vehicles a shocking eight times … . But the number of people dying prematurely due to air pollution went up by almost 30 per cent in four years between 1991 and 1995. An estimated 52 000 people are dying due to air pollution every year – about 10 000 of them in Delhi itself. (CSE 1998)

Bronchitis, pneumonia and asthma are all common and the endemic tuberculosis is worsened by the air quality. Harsh Vardhan, the Health Minister for Delhi, confidently pronounced in June 1998 that there was no evidence to link pollution to heart and lung diseases (*The Hindu* 18 June 1998). (Oxygen bars have recently been set up to cater to people who disagree with him and are gullible enough to think they might counteract the filthy air.)

In the past few years air travellers have become accustomed to the inconvenience of too many winter-time flights being delayed at Delhi's Indira Gandhi Airport because of smog, and residents are used to not seeing the bright blue skies that used to be associated with the cold weather. The air pollution is visible, makes one's eyes run and throat hurt. That is the least of it: 'The air concentration of benzene in central Delhi exceeds the air quality standards of the European Union by as much as 10 times. The air quality samples were taken in 1996. Since then the situation may well have worsened' (Roychowdhury 1998).

Benzene is a carcinogen which causes blood cancers. The World Health Organisation says that there is no safe level for it. It is released into the air from the (cheaper) type of unleaded petrol used in India, which has five times the level of that used in the EU. Not all petrol is unleaded: tests carried out in Delhi and Hyderabad on placenta have revealed abnormal levels of heavy metals, particularly lead and cadmium, indicating build-up of these in unborn babies. The buses, trucks, auto-rickshaws and many of the scooters and motorcycles use the cheaper diesel – a diesel which, according to CSE, is '250 times dirtier than the world's best' (CSE Public Advertisement 1998). 'Vehicular pollution accounted for 64 per cent of the total air pollution in Delhi. It is likely to go up to 72 per cent by 2000' (Tiwari and Roychowdhury 1998). The volume of motorized transport on the streets of Delhi (and other cities) has increased dramatically, by about 13 per cent per annum, through the 1990s. The level of production of cars and two-wheelers has increased steadily with the liberalization of the economy and loans to purchase them have become more easily available. Public transport is so crowded, unpleasant and unreliable that anyone who can afford to travels to work by private transport. Tiwari and Roychowdhary report that between 1993 and 1998 the share of public transport dropped from 62 per cent to 58 per cent of all passenger trips.

Delhi Transport Corporation seriously attempted to make a contribution towards reducing the levels of pollution by introducing fuel-efficient, larger, more comfortable but imported buses. It was prevented by the outrage of the *swadeshi* lobby, strong in BJP-governed Delhi, which forced the purchase of more expensive and less efficient Indian-made Ashok Leyland and TELCO buses. This provoked the exasperated outburst from Ajay Singh, the Director of Delhi Transport Corporation, who said, 'The government is not looking for long term solutions …. It seems that by the time a proper transport system is introduced, Delhi will be dead already' (interview. Tiwari and Roychowdhury 1998).

In November 1996, the Supreme Court took the unprecedented and high-handed step of banning all factory operations in Delhi on the grounds that it was the second most polluted city in the world. The factories, in fact, accounted for only 12 per cent of the air pollution and thousands lost their jobs, but the courts had been unable to make the ample environmental legislation stick and these draconian measures had a simple, if brutal, logic (Halankar 1997). In 1998 it was revealed that industrial workers had neither been compensated nor found new jobs, as had been promised under the Master Plan of Delhi 2001. As Rajalakshmi (1998) points out, as usual some benefit, others pay the price.

In May 1999 the Supreme Court delivered a similar bomb-shell to the car industry and motor dealers by ruling that from June 1999 only cars which achieve Euro I standards of emission could be licensed in the National Capital Region and from April 2000 only those meeting the more stringent Euro II standards. The popular Maruti will fail until quite substantial modifications are made. (Of course people will get around the law by registering their cars at false addresses outside the capital, but it is a start.)

Pollution in paradise

It is not just people who suffer from air pollution – think for a moment of the Taj Mahal, that universally recognized symbol of India. 'The Taj Mahal has suffered much more damage during the past 20 years than in the previous 300 years of its existence, due to alarming air pollution in the Agra region' (Mehta 1994, p. 59). The white marble of the Taj is turning yellow and becoming pitted by acidic pollutants. Mehta points the finger of blame at the nearby Mathura Oil Refinery, allowed to release (an unregulated) 24 000

kilograms of sulphur dioxide a day into the air, but also draws attention to the many factories, often small and unofficial, in the town of Agra itself. Although the Taj has a special sentimental place, other invaluable monuments, such as Fatepur Sikri, are equally threatened by pollution but likely to receive far less in the way of conservation work. When the wind from Mathura does not blow towards Agra, it blows over the wonderfully rich Bharatpur Bird Sanctuary in Rajasthan, where ornithologists are reporting 'the near total absence of Siberian Cranes ... in recent years' (ibid., p. 61).

Thousands of foreign tourists flock into the tropical 'paradise' of Goa, lured by the pictures of white sand, blue sea and palm trees. What the brochures of the holiday firms do not tell them is that the rapid development of seafront hotels has strained the water supply, sewage system and garbage disposal facilities well beyond breaking point; if they want to continue to believe that they are in paradise, it would be best that they do not look too closely. For Goa's residents, the environmental implications of the tourist influx are constant, but it is undeniable that many jobs depend upon the trade. It needs to be asked whether Goa can afford to impose an adequate infrastructure to deal with the water and waste disposal demands of a large-scale tourist industry and, if it cannot, just how much its population should be expected to pay in environmental costs. Sim-

FIGURE 10.7 The Taj Mahal is suffering the effects of air pollution

ilarly the romantic city of Udaipur is being overrun by illegally constructed hotels whose sewers go straight down into the lakes they cluster around in defiance of planning permission (Iqbal 1998). The hill stations, too, are groaning under invasions they can scarcely support now that tourism has become fashionable amongst the urban élites.

GARBAGE

Not so very long ago, virtually everything thrown away in India was recycled. Sweepers and second-hand dealers sorted every scrap of rubbish and allocated it to its most profitable end. They still do this, but an increasing amount of India's rubbish is not recyclable. Flimsy blue bags, apparently the last possible stage in the recycling of waste plastic, have replaced the disposable bags of the past which were stuck or sewn from such materials as redundant government forms and old exam papers. The old disposables were pulpable, biodegradable and even edible to cattle and goats; today's are useless, clogging drains, choking animals, building up in rivers and on waste land and releasing toxic fumes when burned. On journeys, plastic cups have replaced the former clay disposables which returned to the earth from which they were made.

More and more manufactured goods cannot usefully be recycled and are just dumped. Today, hospitals use disposable plastic syringes and other instruments instead of sterilizing and re-using. The waste is dangerous to the rag-pickers – frequently children – who sort through it, rinse it and sell it on to those who pack it up as good as new. On the other hand, the hospitals which incinerate everything release carcinogenic dioxins and furans into the atmosphere and 'of the 34 major hospitals [in Delhi] 11 have installed incinerators which are operated at 400–500 degrees C as against the 1200 degrees C prescribed for complete and proper destruction of pathogens and necessary control of other emissions' (Basu 1998, p. 177).

The task of lifting and dumping domestic refuse falls to the local authorities which are constantly accused of inefficiency and unreliability in their service. Rubbish heaps – attracting dogs, pigs, cows and swarms of flies – accumulate in even the most affluent suburbs of the largest cities. In fact the slums are sometimes cleaner from the point of view of garbage as more is recycled by the poor than by the rich. The *Hindu survey of the environment* published an extensive study of the garbage problem in the major Indian cities, Mumbai in particular emerging as a city which has been unable to divert sufficient resources into refuse collection (Joshi 1995). Bangalore introduced an experimental recycling scheme in 1994, enrolling the assistance of informal sector rag-pickers (Joseph 1994) and in Calcutta a private company converts garbage into fertilizer which is sold to the organic tea producers of North Bengal (*Down to Earth* 1995a)

WILDLIFE

When the cities are expanding and consuming much of the wealth of the rural areas, when the forests are shrinking, the mountains denuding and the air and the water being slowly poisoned, what hope is there for India's wildlife? It is not even easy to campaign for the rights of animals and birds when they are in apparent competition with humans for the dwindling environment. In India there is little tradition of hunting for food – even meat-eaters tend to avoid the flesh of wild animals. Hunting was an aristocratic sport and habitats were maintained for the pleasure of princes and landowners, such that several modern wildlife reserves are the former hunting grounds of maharajas. Under feudal systems, people were excluded from clearing those forests which were set aside for hunting and, whatever one's moral position on the subject of killing for pleasure, this resulted in a conservation of wild species. The total exclusion of the people was not required and the harvesting of minor forest products aided in the management of forest habitats.

With the demise of the princes, the forest department frequently excluded people from the forests altogether, sometimes with unforeseen consequences, as when 'experts' banned cattle from grazing in Bharatpur bird sanctuary, causing grasses to encroach on the wetlands. Land-hungry peasantry often came to see themselves in conflict with wildlife and to resent the apparent protection which it received. That resentment became all the more acute when deer and elephant ate valuable crops.

The wildlife of India has an absolute right to its habitat, in exactly the same way as sub-sistence farmers and gathering peoples, but of course it cannot mobilize and it cannot vote. It often requires that human-centred arguments around the economic benefits of biodiversity or wildlife tourism be mobilized in order for the welfare of animals to be taken seriously. It is well known that the photo-genic animals get the most elaborate protec-tion, with the tiger the most popular and insects hardly figuring at all, even though they have valuable roles to play in integrated ecosystems. Gadgil (1998), arguing for a National Biodiversity Act, refers us to the danger to crops and wild flora when bees are wiped out through the use of pesticides; he also mentions that pharmaceutical companies have started to do research on the potential use of spiders' poison in treating neurological disorders. Gadgil advocates valuing local knowledge to compile inventories of animal and plant life, both wild and domesticated. He recommends that indigenous conserva-tion practices, such as the reverence for sacred groves (Burman 1994) and sacred pools, be respected as an important way of preserving species.

The wildlife of India is under threat from the fall-out of all varieties of development – urbanization, industrial pollution, cash-based farming, the retreat of the forests, tourism and the large dams. Birds are trapped for sale in the markets and shipped overseas to live or die miserably in cages. Tigers are killed for the supposed therapeutic qualities of their bones and for their beautiful coats. Elephants die to yield ivory trinkets and novelty leather goods. Snakes and crocodiles become acces-sories – the list of unnecessary and violent luxury uses of wild animal products is almost unending. Both avarice and poverty lie behind Indians catering to this export trade and only recession in the South East Asian economy seems to make any difference to demand.

Attempts at wildlife conservation through such schemes as Project Tiger have had mixed success. The designation of tiger reserves seems sometimes to have attracted poachers, but anti-poaching units of the police have been formed (*Down to Earth* 1995b) and I know that at least one forest offi-cer co-operates with Naxalite groups in the

---

Box 14 The Bishnois and the blackbuck

In October 1998 the film star, Salman Khan, was arrested for illegally hunting blackbuck in Rajasthan. People of the Bishnois tribe, famed for their protection of nature, reported him.

Salman Khan's nemesis, the Bishnois, are a community of martyrs. Death is a hazard when you protect the things others covet dearly. For more than 500 years the Bishnois sacrificed their lives to protect trees and animals, particularly deer, on their arid lands, a legacy of their guru's word, handed down over generations. In Khejral village, close to where the beefy star and his friends killed two blackbucks, stands a memorial to their fierce commitment to nature. It records a carnage in 1730 when Amrita Devi and 362 of her people were killed over a month, trying to stop a mediaeval chieftain carting away wood for his palace. A State award for conservation is named after her. The 1997 award went to Nihal Chand Bishnoi who was shot while trying to protect deer from poachers ....
Five years ago incensed villagers refused to let an airforce helicopter take off; it had landed after some airborne hunting. Two years ago an army officer caught hunting deer was soundly thrashed by Bishnois. Salman is lucky they never actually managed to lay their hands on him.

Source: Rohit Parihar 1998: Bucking the Law. *India Today International* 23 (43) p. 36

I suggest we kill him too. It should pay for our bail!

RUSTAM VANIA

FIGURE 10.8 Poachers know there are few deterents
Source: Down to Earth (1995c)

war against poachers. After an increase in the number of tigers from 1 827 in 1972 to a high of 4 334 in 1989, there was a worrying (and connected?) post-liberalization decline to 3 750 in 1993 (ibid.). As India's Vice-President, Krishan Kant, pointed out at an International Tiger Millennium Conference in Delhi, 'The local people are the best guardians and we must facilitate their role . . . The protection of the tiger cannot be a function of a few concerned individuals, organisations or a project. It needs to be protected in the very implementation of a country's socio-economic policies and plans', continu-

ing to lay the blame on 'progressive commercialisation of global society' (*The Hindu* 1999).

There is a popular contempt for those who kill for pleasure in India, but many of those who come from the 'princely' castes are immune to this feeling. There was outrage in the press in late 1998 when a party of film stars went hunting blackbuck (illegally) in Rajasthan and an exposé of the fad for hunting among the new urban élite. (Delhi's Minister of Health, Harsh Vardhan, a Rajasthani who is famous for putting his foot in his mouth, said that sensible blackbuck ought to make sure that they stay in Bishnoi villages.)

ANY HOPE?

It is easy to be pessimistic for India's environment and we must constantly remind ourselves that, though it is easy to blame local corruption and profiteering, most of the blame rebounds right back on the 'omnivorous' peoples who think that they do not pollute in as gross a fashion as can be found in Gujarat. Gujarat is doing the West's polluting for it and those of us who are fortunate to drink clean water and breathe clean air need to ask a few more questions about where the products we consume come from and how they are made. As the *Narmada Bachao Andolan* showed, international pressure can make a difference.

Much hope lies in the many local movements to cherish the environment in India. I shall name just a few. The People's Science Institute in Dehra Dun provides technical advice to small local schemes such as water-harvesting all over the country. It does not just provide the technical know-how, it helps villagers to mobilize the development funds they are entitled to and to stand up to contractors and Block Development Officers who have everything to gain from preventing self-help. The Tilonia Barefoot College in Rajasthan has pioneered affordable solar power for rural areas, among a wide range of other conservation orientated techniques, by drawing upon the knowledge of local people in conjunction with volunteer scientists and

technicians. The Centre for Science and Environment in New Delhi is a more affluent NGO, which concentrates on collecting and propagating information and putting pressure on government and international agencies on environmental matters. Lokayan in Delhi serves to co-ordinate and facilitate communication between hundreds of small local social movements across the country. It raises consciousness abut the environment by relating it to other social and economic issues. There are many, many more.

The state

State governments sometimes launch comprehensive environmental programmes. Prem Kumar Dhumal tackled environmental issues with considerable success as soon as he came to power as Chief Minister in Himachal Pradesh. This mountain State has a particularly fragile eco-system and suffers from deforestation and soil erosion. A programme of community forestry was launched, a law regarding waste disposal was passed and, incredibly, the use of plastic bags in shops was banned. However, it appears to be individually driven and dictatorial (Martin 1999). The *Janmabhoomi* Development Programme in Andhra Pradesh has a considerable environmental component and throughout the country there are many such piecemeal efforts made by enthusiastic government officers.

FIGURE 10.9 Solar panels for rural technology, Tilonia, Rajasthan

FIGURE 10.10 The fragile Kerala backwaters

The environment comes under the general authority of the Department of Forestry and Environmental Affairs, which undertakes very substantial work. However, there are frequent conflicts of interest between the commercial and environmental wings of forestry.

The international agencies are there, too, in a pro-active fashion. Regrettably, for all their enormous expenditure and their highly-paid teams of professional advisors, they often manage to get things wrong. CSE launched a debate on the Ecodevelopment Project (Eco-P) funded by the World Bank (in the form of a $27 million loan) and the Global Environmental Facility (in the form of a $20 million grant) to reduce 'human-induced negative impacts' on 'globally significant biodiversity' (CSE 1998, p. 1). This boiled down to a plan for 521 parks and sanctuaries where local people were intended to contribute in cash terms as well as participating joyfully in setting up something they did not know they wanted:

All the conservation-based research and management strategies have been planned by project officials and forest officials. Local populations like tribals and villagers can only contribute by acting as guides, leading learned naturalists through the forest to a plant or a weed, or some animal hideout. (ibid., p. 4)

NGOs were supposed to be drafted into the day-to-day administration of Eco-P:

but the project only recognises NGOs that are registered, have proper systems of accounting and auditing, a proven track record, are secular and apolitical, have adequate field level staff and training facilities, understand the social and political situation and share a rapport with the community. (ibid., pp. 5–6.)

NGOs stayed away in droves. As CSE points out, insensitivity and bureaucratic high-handedness prevailed where there could have been genuine local co-operation over this issue of the *global commons*.

11

A STEEL FRAME?

For the first four decades after Independence, one of the best careers an educated young person could aspire to was in the Civil Service. Every year hundreds of thousands of new graduates presented themselves for the combined services entrance examinations, though only a fraction of them would be successful in landing places as trainees in All-India Services, which constitute the officer grades of the senior services. Beyond these relatively few officers, in 1983 16.2 million people were employed by the Government of India, the States governments, public sector units and local government combined (it sounds very high, but one needs to remember the size of the population of the country). Government service, at whatever level, was popular because it was secure, relatively well remunerated and the source of unofficial additional income. In addition, in the élite services there was also scope for considerable influence.

THE ALL-INDIA SERVICES

The Civil Service operates according to a system it inherited from the British raj. As its critics constantly point out, it is still a colonial civil service. This system deploys a very small number of highly-trained, fast-track officers to take responsibility for the work of vast ranks of lesser functionaries. The Union Government of India and the governments of the individual States draw their senior staff from the All-India Services, paid by the Union Government. These are the Indian Administrative Service (IAS), the Indian Police Service (IPS) and the Indian Forest Service (IFS). (The tiny Indian Foreign Service is also an All-India Service, but it obviously does not have any State functions.) All-India officers are attached to the *cadre* of just one State and, except when on a Union Government or diplomatic posting or secondment, will work only in the service of that State. At State level, there are also lower ranks of government employees in a host of government departments; these are employed and paid by the State government. They can only in very exceptional cases rise, through special promotion (often involving very close relationships with politicians), to All-India status.

Members of the All-India Services are not merely given highly focused training for their careers, they also undergo a socialization process which is designed to build up an *esprit de corps*. Young IAS officers are left in no doubt that they constitute a separate and special category of society after their sojourn at the National Academy of Administration. They have splendid accommodation on the edges of a popular hill-station. Here, in addition to learning about development, law and management, they learn protocol and etiquette, riding and shooting. They play cricket, go climbing and trekking in the Himalaya. They follow crash courses in music and the arts and film appreciation; they learn how to make polite conversation

FIGURE 11.1 The first stage in a Civil Service career

and put guests at ease. The idea is that they become accomplished, confident and able to cope at a garden-party as well as in a crisis. They become a sort of club.

In every aspect of government, whether we are talking about the administration of a district, running a State-owned industrial unit, or advising the Prime Minister, a member of the Indian Administrative Service will be ultimately responsible.

Virtually all IAS officers begin their careers in the districts. The States of India are divided for administrative purposes into districts and virtually all rural administration and development work is a district matter. The Collector is the senior IAS officer at district level but it is unlikely that he/she will have more than two junior IAS officers to work with. He/she will take responsibility for the many functionaries who deal with the government of about two million people but is unlikely to be more than about 35 years of age. The Collector acts as District Magistrate for certain types of legal cases, particularly those relating to land disputes; is responsible for rural development, education, health services and welfare work; supervises the collection of taxes. Much of the work is desk-bound but the Collector co-ordinates the government response in the event of earthquakes, droughts, famine, floods, civil disorder. His/her closest aid is the Superintendent of Police who takes charge of law and order matters, including civil unrest, but it is the Collector who (literally) reads the

Riot Act to a crowd to sanction the use of police action and is expected to be willing to use a revolver if necessary. There is clearly a lot of glamour attached to the district phase of the IAS officer's career and there are many intrinsic rewards.

After district service, IAS officers go on to duties at State level; these can include running a public sector industrial or trading unit or working in a department of a ministry. The work becomes much more routine and at this stage of their careers they come more closely into contact with State-level politicians and the business community. This means that they are likely to come into contact with very high levels of persuasion and corruption. Later there may be a Delhi posting or a secondment to an international organization.

Because the Establishment varies from year to year there is no fixed number of vacancies for the civil services generally; in the early 1980s recruitment into the IAS was at its highest at around 150 per anum; today, in a climate of retrenchment, only about 80 join the Service as trainees each year and the competition for places is as fierce as ever. The total establishment of the IAS is just over 5 000 in all grades, from trainee to Secretary.

THE IAS AND LIBERALIZATION

It is obvious that even the youngest IAS officers have considerable influence. In the era of 'licence/permit/quota raj' – before liberalization – nothing could move without government permission. Many people were very jealous of the extent of the power of these unelected officers and were jubilant at the thought of their exclusion from economic life with the onset of the new economic policy.

Bureaucracy is, almost by definition, irritating for those who have to confront it. Everyone who has ever visited India has stories to tell about time wasted by obstructive procedures. It is even more irritating for those whose profits depend on getting the right stamp in the right place in order to locate a plant, obtain raw materials or get permission to move finished products, etc. These mundane chores are handled much lower than the levels of the IAS, but it is these lower ranks which caused the wheels of government to turn very slowly indeed. It was obvious that a system like this would have to have been staffed by saints if it were not to be seduced into taking the 'speed money' it was offered by impatient clients. It was equally obvious that, once the system had been corrupted, it was in the interest of minor officials to slow things down as much as they could and of more senior officials to be discriminating in granting their favours.

Chapter Seven has already looked at corruption and only the very naïve would believe that it does not take place right up to the highest levels of government service; however, it is not universal. The corruption needs weeding out and the bureaucracy needs streamlining but, perhaps controversially, I maintain that a well-run state structure, such as seems to be struggling into existence in Andhra Pradesh, is the only realistic way of delivering economic development to the poorest people in India. It is generally acknowledged that some services are more prone to corruption than others (the Revenue Service, for example, is notorious, as is the Public Works Department). Whilst senior officers may sin spectacularly, it is the junior and middle ranks who are more persistent in their offending.

The IAS is relatively free from active corruption; Das, himself a senior IAS officer, states quite incontrovertibly 'there is rampant corruption in the Civil Service as a whole', but then he goes along with the Cabinet Secretary's estimation that somewhere in the region of 10–15 per cent of the IAS is corrupt (1998, p. 167). This is of course not something one can conduct a survey on and the figures are too conveniently round to mean anything more than 'a significant amount, but not a great deal'. It is the same guestimate that N.C. Saxena, then Director of the Lal Bahadur Shastri National Academy of Administration, gave me for his *cadre* of Uttar Pradesh, which he was at pains to stress was one of the worst. (On the other hand, Aruna Roy, a leading social activist who had left the IAS because she felt confined by its structure, expressed the opinion that not more than 10 per cent of the people who had entered the service with her were still straight). The Service itself is conscious of the need to clean up its image. As previously mentioned, in 1995 the Uttar Pradesh IAS Association carried out a poll to list its most corrupt officers with the intention of publicly naming and shaming them. The list has never been published, but there are several rather uncomfortable people in the *cadre*. The Lal Bahadur Shastri National Academy of Administration has launched a programme to campaign from the inside for Civil Service reform (you can visit its website). The LBSNAA preliminary report on Civil Service reform states quite unequivocally:

Unfortunately, many IAS officers are accepting a diminished role for themselves by becoming agents of exploitation in a state structure which now resembles more the one in the mediaeval period – authoritarian, brutal, directionless and callous to the needs of the poor. (Sen 1995, p. 18)

Within this system of political corruption there are many IAS officers with deep commitment to fair play and to alleviating the conditions of the poor in India. Certainly there is also a lot of hot air, with people posturing in print and at endless conferences about their commitment to the poor and their incorruptibility; but behind this, there is also action and considerable personal bravery, like that of Dasharath Prashad, whom I have already mentioned in Chapter Seven. He was not the first honest officer to be murdered.

INTERACTING WITH POLITICIANS

The conventional practice for State politicians who resent the actions of professional officers is to have them constantly transferred around the State so that their work and their families' lives are disrupted. The same practice of transfer can take place right up to Secretary level if a minister of the Union Government is displeased by the lack of compliance of his/her senior civil servant. There is considerable malaise amongst the honest and hard-working members of the Service and when the BJP Government, with its overtly communalist backers, came to power in 1998 there were several who felt that the final crunch had come and that they needed to consider whether they could continue to act as the servants of those they did not approve of.

In the past, the Civil Service had almost unlimited powers; in the present, it submits to other forces. Members of the All-India Services are beleaguered, whether they are straight or corrupt. They no longer command an unambiguously high status and some politicians delight in publicly humiliating them to amuse their electorates. They are caught between the service of the people and the service of political masters and mistresses. Their unease can be traced back to Indira Gandhi's Emergency, when they found themselves ordered to implement harsh and erratic policies and many tried to resolve their conflict of interest by keeping their heads down; when Indira Gandhi returned after the intervening period of Janata rule she clamped down on those civil servants who had demonstrated their 'disloyalty' once the pressure was off. As the Rudolphs (1987) say, 'Unmediated exposure to power left many civil servants intimidated and cautious.' If they were 'intimidated and cautious' in 1980, many were running scared of politicians by the late 1990s.

PRESTIGE

In relative terms, civil servants are not as wealthy as they once were (despite a generous revision of their pay scales in 1998). With the growth of opportunities for highly educated people in the private sector, government service is losing its appeal. A career in the private sector offers much better pay with considerably reduced attendant problems. In the mid 1990s, senior management jobs in the private sector were commanding salary increases of an average of 17 per cent per anum and the perks were considerable. Das (1998, p. 165) provides a table of typical remuneration of different categories of employment in India and shows that a manager with an MBA can expect a starting salary two-and-a-half times as high as a bureaucrat, whereas managers' retirement level salaries are 200 times those of senior civil servants. As Chapter Two has shown, the high-class, high-caste young men who formerly dominated the All-India Services have been attracted into the private sector and emigration. Young IAS officers from the *mofussil* towns sometimes see the Service as a springboard to a post in the private sector, since the training, early experience and networks are second to none.

The senior ranks of the services still reflect the old élites, extant at the time of their recruitment; new recruits demonstrate the transformations. Mandalization is obvious: from 1995 onwards, 50 per cent of the intake to the All-India Services was reserved. (In reality a slightly higher proportion than this was recruited from SC/ST/OBC because anyone from those categories who won a place in the 'open' category did not count against the reserved quota.) Since there has been an increase in the power at State level of politicians from the same sections of society, many members of old élites see a dangerous alliance emerging as they witness yet another contributory factor to their exclusion from the public realm. Reservation was necessary so that the hold of traditional élites could be broken, but its outcome is not always the general improvement in the condition of deprived sections that was intended. Whatever their caste background, only highly educated people can aspire to recruitment, and though good people can come through as a result of ability and hard work, most recruits come from the so-called 'creamy layer'. These people are often more concerned to draw close to politicians of their own community than to work with the poor.

The recruitment of members of higher castes has changed in nature. Although there is no quota relating to gender, increasing numbers of English-educated cosmopolitan young women have been attracted to the Services. Whereas males of the upper castes used to dominate the Service, they now make up rather less than a third of the intake. This diminished share does not consist of the same kind of men as joined in the past; the super-élite rarely applies now that the nature of the work, its integration into society and its prestige rating have changed so radically. Praful Bidwai started a major press debate about the IAS with a *Times of India* article in 1994 (29 July), in which he revealed that few current officer-trainees were liberally educated urban men from the best public schools. Instead, they came from the wealthier sections of the smaller towns of the poorer northern states – a section of society particularly associated with the forces of *Hindutva*. He had found an enthusiasm for right-wing politics, and that some had even held a private celebration on the campus for the anniversary of the demolition of the *Babri Masjid*. The Academy countered that one would expect recruitment to reflect trends in society, but that the training was designed to counter communalism. Then *India Today* published a lengthy piece on dowry taking by IAS officers (dowry is illegal and the IAS is supposed to implement the law) indicating that the first bribe a young IAS officer was likely to take was the dowry paid by affluent parents-in-law who believed that a connection into the bureaucracy would be valuable.

As the Academy realized, the IAS is not immune to the processes of Indian society. Real wealth and influence are global and the super-élite is turning its back on the state, works in the private sector and lives an increasingly privatized existence in its gated colonies and westernized social capsules. To some extent, the public domain is left to be battled out between two major camps: on the one hand there is the rank-and-file of the higher castes, who oppose Mandalization and rally behind the forces of *Hindutva*; on the other, the mass of *dalit–bahujan* India, internally significantly divided by class.

Yet the Civil Service remains very important. The amounts spent on development projects are such that no one should write off the state as the prime player in the economy. Those high dowries (paid by all castes) demonstrate that there is still widespread desire to make links into the structure of the bureaucracy (a powerful family aims for a portfolio of sons-in-law spread over the main fields of influence). The Service is important for a reason it inherits from the British raj: it is the most resilient and flexible structure to be found in India. It has the famous 'steel frame' – the grid of personal contacts, forged through the emphasis on *esprit de corps* at the training stage. To talk to an IAS officer is rapidly to become aware of an India-wide network of contacts, and information flows that no other institution can match. The Service has hitherto been flexible in its functions, recruitment, methods and style and it is unlikely that the structure which weathered the demise of British imperialism will buckle under the current round of change. The high-fliers in the middle ranks of today's service are eagerly espousing liberalization, are extending their global networks, and are also trying to keep themselves from being sucked into the power games of parochial politicians. They also appreciate that, for all the immediate power of politicians, it is the permanent civil servants who have the greater knowledge and a stronger structure.

Until recently the Indian military was always seen as outside political considerations. The armed forces have been exempted from the quotas of Mandalization and the officers have continued to be drawn from what the British liked to call the 'martial castes' – members of the *kshatriya* communities and Sikhs. There has, however, been an increasing tendency for the military to become politicized and the controversial nuclear tests carried out in 1998 have brought many army officers into the right-wing

Hindu nationalist fold. The aloofness of the military from politics received an abrupt jolt in December 1998 when the Minister of Defence dismissed Admiral Bhagwat, the Naval Chief of Staff, for his insubordination, outspokenness and, some say, politically active lawyer wife. Although Bhagwat had little personal popularity, there was a fairly widespread feeling amongst the establishment that politicians had gone too far.

One occasionally hears rumblings amongst the élites that the chaos of Indian political life could be cured by an appeal to the generals, but independent India's greatest salvation has always hitherto been its democratic system, combined with its independent Civil Service, its judiciary and its apolitical armed forces. Unpopular politicians can be brought down at election time and their power, though far too great, is not unlimited. When one hears criticism of India's democratic system in practice, one should remember that the alternative is infinitely more dangerous.

12

INDIA AND HER DIASPORA

Arjun Appadurai's *Modernity at large* begins with an account of his adolescence in Bombay which was already preparing him for migration – a sense that the world was outside India. He tells how subtly his view of the centre of existence had shifted from Britain the former colonizer (whose culture had coloured his upper middle class childhood with Billy Bunter, Biggles and Enid Blyton and then generated fantasies about debates in the Oxford Union), to 'the harsher, sexier, more addictive New World'. By the late 1960s, 'the American bug had bit me. I found myself launched on a journey that took me to Brandeis University', and a career in the West (Appadurai 1996, p. 2). This trend has snowballed among the educated élites and it is sobering to know that virtually the whole of the youth of a social fraction in India is now craving to live outside its own country and that this obsession has been largely constructed by the power of the international media.

Appadurai's book is concerned with 'a theory of rupture that takes media and migration as its two major, and interconnected, diacritics' (p. 3); to develop this he opts to 'situate [his] genealogy of the global present in the area [he] knows best: India' (p. 16). But, as I pointed out in my Introduction, India is not just a fortuitous choice, it is an excellent point from which to survey global modernity. It is a country in which the élites are open to the influences of the rest of the world, where foreign travel is normal and

families are flung across continents, where globalization is a word in everyday use. It is also a country in which the rest of society is trapped in the local – grounded, consuming local products, speaking a local language. This global–local distinction along class lines is one of the main reasons for the enthusiastic westernization of those who are competitively ambitious.

There has been a long history of migration from India which has been a function of colonial and postcolonial relations. In the nineteenth century the main migration was of labourers, often indentured, to the plantations and railways of the British Empire; after Independence it was predominantly the migration of industrial workers to Britain. In the new round of globalization there are two main kinds of migration: that of professionals, to the whole of the English-speaking world, but predominantly to Britain and the USA and, by contrast, the migration of unskilled and semi-skilled manual workers to the Gulf and the Far East (Jain 1998). The legacy endures in each location, so that only slight upward mobility takes place over one generation; descendants of labourers become small shopkeepers and clerical workers (Tambs-Lyche 1980); the 'twice migrants' from Africa encourage profitable skills which are highly portable (Bhachu 1985).

It is not the aim of this chapter to try to summarize the situation of India's diaspora world-wide, but to consider the impact of that diaspora upon India itself. Appadurai

FIGURE 12.1 Education for emigration
Source: SSi Ltd, Chennai

(1990) laid down a useful schema for thinking about globalization (unfortunately, he invented some ugly words at the same time), seeing it as interrelated *flows* of varying speed and intensity: of people ('ethnoscapes'), finance ('finanscapes'), technology ('technoscapes'), mediated messages and images ('mediascapes'), and ideologies ('ideoscapes'). The important thing to stress is the notion of flow, that configurations are never static. I shall borrow Appadurai's categories to structure this chapter.

ETHNOSCAPES

The frequency of flights to and from India worldwide has increased at the same time as their real cost has declined. Whereas 20 years ago a flight between London and Delhi would usually be half empty and the passengers predominantly westerners, mostly travelling as individuals, today flights are full, mostly of Indians, a high proportion of whom are travelling as families. In addition to the obvious business travel, lengthy holidays taken on retirement from a British job, and taking young children to see their 'home', attending weddings has become a major reason for travel. Just as wedding parties make block bookings on Indian trains, they do the same on international airlines. These are the 'ethnoscapes' – people travelling thousands of miles for business deals, tourism, education and just ordinary family reasons. Migration is no longer the once-and-for-all-time severance and replanting it used to be; travel is coming to be built into the family budgets of India's migrants.

However, ethnoscapes do not just signify the physical movement of people. People keep in direct touch by telephone and e-mail, replacing the anxiety of long waits between letters from home. The élite diaspora are in constant contact with family, friends and useful associates too. Contact is essential, since there is an assumption that a return will be made. However, it is becoming increasingly clear that, on retirement, many old people decide to stay close to their children and grandchildren, rather than to make the intended return migration.

Many migrants prefer to arrange the marriages of their children in India and a network of contacts is essential to making a suitable match. Advertisements are also placed in Indian newspapers for sons- and daughters-in-law but advertising has always been seen as inferior to personal contacts. There has recently been a spate of scandals in the Punjab about NRI ('non-resident Indian') men marrying for very large dowries and then returning to the United States without their wives; often they are found already to be married. The interpretation is that the marriage of one's daughter overseas can be a valuable but risky investment.

Universities in the West are keen to recruit students from overseas, and advertise regularly in the English-language newspapers. One British university in a region with a high Indian immigrant population made the whole venture seem less expensive by publishing a version of its breakdown of costs which assumed that the prospective student could live free with relatives. Much of the very expensive overseas education which is the prerogative of the upper classes is financed through diasporic families, with successive waves of young people being sponsored by a family which is similar in many ways to a multinational firm. In behaving in this way the family is, of course, reproducing and increasing its initial advantage and it becomes ever more difficult for others to break into the charmed circle.

When one remembers the NCAER calculation that only about 650000 households in India come into the upper part of the category 'Very Rich' (i.e. those with incomes of more than a million rupees per annum), it is becoming quite worrying in social and cultural terms that in 1997–98 33818 students left for the United States, 4500 went to Britain and 4100 to Australia.

However, not all migrants are from the educated élites. If you travel from Delhi by any of the Gulf airlines you will notice a special queue to one side at immigration; if you join it by mistake you will be told to go to one of the others. Everyone in that queue will be male, there will be no children, the clothes and the luggage will be shabbier, and most of the people, small in stature. These are people

Box 15 A foreign MBA

Monica Mehta is your typical overachiever. Armed with a Masters in commerce from Bombay University the 28-year-old worked in a stockbroking firm for four years before setting out on her own last year. It wasn't enough. In the next few weeks she will be flying out to the US for an MBA. 'In any business, international exposure is a must. My basic Indian qualifications have not given me a global focus in the profession,' Mehta explains. 'Global focus' won't come cheap: Mehta will fork out $45 000–50 000 over the next year for the course; it will take her close to eight years to recover that amount. But Mehta isn't counting the cost, she is looking at the intangible benefits of an internationally accepted degree.

Source: N. Chowdhury, *India Today* 15 March 1999

going to work as labourers in the Gulf. Their papers are being processed *en masse* as they have been recruited by agents. Although they look poor, they will probably have paid more for their tickets than the people in the fashionable clothes in the other queues because they are buying a package which is supposed to transform their lives; to do this many will have taken out loans at punishing rates, often with the same agent. One sees the advertisements in the papers and over travel agents' doors, promising travel, visas, work permits, work – all in one package. Sometimes it is legal, sometimes it is not. Shah (1999) demonstrates that about 50 per cent of the migrant labour to the Gulf is arranged through agents, 34 per cent through friends and relatives already working there, and the remainder is directly recruited. Nair (1999) notes that the returning Gulf migrants into Kerala do not always fare as well as they had anticipated; they find it difficult to obtain waged employment and frequently set up small business which fail.

The trade in illegal immigrants from India is one of the most deplorable transactions since the abolition of the slave trade. For high

premiums (last heard of, about $4 000 from the Punjab to Europe), an illegal immigrant is guaranteed nothing, not even his life. The last stage of the journey, from North Africa into Europe, is the most dangerous as illegal migrants are wedged into freight containers, the holds of ships and into unseaworthy boats sailed by pirates who, when sighted by patrol boats in the Mediterranean, are liable to demand that their human cargo jumps overboard. On Christmas Day 1996 somewhere in the region of 300 South Asian young men were drowned in the Ionian Sea. Many of the Indians among them came from the same region of the Punjab where there is a long tradition of emigration by the sons of Jat farming families. They were recruited by an agent from the predominantly Punjabi Karol Bagh area of Delhi who had a long-standing reputation in the villages from which his clients came. Some 450 people had been wedged into a vessel with a limit of 100 which sank. There are frequent similar but smaller scale disasters and, it is assumed, many one does not hear about (Swami 1997a). In an interview with families of the victims, the motive for illegal migration of Sikh Jat men was revealed as residing in the way in which the benefits of the Green Revolution were diminishing – smaller farmers' land holdings were fragmenting on inheritance and former prestige was being forfeited in the new economy: 'The tenth class educated Amrik Singh now had relatively low status. Since he was not equipped to compete for white collar jobs or to run a lucrative business, the only way to regaining lost family honour lay in making his way abroad' (Swami 1997b).

Martin and Schumann (1997) refer to the ready market for software engineers from India in the United States and parts of Europe, but there are also visa controls and competition for places. In July 1999 the American Visa Office stopped issuing any more visas for workers for the year. India has started to become conscious of the way in which it trains highly skilled young people only for them to leave (with no apparent conscience). There have been recent suggestions that India should be compensated for the 'brain drain' by the receiving countries, not in money, but in a reverse flow of expertise.

FINANSCAPES

Appadurai's 'finanscapes' include flows of wealth from migrants back 'home'. In 1996–97 NRI deposits amounted to Rs 12 208 crores, up from just Rs 1 008 crores in 1991–92 (*Statistical outline of India* 1997–98, p. 108) There are government induced investment schemes and the overseas editions of Indian journals carry articles on investing in shares in Indian companies; however, there is also direct investment in business, remittances to relatives and the purchase of land and houses. Advertisements for expensive housing complexes which boast clubs, swimming pools and security systems are targeted quite explicitly at NRIs, but there is also routine improvement of housing in areas with high rates of migration; many villages in the Punjab, Gujarat or Kerala have pockets of very high standard housing which represents small-scale personal investment. As Appadurai points out, this impacts on the incomes of local builders. In an interesting reversal of the flow of university students from India to the West, private schools in India are appealing to NRIs who would not be able to afford the exorbitant costs of an élite school education in the West. India, officially, corporately and individually is aware of the foreign-earned wealth of its expatriates. Part of the reason for the deepening of the balance of payments crisis of 1991 was that many NRIs took fright and withdrew their assets, demonstrating the depth of their 'solidarity' with the home country (Bhaduri and Nayyar 1996).

However, the flows of finance are also simple imports and exports initiated through NRI firms, as trade obviously follows personal knowledge and experience. This will not show up in the national accounts as NRI transfers, but the link is there. This can be at all scales and the flow of money can make changes at levels one might not anticipate; for example, fish, the mainstay of the diet in Kerala, has become very expensive, partly because remittance money gives some people increased buying power, partly because Keralan migrants in the Gulf are importing fish from their home region (and partly because of over-fishing caused by both). The alphonso mango in Gujarat has suffered exactly the same fate, this time because it is air-freighted to Britain where one can buy boxes in Indian-owned shops. The flow of people hastens the global uniformity of price, obviously to the disadvantage of the poor but to the great advantage of the local trader.

TECHNOSCAPES

'Technoscapes' are obvious – technology transfer is speeded by personal experience and contacts. The diaspora is certainly not the sole (or even main) reason for flows of technology from the West, but it does facilitate it. Before the liberalization of Indian markets and the consequent consumer boom for the upper classes, overseas travel was a major source of modern household consumer durables in India – but this is no longer the case.

MEDIASCAPES

'Mediascapes' are crucial to the globalization process. Throughout this book I have made constant reference to my favourite Indian newspapers and journals; some arrive by airmail, some I access on the Internet. Satellite TV, too, allows NRIs to watch some of the same programmes as their relatives at home and video shops and cinemas keep people abroad immersed in Indian cultural products. When I returned from a recent visit to rural India, I realized that I was more out of touch with the details of Indian current affairs than I am when I stay at home. But the media is not the same as life – the media glosses meanings too much; it is selective and seductive in its images and different things seem important when they are experienced from afar. A mediated view of India can be dangerously deceptive, given the way in which it so routinely edits out the poor.

Expatriate Indians not only receive media products from India, they generate images for themselves and for repatriation. The organization, Living Media, which owns *India Today*, the music company Music Today, an art dealership Art Today, and also produces TV current affairs programmes, is conscious that these are not just for home consumption. It is clear from its marketing that it sees itself catering to a global Indian clientele as it features items on Indians who are successful abroad, such as the profile of London-based L.N. Mittal and his global empire (Aiyar 1998b), and produces British and American *India Today* supplements which reflect back the image of themselves that NRIs wish to consume (Mitra 1999). But those supplements also contain advertisements for cheap phone calls home, florists' delivery services, investment opportunities and luxury housing complexes in Indian cities.

A third of the revenue from Bollywood movies is derived from NRI takings and *India Today* reports that the overseas tastes seem firmly 'to favour mush over violence or low brow comedy' (*India Today International* 1999, p. 47). This taste can be seen to coincide with (or influence?) the current preferences of middle-class India too. Patricia Uberoi's (1998) interpretation of two recent Hindi movies, *Dilwale dulhania le jayenge* (Director: Aditya Chopra) and *Pardes* (Director: Subhash Ghai), shows how the lives of NRIs have become a feature of a genre of popular cinema in India. She notes how Indian family values relating to arranged marriages are worked out through the theme of young NRIs resolving the contradiction between duty and personal choice and introduces a device which she calls 'the arranged love marriage'. The films were popular both in India and overseas for their mixture of modern imagery and setting with extreme conservatism, including strong patriotic themes.

Kuch Kuch Hota Hai (Director: Karan Johar), a film released in 1998, was a box-office hit in both India and Britain. It can be seen as yet another twist in mediatized Indianized-westernization for it is possible to see it as an NRI film set mainly in India. It picks up all the seductive images of the NRI film - designer fashion, college, youthful fun, the beach scene and drops them down in Mumbai. It is not remotely like Indian student life but works to transmit a message all the more powerfully for that. *India Today* quotes its director as saying, 'I shopped for twelve days in London. I make no bones about the fact that I wanted to show a Polo Sport, a Ralph Lauren or a DKNY, show them loud.' The film started a fad in India for major brands – 'The international up-market label, the ultimate cool, is all over Janpath in Delhi and Linking Road in Mumbai' (Joshi and Chowdhury 1998, p. 52–5). In 1999 the popular film with the élite young was *Hyderabad Blues*, which has already been mentioned in Chapter Two. It was targeted directly at the market niche consisting of English-speaking young Indians, and unusually for a film which was not seen as arthouse, it contained no singing and dancing. It catered to westernized preferences, but took as its theme the problems of a boy returning from America to confront his own westernization, and had him settle down to one of Uberoi's 'arranged love marriages'.

Young film makers find it almost obligatory to shoot one or two scenes of their Bollywood movies in Europe – Switzerland or Scotland taking the place of the conventional Himalayan scenes. It is interesting to note that this genre of 1990s film is unrelentingly 'nice', clean, and depicts affluent people – going right against the trend of gangster movies which had previously dominated Bollywood. It is reclaiming globalization and westernization for 'traditional' Hindu values at the same time as it familiarizes middle India with images of the world.

The Hindi movie is one of the main ways in which second and third generation Indian diaspora maintains a dialogue with India. Ziauddin Sadar (1998) gives a graphic description of the way in which films from home reinforced the Indian community in London, how viewing them was an opportunity to get people together and how their morality would be pored over in conversations for the next week. But another important value of film and TV is that they revitalize language amongst young NRIs; they offer more incentive for using Hindi than just talking to one's grandparents and it is important to note that they do prioritize Hindi over other Indian languages. Magic

Software Ltd produces a CD-ROM for learning Hindi. It advertises it in Britain as 'a good buy for people looking for their roots'. Flowing in the other direction, 'Hinglish' (using Hindi and English words as one language) is increasingly spoken by the educated young in the streets and in films.

IDEOSCAPES

Media constructions bring us close to Appadurai's last 'scape', that of ideology. I would not go so far as to say that films like *Dilwale dulhania le jayenge* have an overt *Hindutva* message, but I would say that they reinforce a view of life which finds the ideology of the Hindu Right appealing.

It is conventional to see the Indian diaspora as nostalgic for an idealized India and to assume that this nostalgia lends itself to fundamentalism and conservatism. Whilst I recognize this impulse, my own view is that one finds that the diaspora is politically to the Right for exactly the same reasons as British colonials were right wing, that is, that the class from which they are recruited is inherently conservative in politics. When one talks to the young people who are contemplating a move to the West, one finds them already imbued with ideologies of individualism and competition and the culture of the diaspora. But the overly mediatized view of India upon which the diaspora sustains itself does often foster a self-conscious orientation towards ideology. The Internet abounds with politico-religious sites generated by and for Indian expatriates. Almost invariably these suggest donations to further the cause and NRIs are a major source of finance for a range of temples, training camps, propaganda campaigns and so on.

The *Vishwa Hindu Parishad* (VHP), as its name (World Hindu Council) suggests, is aimed at spreading the *Hindutva* message worldwide, particularly in the United States. Shashi Tharoor (1997) begins his chapter on NRIs with a warning about the VHP and refers to its American members as 'a coven of well-heeled Hindu professionals from Southern California'. He is particularly scathing about those who have left India only to pre-

tend to be more Indian and divides NRIs into those who 'never relinquished India' and those who are 'not really Indian' (he is himself an NRI).

Certainly the RSS has a global policy which it targets through the NRI population. The overseas wing of the RSS is known as the *Hindu Swayamsevak Sangh* and has its headquarters in London. It has an active presence in 92 countries and holds periodic training camps in India for RSS workers abroad. One of its major activities is to recruit student members and it claims to have a presence in virtually all British universities where, according to the overseas co-ordinator, 'our *swayamsevaks* inspire them with our ideology' (Unnithan 1998). In Britain the student RSS organization is known as the National Students' Forum and in the United States it is the Hindu Students' Council. In 1998 the BJP launched the Overseas Friends of the BJP (OFBJP) with the aim of maintaining a following with NRIs (amongst other things, it encourages them to e-mail their contacts in India at election times asking them to be sure to vote BJP). Even more significantly, it lobbies for right-wing Indian issues in other countries and, according to a member who lectures at the London School of Economics, it campaigns 'to remove misconceptions about the BJP, that it is a communal or fascist party' (Suri and Keshavan 1998).

It was reported that in the 1998 general elections, Punjabi NRIs, particularly those from Canada, were sufficiently enthusiastic not just to watch from afar. Substantial numbers were actively electioneering in the Punjab across the range of political parties. There was every indication that their activities in the Punjab were prompted by Canadian Sikh community factionalism, where rival groups of reformists and fundamentalists vie for control and where the latter try to regulate academic research on Sikh scriptures, modes of worship and communal eating (Pandher 1998b). Tharoor with his customary bluntness comments on 'the irony of political extremism being advocated from ivory towers of bourgeois moderation' and their leaders 'deriving sustenance almost entirely from clean-shaven expatriate co-religionists largely

Box 16 Non-resident Sikhs

Sikh communitarian politics is influenced not only by developments in the Punjab or internal caste/class cleavages. As a global community, with substantial numbers settled in the West, the overseas Sikh community – the NRS – has come to play an important role in Sikh affairs. In the manner of distanced outsiders, NRS constructions are not just marked by nostalgia and longing, they seem to favour more textual, if not fundamentalist, interpretations. Given their greater financial clout, the support they can and do extend to different formations can and does cause problems.

Source: anonymous editorial of *The Sikh Spirit*, a special issue of *Seminar*, to mark the 300th anniversary of the *Khalsa*, 476, April 1999

unfamiliar with the prohibitions and injunction of their faith' (Tharoor 1997, p 141).

However, it is not only the forces of Sikh fundamentalism and *Hindutva* which propagate their ideology amongst the overseas Indian community. *Ghadar* is an example of a far Left organization of expatriate Indians, mostly based in North America, which resurrected the name of an organization of *dalit* labourers in San Francisco in the 1920s. (The name *Ghadar* means 'mutiny'.) It seeks to mobilize a power base among Indians abroad for such issues as awareness of untouchability and the many Indian social movements (it has nothing like the base of its rivals).

There is no simple unidirectional flow of ideology from India to the West or from the West to India. I have never liked the term 'hybridity' because it conjures up ideas of pure breeds mating, when it is more appropriate to think about volatile ideas and practices which emerge out of new economic and political formations. These draw upon old symbolic systems because culture always works with what it has to hand.

CITIZENSHIP

India does not allow its citizens to take out dual nationality (although it is willing to allow naturalized Indians to retain the citizenship of their birth). This means that if migrants from India wish to acquire citizenship of their country of residence, then they must relinquish their Indian citizenship (people often get around the practical problems posed by this by dividing nationality between spouses). Those who retain Indian citizenship are granted the special legal status of non-resident Indian which entitles those who do not reside in India for more than six months in the year favourable rates of interest on bank deposits, rights to take such interest out of the country, and advantageous rates of tax. (With relaxation of exchange controls these advantages are not as valuable as once they were, but a registration as non-resident allows many people to divert money outside India, sometimes for themselves, sometimes for others, as one of the many ways in which 'black' money could be laundered. This can be used for bribing politicians and officials with payments made directly into overseas banks; some NRIs are really international operators with their base in India rather than genuine diaspora.)

There has been a long campaign for dual nationality by those who have given up their Indian citizenship and the forces of Hindu nationalism have lent their support to this. The current (BJP) government has gone some way down the road of dual nationality by instituting the category 'person of Indian origin' which is extended to persons born in India or the child or grandchild of a person born in India. Identity cards are being issued to these people on payment of $1 000. The new status will extend the right to stay in the country for 180 days without a visa, to buy houses, and to take advantage of the financial privileges of NRIs (Bhaumik 1999).

NERVOUSLY RETURNING

India is ambivalent about the NRIs; people can be scathing about the opportunism of those who leave and they can also feel hurt by the condescending attitudes they seem to display when they visit. In 1996 *India Today* ran a feature caricaturing the 'nervously returning Indians', 'not really Indians' who had come back to India when it opened its doors to TNCs (Transnational Corporations). The target was the families of managers, employed on overseas salaries with hardship allowances for their displacement, who lived in special enclaves where they complained about the lack of infrastructure and the shortage of their favourite products and struggled to get their children into the American schools. They were probably largely imaginary, but they drew upon local upper-middle-class resentments I have often heard expressed (Jain 1996).

It ran a similar story in February 1999, this time about more ordinary professionals who had returned to the new India and been so disappointed that they were setting off abroad again, this time for good. It quoted interviewees as saying that they could not make their mark in India because all niches were sewn up by local networks of influence; they complained about rote learning in schools, about chaotic structures (Aiyar 1999). It is a story that was familiar amongst British colonials – out of place away, even more out of place back 'home'. It is the diaspora itself which offers the sense of belonging, not in a place but in a cultural network. It will be interesting to try to understand the politics of this transnational community in the future, to contemplate its symbolic relationships with India.

CONCLUSION

How can anyone presume to come to 'conclusions' about India? Each commentary can be no more than a pause in a stream of interpretations and understandings and to presume to explain is rash. What I have offered here is my own overview of the way that India is now. This cannot help but be partial in both senses of the word. I have prioritized the views of Indian academics, activists and journalists over western Indianists and, in doing so, I shall doubtless be criticized by those who think that western academic constructions have a special place in the hierarchy of knowledge. I have been trying throughout to take my reader as close to India as I can and the theoretical concerns of western intellectuals, valid as they are in their own right, have rarely been useful to me in this task. This journey has been mediated through my own outsider position; to obscure things by pursuing a debate between outsiders seemed not to be useful.

India is fortunate to have a free press of a remarkably high standard. The very best academics do not believe that there is anything demeaning about writing for the media and in the best journals there is a standard of analysis and writing in English which cannot be bettered. There is also no fear about publishing long pieces, such as Arundhati Roy's two manifestos on nuclear weapons and on big dams, in magazines. Public service television has always served government interests, both political and educational, and the new satellite stations are mostly trivial and con-

sumerist, as in the rest of the world; but the print medium is varied and combative, ranging across the full political spectrum, operating in all languages, nationally and locally based. In addition to the newspapers and journals, book publishing thrives in India and the small publishing houses have not yet fallen to large international conglomerates. The population is large enough for minority concerns to be worth publishing. Then there are all the 'little' publications, emerging from groups of activists of all political persuasions. The printed word is still exciting in India and it is a pity that so little of the product is read outside the country. Indian books deserve to be read other than by Indianists.

It is, however, in the nature of critical writing that it tends to concentrate upon the faults of a society rather than its positive aspects. I am conscious that, partly as a consequence of what I read and who I talk to, I too have emphasized India's problems. Many people in India are acutely worried about the changes that are occurring as a consequence of the current wave of globalization; they see the market intruding into areas of life which they thought they could control at the level of interpersonal relationships. These anxieties relate to the most fundamental aspects of life – the ability to earn a decent living, to expect a reasonably secure future for one's children. They emerge constantly, but they take very different forms and polarize people into opposing camps. Sometimes there is little real difference in the underlying fears of people who take the *Hindutva* route and those who support the new social movements in their opposition to large-scale changes. However, the choice of direction will ally individuals with very different structures.

One is bound to take sides, even if one can understand other positions. I can empathize with the concerns of old élites who fear for the work prospects of their children. I know why they oppose reservation, with whatever arguments come to hand, at the same time as trying to achieve new exclusive niches for themselves by working with their international contacts. I can also feel for their quest for the moral high ground that comes with religious certainty as they work out strategies which best protect their interests. I understand it, but I wish that it was not so.

The changes which are occurring in the new India seem to me to be predominantly a matter of differentiation and polarization. Categories are hardening out and continuities are being severed. The underlying theme of Deleuze and Guattari's *Capitalism and schizophrenia* (1984, 1987) has never seemed more valid – that modernism creates breaks, ruptures, discontinuities, chasms, with the result that oppositions become more convincing than continuous flows. Even Hinduism, the religion of continuity and unity, has taken an oppositional form. Perhaps in the long run, this is all to the good. Perhaps, in recognizing rather than blurring conflicts, people can come to better understanding of their world – but it is a very great risk. India is coming to see violent communalism as almost normal and the wealthy increasingly hide away from the mass or flee the country altogether.

It has become something of a cliché for a particular type of westerner to look to India for enlightenment. At religious gatherings such as the *Kumbh Mela* it is common to see earnest young Europeans and Americans, clad in brand new saffron robes, convinced that they have glimpsed an escape from the nastiness of materialism. They may well have, but few realize the depth of the relationship between the *sadhus* and the politics of the Right or the ways in which this connects right back into the new globalization. And yet, I do believe that India has many things to teach the rest of the world about its present-day condition and that some of these do emerge from a philosophical position which assumes relationships based upon giving rather than bargaining. However, I believe that the main lesson India has to teach the rest of the world is the need never to give up the struggle for human dignity.

GLOSSARY

Adivasi	Person who belongs to a tribal community
Agarbattis	Incense sticks
Andolan	Association/movement
Arrack	Country liquor (sometimes used generally to include both legal and illegally distilled alcohol, other times restricted to the legal in opposition to the illegal *hooch*).
Avatar	Incarnation
Babri Masjid	The mosque at Ayodhya demolished by right-wing Hindu vandals.
Bahujan	Masses, common people. Often used to refer to the category 'other backward classes' (OBC).
Baniya	A trader caste
Bidis	Rolled leaf cigarettes
Brahmin	Traditionally the priestly caste. Tends to specialize in the knowledge-based businesses and professions.
Bustee	Shanty town
Chuprassi	Office messenger (especially in government service)
Dacoit	Brigand
Dada	Literally, 'paternal grandfather', but used of a criminal slum lord who offers 'protection'.
Dalit	Literally, 'oppressed'. The term is used by and of people who belong to the castes formerly known as 'untouchables'. (Gandhi referred to them as *harijans*, 'children of God', but today this term is regarded by *dalits* as patronizing.)
Deshi	Literally, 'of the country'. Has come to mean folksy, traditional or unsophisticated. (See *swadeshi*, which has not taken on these latter meanings.)
Devadasi	A woman given to a temple as a bride of the god – however, she is far from being a nun. Often translated as 'temple prostitute'.
Dvija	The 'twice born' – *brahmins*, *kshatriyas*, *vaishyas* taken together.
Grameen Bank	A network of local women's-run credit associations. Established in Bangladesh but much imitated in India.
Gram	Village (as in *gram panchayat* – village council)
Goonda	Violent urban criminal, mobster
Haat	Market
Harijan	Gandhi's term for 'untouchables'. Now generally rejected as patronizing (and because it also means the child of a *devadasi*).

Hawala	Money laundering
Hindutva	Hinduism as a way of life. Hindu culture. Supporters of *Hindutva* say that it applies to the Indian way of life, regardless of religion. Others see it as a form of religious chauvinism similar to the idea of fundamentalism in other religions.
Jajmani system	*Jati*-based system of division of rural labour focusing on a feudal landlord.
Jati	A hereditary corporate group, associated with traditional occupations. Acts as a community/interest group; likely to have strong political identity. In theory, hierarchically arranged according to degrees of ritual purity. The grouping generally implied when the term 'caste' is used.
Jhuggi	Hut (used of slum dwellings)
Kayastha	Traditionally a *kshatriya jati* which specialized in record-keeping and accounts for the landlords. Today its members tend to be employed in administration, management and education.
Khadi	Hand-spun and woven fabric. It has an ideological significance since Gandhi fostered the production of *khadi* as a village industry in opposition to the British cotton industry. Today politicians still wear *khadi* as a mark of their adherence to the original Independence principles. Every town has a highly-subsidized, state-run *khadi* shop.
Kshatriya	Traditionally the category of castes of landowners, rulers, warriors.
Lathi	A pole used as a weapon, particularly by police in riots.
Lok Sabha	Lower house of Parliament

Mahila Mandal	Women's association or club
Mandalization	The implementation from 1990 onwards of the recommendations of the Second All-India Backward Classes Commission, chaired by B.P. Mandal and known as the Mandal Commission. Reserves a varying proportion of jobs in the state sector for 'backward classes' in addition to those already reserved for Scheduled Castes and Tribes. Prompted an upper-caste backlash.
Mandir	Hindu temple
Masjid	Mosque
Mofussil	Provincial. Generally used as '*mofussil* towns', smaller towns which are not the State capital.
Naxalites	Marxist guerilla groups. Named after the village of Naxalbari where the movement began.
Om	The last letter of the alphabet. A Hindu symbol of infinity.
Panchayat	Literally, a group of five people. Means a local council (can be any number of members)
Panchayati raj	Literally, rule by the council. Means a system of local government introduced by the 73rd Amendment to the Constitution whereby authority is transferred from the bureaucracy to locally elected representatives.
Pandit	*Brahmin* priest/scholar in northern India. Originating in Kashmir.
Parivar	Family
Patta	Certificate of entitlement to land
Purdah	Seclusion of women
Raiyat	Wealthy peasant
Raj	Regime, authority, rule
Rashtra	Nation
Sadhu	Holy man who has taken a vow of poverty.

Samskaras	Life rituals
Sanskrit	Ancient language of northern India, no longer spoken. The language of the scriptures and, thus, the brahmins. (Roughly the same status as Latin in Europe. Until recently members of lower-caste groups were forbidden to learn it.)
Sanskritization	Term generally attributed to M.N. Srinivas to describe the process whereby a jati could attempt to negotiate an improvement in its status by emulating the behaviour of brahmins (typically through ritual observances and by becoming vegetarian and teetotal).
Sangh Parivar	The association of right-wing Hindu organizations.
Sarpanch	Head of local council
Sathin	Friend, used particularly of a befriending scheme for women's welfare in Rajasthan.
Satyagraha	Ghandi's term for peaceful resistance. Literally, 'truth force'.
Sena	Army (in the sense of a private army)
Shakha	The physical fitness and prayer meetings of the RSS.
Shiv Sena	A right-wing political party based in Maharashtra.
Shudra	Traditionally the category made up of artisan castes.
Swadeshi	Support for nationally produced goods and avoidance of imports. Originally an important part of the Independence movement, associated with Gandhi, whereby British goods, particularly cloth, were boycotted. It has become associated with modern Hindu nationalism as one of the planks of resistance to the westernization of culture.
Tandoor	Clay oven
Vaishya	The category of castes traditionally associated with taking profit from trade or usury.
Varna	A hierarchical category (but not group) taking its justification from Vedic scriptures. Literally means 'colour', but this should not be interpreted as implying historic racial differentiation. Varnas have no corporate identity. Often translated as 'caste'.
Vaishnavite	Division of Hinduism focusing on the adoration of Vishnu and his avatars, especially Ram.
Yatra	Pilgrimage. Rath Yatra are the journeys taken by chariot to raise consciousness of militant Hinduism.
Zamindar	Feudal landlord

ACRONYMS

AIADMK	All-India Anna Dravida Munnetra Kazhagam (Tamil political party)
BJP	Bharatiya Janata Party (national political party)
BSP	Bahujan Samaj Party (Uttar Pradesh political party)
CPI(M)	Communist Party of India (Marxist) (national political party)
DMK	Dravida Munnetra Kazhagam (Tamil political party)
ISI	(Pakistan's) Inter-Services Intelligence
JMM	Jharkhand Mukti Morcha (tribal State movement)
NGO	Non-Governmental Organization
NRI	Non-Resident Indian
OBC	Other Backward Classes
PIO	Person of Indian Origin
RJD	Rashtriya Janata Dal (Bihari political party)
SC	Scheduled Caste
ST	Scheduled Tribe
RSS	Rashtriya Swayamsevak

Sangh (right-wing Hindu organization)

VHP   Vishwa Hindu Parishad (Right-wing Hindu organization)

MONEY, NUMBERS, ETC.

Money
The rupee is the unit of currency. It is divided into 100 paise. (Colloquially, some people still divide the rupee into 16 annas; so 8 annas = 50 paise.)

Numbers
1 lakh = 100 000
1 crore = 10 000 000 (the term million is not much used)

An Indian billion is the same as the American (not British) billion (i.e. 1 000 000 000)

Distance
Distances are usually officially cited in kilometres in India; however, miles are still often used in everyday speech.

SPELLING

India spells English words in the British manner, so generally ends words in 'ise' rather than 'ize'. When citing Indian works I have followed Indian conventions regarding spelling. For transliterated words I have followed the most common Roman script spellings (though there are invariably alternatives).

BIBLIOGRAPHY

Agarwal, A. 1986: The fifth World Conservation Lecture: human–nature interactions in a Third World country. *The Environmentalist* **6**(3): Republished as An Indian environmentalist's credo in Guha, R (ed.) 1998: *Social ecology*. Delhi: Oxford University Press, 346–84.

Agarwal, P. 1995: Feminist environmentalism or ecofeminism? *The Hindu Survey of the Environment* 1995. Chennai, 7–14.

Agha, Z. 1996: Explosive fallout. *India Today International* **21**(3), 22–7.

Agnihotri, I. and Mazumdar, V. 1995: Changing the terms of political discourse. In Agnihotri, I. and Mazumdar, V. (eds), *Women towards Beijing: voices from India*. Delhi: Lokayan.

Agnihotri, V. (ed.) 1995: *Skills for effective administrators*. New Delhi: Vikas.

Agnihotri, V. and Mittal, R. 1995: Managing personal affairs. In Agnihotri, V. (ed.), *Skills for effective administrators*. New Delhi: Vikas.

Agnihotri, V. and Ramachandran, H. (eds) 1996: *Dimensions of the new economic policy, Vol. I: economic sector,* Vol. II: social sector. New Delhi: Concept Publishing.

Ahmad, A. 1994: Structure and ideology in Italian Fascism. *Germinal* **1**, 26–60. (Also reprinted in modified form in Ahmad, A. 1996: *Lineages of the present: political essays.* Chennai: Tulika, 320–68.

Ahmad, A. 1996a: Fascism and national culture: reading Gramsci in the days of Hindutva. In *Lineages of the present: political essays.* Chennai: Tulika, 221–67.

Ahmad, A. 1996b: In the mirror of Urdu: recompositions of nation and community. In *Lineages of the present: political essays.* Chennai: Tulika, 191–220.

Ahmad, A. 1996c: On the ruins of Ayodhya: communalist offensive and recovery of the secular. In *Lineages of the present: political essays.* Chennai: Tulika, 267–319.

Ahmad, A. 1999: The many roads to Kargil. *Frontline* **16**(14), 18–25.

Ahmed, F. 1998: Crime on the campus. *India Today International* **23**(19), 22–3.

Aiyar, V.S. 1998a: Ransom city. *India Today International* **23**(48), 20–4.

Aiyar, V.S. 1998b: Richest Indian in the world. *India Today International* **23**(16), 26–31.

Aiyar, V.S. 1999: The dream that died. *India Today International* **24**(6), 36–40.

Amin, S. 1997: *Capitalism in the age of globalization: the management of contemporary society.* London: Zed Books.

Anant, V. 1991: Indomania. *Race and Class* **33**(2), 59–63.

Appadurai, A. 1990: Disjuncture and difference in the global cultural economy. *Theory Culture and Society* **7**, 295–310.

Appadurai, A. 1991: Global ethnoscapes: notes and queries for a transnational anthropology. In Fox, R.G. (ed.), *Recapturing anthropology: working in the present.* Santa Fe: School of American Research Press.

Appadurai, A. 1995: The production of locality. In Fardon, R. (ed.), *Counterworks:*

managing the diversity of knowledge. London: Routledge.

Appadurai, A. 1996: *Modernity at large: cultural dimensions of globalization.* Minneapolis: University of Minnesota Press.

Arora, K.C. 1996: *The steel frame: Indian Civil Service since 1860.* New Delhi: Sanchar Publishing House.

Asser, E. 1998: A new service class? Software workers in Bangalore (unpubl.) Conference paper presented at Institute of British Geographers Annual Conference, Guildford, UK.

Asthana, S. 1993: Urban community development in the Third World: lessons from Visakhapatnam, India. In Mukherjee, A. and Agnihotri, V. (eds), *Environment and development: views from the East and the West.* New Delhi: Concept Publishing, 505–24.

Athreya, V. and Chunkath, S. 1998: Maternal mortality in Tamil Nadu. *Frontline* **15**(2), 71–4.

Awasthi, D. 1997: Crisis of credibility. *India Today International* **22**(5), 24–5.

Bacchetta, P. 1996: Hindu nationalist women as ideologues: the *Sangh*, the *Samiti* and their differential concepts of the Hindu nation. In Jayawardena, K. and de Alwis, M. (eds), *Embodied violence: communalising women's sexuality in South Asia.* New Delhi: Kali for Women, 126–67.

Bagachi, A. 1995: Dialectics of Indian planning: from compromise to democratic decentralization and threat of disarray. In Sathyamurthy, T. (ed.), *Industry and agriculture in India since Independence.* Delhi: Oxford University Press, 46–93.

Bailey, F. 1957: *Caste and the economic frontier.* Manchester: Manchester University Press.

Banerjee, S. 1980: *In the wake of Naxalbari: a history of the Naxalite movement in India.* Calcutta: Subarnarekha.

Banerjee, S. 1995: Hindu nationalism and the construction of women: the *Shiv Sena* organizes women in Bombay. In Sarkar, T. and Butalia, U. (eds), *Women and the Hindu Right.* New Delhi: Kali for Women, 216–32.

Bardhan, P. 1984: *The political economy of development in India.* Oxford: Blackwell.

Basu, A. 1995: Feminism inverted: the gendered imagery of real women of Hindu nationalism. In Sarkar, T. and Butalia, U. (eds) *Women and the Hindu Right.* New Delhi: Kali for Women, 158–80.

Basu, A. 1996: Mass movement or élite conspiracy? The puzzle of Hindu nationalism. In Ludden, D. (ed.), *Making India Hindu.* Delhi: Oxford University Press.

Basu, S. 1998: Medical waste disposal: burning problem. *The Hindu Survey of the Environment 1998.* Chennai, 175–8.

Basu, T., Datta, P., Sarkar, S., Sarkar, T. and Sen, S. 1993: *Khaki shorts and saffron flags: a critique of the Hindu Right.* Delhi: Orient Longman.

Bavadam, L. 1996: The stakes in Vidarbha. *Frontline* **13**(23), 41–2.

Bavadam, L. 1998: Crime and punishment. *Frontline* **15**(23), 113–4.

Baviskar, A. 1997: *In the belly of the river: tribal conflicts over development in the Narmada Valley.* Delhi: Oxford University Press.

Baweja, H. 1998: ISI spreads its net. *India Today International* **23**(49), 12–15.

Baweja, H. 1999: Wanton ways. *India Today International* **24**(22), 40–1.

Baweja, H. and Chakravarty, S. 1999: Murder of a model. *India Today International* **24**(20), 26–32.

Beteille, A. 1997: Caste in contemporary India. In Fuller, C. (ed.), *Caste today.* Delhi: Oxford University Press.

Bhachu, P. 1985: *Twice migrants: East African Sikh settlers in Britain.* London: Tavistock.

Bhaduri, A. and Nayyar, D. 1996: *An intelligent person's guide to liberalization.* New Delhi: Penguin.

Bhagwati, J. 1998: The design of Indian development. In Ahluwalia, I. and Little, I. (eds), *India's economic reforms and development: essays for Manmohan Singh.* Delhi: Oxford University Press, 32–9.

Bhattacharjea, A. 1998a: Right to Information: the Indian experience. *Vidura: Journal of the Press Institute of India* **35**(3), 15–19.

Bhattacharjea, A. 1998b: Pressures on a profession. *Vidura: Journal of the Press Institute of India* **35**(4), 25–6.

Bhaumik, S. 1996: Robbing the poor. *India Today International* **21**(21), 76–81.

Bhaumik, S. 1999: *Privileges at a price. India Today International: UK Special* **24**(15), 24b.

Bidwai, P. 1994a: High cost of provincialization in the Civil Services. *The Times of India* 29 July.

Bidwai, P. 1994b: Are we killing the IAS? *Tribune* 2 August.

Bidwai, P. 1995: Making India work – for the rich. *Multinational Monitor* 16(7/8). Http://gopher.essential.org/monitor/hyper/mm0795.04.html

Bidwai, P. 1996: Toxic waste disposal: a ready, dumping lot. *The Hindu Survey of the Environment 1996*. Chennai, 185–91.

Bidwai, P. 1997: Destitution driving the poor to death. World News Inter-Press Service. Http://oneworld.org/ips2/may/india2.html

Bidwai, P. 1998: Hindutva's fallacies and fantasies. *Frontline* 15(24), 104–5.

Bidwai, P. 1999: The unending cost. *Frontline* 16(16), 103–5.

Bose, S. and Jalal, A. 1997: Modern South Asia: history, culture, political economy. London: Routledge.

Brass, P. 1984: National power and local politics in India: a twenty year perspective. *Modern Asian Studies* 17(1), 89–118.

Brass, P. 1994: *The politics of India since Independence*. 2nd edn, Cambridge: Cambridge University Press.

Brass, P. 1997: *Theft of an idol: text and context in the representation of collective violence*. Princeton: Princeton University Press.

Bruno, K. 1995: Gujarat's toxic corridor. *The Hindu Survey of the Environment 1995*. Chennai, 163–6.

Burman, R. 1994: Sacred groves and the modern political economy. *Lokayan Bulletin: Special Issue on Tribal Identity* 5(5/6), 41–52.

Burra, N. 1995: *Born to work: child labour in India*. Delhi: Oxford University Press.

Caplan, P. 1985: *Class and gender in India: women and their organizations in a South Indian city*. London: Tavistock Publications.

Carson, B. 1999: Filling the Bollywood hole in Glasgow. *The Scotsman* 29 July, 17.

Central Statistical Organization (CSO) 1997: *Statistical abstract of India*. New Delhi: Ministry of Planning and Programme Implementation, Government of India.

Chakraborty, S. 1995: Muckraking. *Down to Earth* 4(3), 20–1.

Chakravarti, S., Aiyar, V. and Rekhi, S. 1998: The great depression. *India Today International* 23(36), 26–28.

Chakravarti, S. and Rekhi, S. 1998: Rising prices. *India Today International* 23(29), 19–24.

Chalam, K. 1998: Caste and economic reforms. *Seminar* 471, 33–7.

Chandrasekhar, C. 1996: For India incorporated: big business in search of an agenda. *Frontline* 13(10), 97–8.

Chatterjee, P. 1985: The Indian big bourgeoisie: comprador or national? In *A possible India: essays in political criticism*. Delhi: Oxford University Press, 1–11.

Chatterjee, P. 1993a: The nation and its outcasts. In *The nation and its fragments: colonial and postcolonial histories*. Delhi: Oxford University Press, 171–99.

Chatterjee, P. 1993b: Communities and the nation. In *The nation and its fragments: colonial and postcolonial histories*. Delhi: Oxford University Press, 220–39.

Chatterjee, P. 1994: Secularism and tolerance. *Economic and Political Weekly* 39(28), 1768–77. Reprinted in Bhargava, R. (ed.) 1998: *Secularism and its critics*. Delhi: Oxford University Press.

Chatterjee, P. 1997: The centre crumbles. In *A possible India: essays in political criticism*. Delhi: Oxford University Press, 213–27.

Chatterjee, P. and Mallik, A. 1975, tr. 1997: Indian democracy and bourgeois reaction. In *A possible India: essays in political criticism*. Delhi: Oxford University Press, 35–7.

Chaudhuri, K. 1997: Crackdown on the tea industry. *Frontline* 14(21), 29–30.

Chaudhuri, K. 1998: The Bodo blasts. *Frontline* 15(13), 46–7.

Chaudhuri, K. 1999: Carnage in Narayanpur. *Frontline* 16(5), 28–31.

Chatterjee, U. 1988: *English August: an Indian story*. New Delhi: Rupa & Co.

Chopra, P. 1999: Let it burn up caste. *The Hindu Online* 16 March.

Chossudovsky, M. 1992: India under IMF rule. *The Ecologist* 22(6), 271–5.

Choudhury, S. 1999: The North East: a concept re-examined. *Seminar* 474, 34–7.

Chowdhury, N. 1999: Dipping into India's pocket. *India Today* 24(11), 30–1.

Clark, S. 1998: Dalits and *Christianity: subaltern religions and liberation theology in India*. Delhi: Oxford University Press.

Cohn, B. 1987: The census, social structure and objectification in South Asia. In *An anthropologist among the historians and other essays*. Delhi: Oxford University Press, 224–54.

Corbridge, S. 1997: The merchants drink our blood: peasant politics and farmers' movements in post-Green Revolution India. *Political Geography* **16**(5), 423–34.

CSE 1991: *Floods, flood plains and environmental myths*. New Delhi: Centre for Science and Environment.

CSE 1995: Debate: planters' devils? *Down to Earth* **4**(7), 48–55.

CSE 1998: Campaign: people for wildlife. *Nonfense* **1**(1). Http://www.oneworld.org/cse/html/cmp

Dalit Voice 1997: Happiest news of the day: Hindus set up 'Savarna Samaj Party'. **16**(2), 2–3.

Das, A. 1992: *The republic of Bihar*. New Delhi: Penguin.

Das, A. 1996: *Changel: the biography of a village*. New Delhi: Penguin.

Das, P. 1995: Manifesto of a housing activist. In Patel, S. and Thorner, A. (eds), *Bombay: metaphor for modern India*. Delhi: Oxford University Press, 121–42.

Das, S. 1998: *Civil Service reform and structural adjustment*. Delhi: Oxford University Press.

Das, V. 1976: Indian women: work, power and status. In Nanda, B. (ed.), *Indian women: from purdah to modernity*. New Delhi: Vikas.

Das, V. 1990: Our work to cry: your work to listen. In Das, V. (ed.), *Mirrors of violence: communities, riots and survivors in South Asia*. Delhi: Oxford University Press, 345–98.

Das, V. 1995a: National honour and practical kinship: of unwanted women and children. In Das, V. (ed.), *Critical events: an anthropological perspective on contemporary India*. Delhi: Oxford University Press.

Das, V. 1995b: One soap opera: what kind of anthropological object is it? In Miller, D. (ed.), *Worlds apart: modernity through the prism of the local*. London: Routledge.

Dasgupta, B. 1995: State power and indigenous capital development in India. In Sarbadhikari, P. (ed.), *Reconstituting India*. Delhi: Oxford University Press.

Datta-Chaudhri, M. 1999: Some lessons from 1998. *Seminar* **473**, 29–33.

Davis, R. 1996: The iconography of Rama's chariot. In Ludden, D. (ed.), *Making India Hindu: religion, community and the politics of democracy in India*. Delhi: Oxford University Press, 27–54.

de Haan, A. 1997: Unsettled settlers: migrant workers and industrial capitalism in Calcutta. *Modern Asian Studies* **31**(4), 919–49.

Deleuze, G. and Guattari, F. (tr. Hurley, R. Seem, M. and Lane, H.) 1984: *Anti-Oedipus: capitalism and schizophrenia*. London: The Athlone Press.

Deleuze, G. and Guattari, F. (tr. Massumi, B.) 1987: *A thousand plateaus: capitalism and schizophrenia*. London: The Athlone Press.

Department of Rural Development, Ministry of Agriculture 1991a: *Manual for integrated rural development and allied programmes of TRYSEM and DWCRA*. New Delhi.

Department of Rural Development, Ministry of Agriculture 1991b: *Manual for Jawahar Rozgar Yojana*. New Delhi.

Desai, K. 1999: *Hullaballo in the guava orchard*. London: Faber.

Dey, N., Roy, A., Singh, S. and Srivastava, K. (eds) 1995: Public hearing: a mode for people's monitoring. *Proceedings of a workshop on the Right to Information*. Mussoorie: Lal Bahadur Shastri National Academy of Administration.

Dhesi, A. 1998: Caste, class synergies and discrimination in India. *International Journal of Social Economics* **25**, 1030–48.

Dhillon, A. 1997: Antisocial service. *India Today International* **22**(34), 38–9.

Dogra, B. 1998: *A red–green movement: Shankar Guha Niyogi and the struggle of Chhatisgarh people*. New Delhi: Highly Relevant Books.

Dogra, B. undated: *The non-party process: profile of a people's organisation*. Nangloi, Delhi: Kulreshi Printers.

Doniger, W. and Smith, B. (tr.) 1991: *The laws of Manu*. Harmondsworth: Penguin.

Down to Earth 1995a: Moneymakers. **4**(3), 7.

Down to Earth 1995b: Stripe strikes. **4**(7), 19.

Down to Earth 1995c: 'Kill him too' (cartoon). **4**(8), 12.

Down to Earth 1999: Analysis: perpetual thirst. **7**(19). Http://www.oneworld.org/cse/html/dte/dte990228

Mitra, S. 1998b: Old parents: unlovingly yours. *India Today International* **23**(28), 47–53.

Mitra, S. and Baweja, H. 1998: RSS on the rampage. *India Today International* **23**(39), 12–17.

Mitra, S. and Chakravarty, S. 1999: Hello from hell. *India Today International* **24**(4), 28–32.

Mitra, S. and Rekhi, S. 1998: The great disclosure. *India Today International* **23**(42), 26–31.

Mohan, S. 1998: The changing political scenario. *The Hindu Online* 6 January.

Monteiro, A. 1998: Official television and unofficial fabrications of the self: the spectator as subject. In Nandy, A. (ed.), *The secret politics of our desires: innocence, culpability and Indian popular cinema.* Delhi: Oxford University Press, 157–207.

Morris-Jones, W. 1971: *The government and politics of India.* London: Hutchinson.

Muralidharan, S. 1996: Lengthening list: the *hawala* scandal rolls on. *Frontline* **13**(3), 4–10.

Muralidharan, S. (co-ordinator) 1998a: Cover story: Who's afraid of Article 356? *Frontline* **15**(14), 4–32.

Muralidharan, S. 1998b: The *Hindutva* takeover of ICHR. *Frontline* **15**(14), 105–7.

Muralidharan, S. 1998c: Food economy: a price to pay. *Frontline* **15**(24), 109.

Muralidharan, S. 1998d: For four new States. Frontline **15**(15), 31–4.

Muralidharan, S. 1999: A bitter aftermath. *Frontline* **16**(4), 22–3.

Muralidharan, S. and Pande, S. 1998: Taking *Hindutva* to school. *Frontline* **15**(23), 4–10.

Nabar, V. 1995: *Caste as woman.* New Delhi: Penguin Books.

Nair, P. 1999: Return of overseas contract workers and their rehabilitation and development in Kerala (India): a critical account of policies, performance and prospects. *International Migration* **37**(1), 209–42.

Nandy, A. 1983: The uncolonized mind: a post-colonial view of India and the West. In *The intimate enemy: loss and recovery of self under colonialism.* Delhi: Oxford University Press.

Nandy, A. 1994: *The illegitimacy of nationalism.* Delhi: Oxford University Press.

Nandy, A. 1995a: An intelligent critic's guide to Indian cinema. In *The savage Freud and other essays on possible and retrievable selves.* Delhi: Oxford University Press, 196–236.

Nandy, A. (1995b) *Sati* in *Kali Yuga*: the public debate on Roop Kanwar's death. In *The savage Freud and other essays on possible and retrievable selves.* Delhi: Oxford University Press.

Nandy, A. 1998a: Indian popular cinema as a slum's eye view of politics. In Nandy, A. (ed.), *The secret politics of our desires: innocence, culpability and Indian popular cinema.* Delhi: Oxford University Press, 1–18.

Nandy, A. 1998b: The politics of secularism and the recovery of religious toleration. In Bhargava, R. (ed.), *Secularism and its critics.* Delhi: Oxford University Press.

Narasimhan, R. and Sattiah, D. 1997: Pudupalakshmi groups in Nellore (AP). In Mathew, A.S. (ed.), *Promoting livelihoods for the rural poor: a source book for development administrators and NGOs.* Mussoorie: Softrain, Lal Bahadur Shastri National Academy of Administration.

Nayyar, D. 1996: *Economic liberalization in India: analytics, experience and lessons.* Calcutta: Orient Longman.

Ninan, T. 1999: A year in purgatory. *Seminar* **473**, 24–9.

Noronha, F. 1995: A shredded project. *Down to Earth* **4**(7), 22–3.

Olsen, W. 1996: *Rural Indian social relations: a study of southern Andhra Pradesh.* Delhi: Oxford University Press.

Omvedt, G. 1995: *Dalit visions: the anti-caste movement and the construction of an Indian identity.* Hyderabad: Orient Longman.

Ould-Mey, M. 1999. The new global command economy. *Environment and Planning D: Society and Space* **17**(2), 155–80.

Padmanabhan, R. 1996: An odious gathering: Godses felicitated in Pune. *Frontline* **13**(13), 79–80.

Pahl, R. 1984: *Divisions of labour.* Oxford: Basil Blackwell.

Panchu, S. 1998: Fighting corruption: SC shows the way. *The Hindu Online* 13 January.

Pande, S. 1995: Uttarakhand again: a new phase in the agitation. *Frontline* **12**(20), 26–7.

Pandher, S. 1998a: Changing political equations. *The Hindu Online* 6 July.

Pandher, S. 1998b: NRIs get into the act in Punjab. *The Hindu Online* 24 February.

Panwalkar, P. 1995: Upgradation of slums: a World Bank programme. In Patel, S. and Thorner, A. (eds), *Bombay: metaphor for modern India*. Delhi: Oxford University Press, 121–42.

Parihar, R. 1998: Bucking the law. *India Today International* **23**(43), 34–7.

Parik, K. 1997: Overview: prospects and retrospect. In Parik, K. (ed.), *India development report*. Delhi: Indira Gandhi Institute of Development Research and Oxford University Press.

Parthasarthy, G. and Murty, C. 1997: Land reform, new economic policy and poverty. In Chadha, G. and Sharma, A. (eds), *Growth, employment and poverty: change and continuity in rural India*. New Delhi: Vikas.

Patel, P. 1999: Difficult alliances: treading the minefield of identity and solidarity politics. *Soundings: Transversal Politics* **12**, 115–26.

Pathak, P. 1993: Urbanisation, poverty and environmental considerations: a micro-level perspective. In Mukherjee, A. and Agnihotri, V. (eds), *Environment and development: views from the East and the West*. New Delhi: Concept Publishing, 449–68.

Patnaik, P. 1998: Some Indian debates on planning. In Byers, T. (ed.), *The Indian economy: major debates since independence*. Delhi: Oxford University Press, 159–92.

Pattabhiram, M. 1997: The genesis of Article 356. *The Hindu Online* 26 June.

Pavarala, V. 1996: *Interpreting corruption: élite perspectives in India*. New Delhi: Sage.

Pendse, S. 1995: Toil, sweat and the city. In Patel, S. and Thorner, A. (eds), *Bombay: metaphor for modern India*. Delhi: Oxford University Press, 121–42.

Phillipose, P. 1997: Time out – tryst with corruption. *Indian Express* 14 August.

Pinch, W. 1996: Soldier monks and militant sadhus. In Ludden, D. (ed.), *Making India Hindu: religion, community and the politics of democracy in India*. Delhi: Oxford University Press, 140–61.

Potter, D.C. 1996: *India's political administrators: from ICS to IAS*. 2nd edn, New Delhi: Oxford University Press.

Prakasam, K. 1992: Ayodhya: questions of history. *Nation and the World* 16 November.

Available at http://muslimsonline.com/babri/babrik pp.htm

Prime, R. 1992: *Hinduism and ecology: seeds of truth*. London: World Wide Fund for Nature.

Quigley, D. 1993: *The interpretation of caste*. Oxford: Oxford University Press.

Racine, J.L. 1997: The roots of man. In Racine, J.L. (ed.), *Peasant moorings: village ties and mobility rationales in South India*. New Delhi: Sage, 329–73.

Rajalakshmi, T. 1998: Capital misery. *Frontline* **15**(10), 120–22.

Rajalakshmi, T. 1999: The woes of a workforce. *Frontline* **16**(8), 119–21.

Ram, D.S. (ed.) 1996: *Dynamics of district administration: a new perspective*. New Delhi: Kanishka Publishers.

Ramachandran, P. 1995: *Public administration in India*. New Delhi: National Book Trust, India.

Ramakrishnan, V. 1994a: Caste cauldron: the politics of polarisation. *Frontline* **11**(19), 10–11.

Ramakrishnan, V. 1994b: Violent games: the Uttarakhand stir and power politics. *Frontline* **11**(21), 24–5.

Ramakrishnan, V. 1994c: The rape story. *Frontline* **11**(21), 26.

Ramakrishnan, V. 1997: March towards Mathura. *Frontline* **14**(6), 28–9.

Ramakrishnan, V. 1999: A dismissal backfires. *Frontline* **16**(5), 16–22.

Rangarajan, M. 1999: Remaking the map of India. *Seminar* **4734**, 39–42.

Rao, L. 1992: Reservation policy and the principle of merit: a study of Indian bureaucracy. *Indian Journal of Political Science* **53**(4), 478–92.

Rao, P.V.R. 1994: Class of '94. *Indian Express* 30 October.

Rao, S. and Natarajan, I. 1996: *Indian market demographics: the consumer class*. New Delhi: National Council of Applied Economic Research and Global Business Press.

Rastagi, R. 1995: Sexism in the Civil Services. *Femina* 8 January.

Rawat, D. 1993: Some environmental challenges of industrialisation in agricultural areas: a case study from the Upper Ganga Plain, India. In Mukherjee, A and

Agnihotri, V. (eds), *Environment and development: views from the East and the West.* New Delhi: Concept.

Ray, R. 1988: *The Naxalites and their ideology.* Delhi: Oxford University Press.

Ray, T. 1995: ULFA, again. *Frontline* **12**(13), 31–2.

Rekhi, S. and Shekhar, G. 1996: Funding the politician. *India Today International* **21**(6), 12–24.

Routledge, P. 1996: Critical geopolitics and terrains of resistance. *Political Geography* **15**(6/7), 509–31.

Roy, A. 1998: The end of imagination. *Frontline* **15**(16), 4–19.

Roy, A. 1999: The greater common good. *Frontline* **16**(11), 4–29.

Roy, S. 1995: 'Liberalization' and the Indian economy: myth and reality. In Sathyamurthy, T. (ed.), *Industry and agriculture in India since Independence.* Delhi: Oxford University Press, 135–49.

Roychowdhury, A. 1998: Breathing benzene. *Down to Earth* **7**(1). Http://www.oneworld.org/cse/html/dte

Rudolph, L. and Rudolph, S. 1987: *In pursuit of Lakshmi: the political economy of the Indian state.* Chicago: University of Chicago Press.

Rushdie, S. and West, E. (eds) 1997: *The Vintage book of Indian writing.* London: Vintage.

Sadar, Z. 1998: Dilip Kumar made me do it. In Nandy, A. (ed.), *The secret politics of our desires.* Delhi: Oxford University Press.

Sainath, P. 1994: *Van samitis* and vanishing trees. *The Hindu Survey of the Environment 1994.* Chennai, 179–81.

Sainath, P. 1996: *Everybody loves a good drought: stories from India's poorest districts.* New Delhi: Penguin.

Sangari, K. and Vaid, S. 1996: Institutions, beliefs and ideologies: widow immolation in contemporary Rajasthan. In Jayawardena, K. and de Alwis, M. (eds), *Embodied violence: communalising women's sexuality in South Asia.* New Delhi: Kali for Women, 240–96.

Saran, R. 1999: Why aren't you spending? *India Today International* **24**(18), 31–5.

Sarkar, S. 1993: The fascism of the *Sangh Parivar. Economic and Political Weekly* **28**, 163–7.

Sarkar, S. 1994: An anti-secularist critique of *Hindutva:* problems of a shared discursive space. *Germinal* **1**, 101–10.

Sarkar, T. 1996: Heroic women, mother goddesses: family and organisation in *Hindutva* politics. In Sarkar, T., and Butalial, U. (eds), *Women and the Hindu Right.* New Delhi: Kali for Women.

Sarkar, T. and Butalia, U. (eds) 1995: *Women and the Hindu Right.* New Delhi: Kali for Women.

Satyamurthy, T. 1996: General introduction. In Satyamurthy, T. (ed.), *Class formation and political transformation in post-colonial India.* Delhi: Oxford University Press.

Saunders, P. 1981: *Social theory and the urban question.* London: Hutchinson.

Saxena, N. 1997: *Policy and legal reforms for the poor in India.* Mussoorie: Lal Bahadur Shastri National Academy of Administration.

Seabrook, J. 1992: The reconquest of India: the victory of international monetary fundamentalism. *Race and Class* **34**(1), 1–16.

Seabrook, J. 1993: Death of a socialist: the Chhattisgarh Liberation Movement. *Race and Class* **35**(2), 1–20.

Sen, Amartya 1987: *The standard of living.* Cambridge: Cambridge University Press.

Sen, Amartya 1992: *Inequality re-examined.* Delhi: Oxford University Press.

Sen, Amartya 1999: *Commodities and capabilities.* Delhi: Oxford University Press.

Sen, Atindra (ed.) 1995: *Civil Service reforms.* Mussoorie: Lal Bahadur Shastri National Academy of Administration.

Seymour, S. 1999: *Women, family and child care in India: a world in transition.* Cambridge: Cambridge University Press.

Shah, A. 1996a: Job reservation and efficiency. Reprinted in Srinivas, M. (ed.) 1996: *Caste: its twentieth century avatar.* New Delhi: Viking.

Shah, A. 1996b: The judicial and sociological view of Other Backward Classes. In Srinivas, M. (ed.), *Caste: its twentieth century avatar.* New Delhi: Viking.

Shah, G. 1997: *Public health and urban development: the plague in Surat.* New Delhi: Sage.

Shah, N. 1999: Chain migration through the social network: experience of labour migrants in Kuwait. *International Migration* **37**(2), 361–82.

Shankardass, R. 1996: The Phoolan syndrome: of crime and politics. *Frontline* **13**(10), 102–3.

Sharma, K. 1995: Chronicle of a riot foretold. In Patel, S. and Thorner, A. (eds), *Bombay: metaphor for modern India*. Delhi: Oxford University Press.

Sharma, M. 1999: A struggle for fishing rights. *Frontline* **16**(14), 65–9.

Sharma, R. 1997: Old game, new pawns: Veerappan strikes again. *Frontline* **14**(21), 122–3.

Shastri, L. 1997: Lake City turns putrid. *The Hindu Survey of the Environment* 1997. Chennai, 91–5.

Shiva, V. 1989: *Staying alive: women, ecology and development*. London: Zed Books.

Shiva, V. 1991: *The violence of the Green Revolution: Third World agriculture, ecology and politics*. London: Zed Books.

Shivalingappa, B. 1997: Mobility and change in the western Ghats. In Racine, J.L. (ed.), *Peasant moorings: village ties and mobility rationales in South India*. New Delhi: Sage.

Shurmer-Smith, P. 1984: The Sikh identity. *Geographical Magazine* **121**, 442–3.

Shurmer-Smith, P. and Hannam, K. 1994: The world as a place: a global culture. In *Worlds of desire, realms of power: a cultural geography*. London: Edward Arnold.

Singh, G. 1997: Understanding political corruption in contemporary Indian politics. *Political Studies* **45** (Special Issue), 626–38.

Singh, K. 1999: Fifteen fateful years: 1984–1999. *Seminar* **476**, 14–16.

Singh, N. 1999: *The politics of crime: a former CBI officer speaks*. New Delhi: HarperCollins, India.

Singh, N. and Ahmed, F. 1995: Crime and politics: the nexus. *India Today International* **20**(16), 26–33.

Singh, P. 1995: *The Naxalite Movement in India*. New Delhi: Rupa.

Singh, R. 1999: Rethinking development in India: perspective, crisis and prospects. In Simon, D. and Narman, A. (eds), *Development as theory and practice*. Harlow: Longman, 55–75.

Singh, S. 1997: Taming the waters: the political economy of large dams in India. Delhi: Oxford University Press.

Singh, T. 1995: Kashmir: a tragedy of errors. New Delhi: Penguin.

Sivaraman, M. 1999: Rising awareness. *Frontline* **16**(14), 96–7.

Spate, O. 1954: *India and Pakistan: a general regional geography*. London: Methuen.

Sridar, V. 1998: Lessons from a tragedy. *Frontline* **15**(19), 48.

Srinivas, M. 1952: *Religion and society among the Coorgs*. Oxford: Oxford University Press.

Srinivas, M. 1962: *Caste in modern India and other essays*. Bombay: Asia Publishing House.

Srinivas, M. 1977: The changing role of Indian women. Man: *Journal of the Royal Anthropological Institute* **12**(2), 221–38.

Srinivas, M. (ed.) 1996: *Caste: its twentieth century avatan*. New Delhi: Viking.

Srinivasan, A. 1990: The survivor in the study of violence. In Das, V. (ed.), *Mirrors of violence: communities, riots and survivors in South Asia*. Delhi: Oxford University Press, 305–20.

Srivastava, R. 1995: India's uneven development and its implications for political processes: an analysis of some recent trends. In Sathyamurthy, T. (ed.), *Industry and agriculture in India since Independence*. Delhi: Oxford University Press, 219–47.

Srivastava, S. 1998: *Constructing post-colonial India: national character and the Doon School*. London: Routledge.

Standing, H. 1991: *Dependence and autonomy: women's employment and the family in Calcutta*. London: Routledge.

State of the forest report for 1997. New Delhi: Ministry of Environment and Forests.

Statistical outline of India 1997–8. Mumbai: Tata Services Ltd.

Subramanian, T. 1995: Cover Story – Rites and wrongs; some protests; taxmen at work. *Frontline* **12**(20), 4–17.

Summers, L. 1991: A widely leaked internal World Bank memorandum. Information found at:
http://jacksonprogressive.com/issues/summersmem/html

Sunderarajan, P. 1998: Officials not sure of meeting water supply target. *The Hindu Online* 30 October.

Surendra, L. 1999: Between nirvana and karma economics. *Seminar* **474**, 38–43.

Suri, S. and Keshavan, N. 1998: Saffron across

the seven seas. *Outlook* 16 March. Http://hindunet.org/hvk/articles/0398/0042.html

Swami, P. 1997a: A passage from India. *Frontline* **14**(2), 115–7.

Swami, P. 1997b: Back from death. *Frontline* **14**(3), 38–41.

Swami, P. 1998a: The Romesh Sharma trail. *Frontline* **15**(23), 110–12.

Swami, P. 1998b: The MEA's children. *Frontline* **15**(2), 68–70.

Swami, P. 1999a: A dangerous drift. *Frontline* **16**(5), 39–41.

Swami, P. 1999b: Broadening the base. *Frontline* **16**(12), 22–4.

Swami, P., Rajalakshmi, T. and Ramakrishman, V. 1998: Elastic standards. *Frontline* **15**(14), 122–4.

Swaminathan, M. 1995: Deprivation and the environment. *The Hindu Survey of the Environment 1995*. Chennai, 21–3.

Tambia, S. 1996: *Levelling crowds: ethnoregionalist conflict in South Asia*. Berkeley: University of California Press.

Tambs-Lyche, H. 1980: *London Pattidars: a case in urban ethnicity*. London: Routledge & Kegan Paul.

Taneja, N. 1994: Populism, *Hindutva*, imperialism: an anti-modernity paradigm for the Third Worlds. *Germinal* **1**, 111–27.

Tendulkar, S. 1998: Indian economic policy reforms and poverty: an assessment. In Ahluwalia, I. and Little, I. (eds), *India's economic reforms and development: essays for Manmohan Singh*. Delhi: Oxford University Press. 280–309.

Thakur, H. 1998: Preface. In Menski, A. (ed.), *South Asians and the dowry problem*. Stoke-on-Trent: Trentham Books, xiii–xxi.

Thapar, R. 1989: Imagined religious communities? Ancient history and the modern search for a Hindu identity. *Modern Asian Studies* **2**(23), 209–39.

Thapar, R. 1990: A historical perspective on the story of Rama. In Gopal, S. (ed.), *Anatomy of a confrontation: Ayodhya and the rise of communal politics in India*. London: Zed Books, 141–63.

Thapar, V. and Parhar, R. 1998: Shikar: savage harvest. *India Today International* **23**(44), 28–34.

Thapar, V. and Ramani, P. 1999: The price of indulgence. *India Today International* **24**(4), 33–6.

Thapar, V., Raval, S. and Chakravarty, S. 1999: Young menace. *India Today International* **24**(3), 30–6.

Tharoor, S. 1997: *India: from midnight to the millennium*. New Delhi: Viking.

Tiwari, M. and Roychowdhary, A. 1998: Left hanging: special report. *Down to Earth* **7**(12). Http://www.oneworld.org/cse/html/dte

Uberoi, P. 1998: The diaspora comes home: disciplining desire in *DDLJ*. *Contributions to Indian Sociology* **32**(2), 305–36.

Unnithan, S. 1998: RSS goes global, chalks out expansion plan. *The Observer* 3 April. Http//www.hvk.org/hvk/articles/0498/0014.html

Vaidyanathan, A. 1995: *The Indian economy: crisis, response and prospects*. Hyderabad: Orient Longman.

Vanaik, A. 1990: *The painful transition: bourgeois democracy in India*. London: Verso.

Vanaik, A. 1995: *India in a changing world: problems, limits and successes of its foreign policy*. Hyderabad: Orient Longman.

Vanaik, A. 1997: *The furies of Indian communalism: religion, modernity and secularization*. London: Verso.

van der Veer, P. 1994: *Religious nationalism*. Berkeley: University of California Press.

Varshney, A. 1995: *Democracy, development and the countryside: urban–rural struggles in India*. Cambridge: Cambridge University Press.

Veham Andhshraddha Virodhi Manch 1998: *Memorandum to the Governor of Gujarat*. Http://www.altindia.net/gujarat/Memorandumtogovernor.html

Venkatesan, V. 1998: Waiting for succour. *Frontline* **15**(23), 106–8.

Venkatesan, V. 1999: Threat of submergence. *Frontline* **16**(14), 35–7.

Vinayak, R. 1997: Victims of sudden affluence. *India Today International* **22**(38), 44–5.

Vinayak, R. 1998a: Ominous intent. *India Today International* **22**(11), 28–9.

Vinayak, R. 1998b: Futuristic farmers. *India Today International* **22**(38), 44–5.

Wadley, S. 1994: *Struggling with destiny in Karimpur 1925–84*. Berkeley: University of California Press.

Warrier, H.K. 1996: The great divide in the Indian administration. *Pioneer on Sunday* 25 February.

World Bank 1997: *India: achievements and challenges in reducing poverty.* Washington, DC: World Bank.

Zerinini-Brotel, J. 1998: The BJP in Uttar Pradesh: from *Hindutva* to consensual politics. In Hansen, T. and Jaffrelot, C. (eds), *The BJP and the compulsions of politics in India.* Delhi: Oxford University Press, 73–100.

SOME USEFUL WEBSITES

Altindia – http://www.altindia.net
('An attempt to create a space on and about the other India.' A really valuable site. Publishes Public Interest Litigation, working papers from major Indian critical theorists, debates on current issues, material from social movements.)

Centre for Science and Environment (CSE) – http://www.oneworld.org/cse/html (An independent NGO specializing in environmental issues. An excellent site with access to its reports and monthly journal *Down to Earth.*)

Lal Bahadur Shastri National Academy of Administration – http://www.lbsnaa.ernet.in (The training establishment of the Indian Administrative Service. A very useful site with links into many government departments, individual officers' home pages and current affairs journals, etc.)

Frontline – http://www.frontlineonline.com (In my opinion by far the best current affairs journal. Part of *The Hindu* group. Published twice monthly. Available in full online.)

Ghadar   –
http://www.foil.org/resources/ghadar.htm (A view of a left-wing expatriate group but also good links into Indian left-wing movements.)

The Hindu – http://www.webpage.com/hindu.index/html
(My favourite daily newspaper. Available in full online. A first-rate site which provides links to journals in its stable.)

India Today – http://www.india-today.com (Major current affairs journal. Published weekly. Available in full online.)

Indian Express – http://www.expressindia.com (Daily newspaper. Rather more 'pacey' than others. Available in full online.)

Narmada Bachao Andolan –
http://www.angelfire.com
(Links to similar organizations)

Planet Bollywood –
http://www.planetbollywood.com
(Interactive, up-to-date information on Hindi films.)

The RSS – http://hindunet.org/rss/RSS (Good for keeping up with the language of *Hindutva.*)

Secular India – http://www.secularindia.com (Fairly conservative approach to secularism. Good links into a range of newspapers and political sites.)

The Times of India –
http://www.timesofindia.com
(Daily newspaper. Available in full online.)

VIDEO

The video *Kaise Jeebo Re! (How do I survive, my friend!)*, directed by A. Singh and J. Jhaveri, is an excellent 80-minute documentary on the people displaced by the Narmada Valley Scheme. It is available in English as well as Bhilali, Gondi, Gujarati and Hindi. It is produced by the socially committed small company Jan Madayam, MD–4 Sah Vikas Society, 68 I.P. Extension, Delhi 110 092, India. E-mail: Jharana Jhaveri <jharana@del2.vsnl.net.in